LOVE · HATE
HOTELS

tony matthews ii

Working in the hotel industry:
We love it.
We hate it.
We can't escape it.

The events and conversations in this book have been set down to the best of the author's ability, although some names and details have been changed to protect the privacy of individuals.

First paperback edition August 2019

Book design by Tony Matthews II
Logo design by Smart Design with Designhill

ISBN 978-0-578-51655-4

www.LoveHateHotels.com

Table of Contents:

Foreword

The hotel industry is a humongous industry, and there is lots of money to be made from it. Companies are coming out of the woodworks trying to get a piece of the hotel industry profit pie. This being said, you would assume it would be a great industry to be working in, right?

Well, hotels are very misleading from the start. You go on vacation and stay at these beautiful properties, and are greeted by these smiling strangers offering to help with your bags, and welcoming you to the "so-and-so" hotel. It makes you feel like the king or queen of the world. From the moment you pull into the parking lot (or Valet loop), the lies, brown-nosing, storytelling, and butt-kissing begins. As a few of my former colleagues would say, "Get your Chapstick ready!"

In this book, I will guide you through my long journey in the hotel industry, and explain to you why the industry seems so great, yet so frustrating to work in at the same time. What some would refer to as a love/hate relationship. I will use mostly false names, and no company names because I valued my time with them and learned tons, whether I liked working for them or not.

CHAPTER 1 - FALLING IN LOVE WITH HOTELS

One way or another, we stumble into the wide world of hotels, and God bless us all! I would guess that the number one reason is likely because we could not get any other jobs out of high school or college, and this was an easy route that didn't require a specific degree, or any at all. As long as you are semi-personable (or the opposite in the case of Night Audit positions), you can be hired at a hotel, even if it is a dumpy little franchise hotel in your friendly neighborHOOD. Don't get me wrong, some brave souls do study Hotel Management in college, and whatever High School Counselors suggested that genius idea should all be fired immediately. Just kidding...or am I?

As most of us graduating college in 2009 discovered, the economy sucked ass, and jobs were few and far between. It was not the greatest time to find a job, especially with a general-ass Business Management degree. What company in their right mind would hire a Manager straight out of college, let alone from party school USA, couch-burning West Virginia University!? And my shitty final grade point average (GPA) was not helping my cause. So I did what any brilliant person would do in tough economic times, and go live on the beach with my sister, not work, and take a real estate licensing course. #Idiot.

Upon successfully completing the Maryland real estate course and emptying my bank account on alcohol, killer seafood, and to-die for bagels at this spot called *A Bagel And...* in Ocean City, I finally passed the exam after about four attempts. And yes, I had to pay over a hundred bucks each damn time! I was never much of a test-taker in school, especially those godforsaken SAT's! I then decided to move back home to Southern Maryland, rent free, with my mom and stepdad to practice my license with potential clients and areas that I already knew. I interviewed with a few different real estate brokers to see which would be the best fit for me and if they even wanted me on their team. I had to make a decision whether to work with well-known real estate companies, like Century 21 and Coldwell Banker, or smaller, more local ones. I actually got a really good vibe from one of the smaller, local brokers and decided to go with them. I felt that the popular real estate companies thought their shit didn't stink and they wanted me to beg to work with them. No thanks. Not my style.

I went and bought all kinds of goodies to make myself feel more professional as an Agent. I got some new, cheap, yet trendy, H&M dress clothes, a laptop, briefcase, and all sorts of office supplies that I assumed I would write-off a portion of as business expenses come tax season. Well, little did I know, I would get paired up with a shitty mentor and pretty much hate working as a Real Estate Agent from the start. She was a super nice lady and seemed super chill (almost too chill, like hippy chill), and she was actually getting back into the real estate game herself. I can't remember why she took a break from it, but she would constantly tell me how broke she was, and make comments about not making money in real estate. Awkwarrddddd! She was definitely not a motivational speaker in her past life. Most experienced Agents will let the newbies advertise for some of their listings because it is great exposure for their properties, free of charge. Then, if someone called about the property, the idea would be that the newbie would be the Buyer's Agent, and the mentor, the Seller's Agent. A win-win situation. Nope, not with dis bitch. I don't know why, but she did not want me doing that. Wtf!? Instead, I had to reach out to another Agent that my mom knew and ask her. I was originally hoping that she would be my mentor because she crushed it in the real estate game, but she was legit too busy to mentor anyone. She had her own Personal Assistant for crying out loud! Living that *Million Dollar Listing* (Bravo TV) dream!

Real estate could be awesome if you had money in your bank account from the start, because you don't make any money until you actually sell something. In fact, you start off in the negatives because you pay for your license test, your memberships, laptop, supplies, and gas to check out listings, etc. It would be wise to get your license when you already know someone looking to buy, and they would be willing to wait for you to get your license and represent them. For example, if your parents, sibling, or best friend are looking for a place. This way you could bank some money on that first sale and grow from there. So let's just say this job was not exactly the best starter job for a broke-ass college kid like me. Not to mention, I was researching houses for clients during the day on weekdays, showing them the houses during the evenings, and then showing some more on the weekends. Basically working 24/7. When exactly was I supposed to have time off!? What's that saying, "You live and you learn?" Well, I lived, and I learned real quick that this was not the career for me at that stage in my life.

All the meanwhile, as I struggled to make it in the real estate game, I had to get a part-time job to float me cash while I tried to make some sales. I decided to test my luck in the restaurant industry because I knew the schedule was flexible, and I didn't exactly have to use my brain. Little did I know, this would be my official entry into the ever-loving hospitality industry. I started with a restaurant that catered to an older-aged clientele, and it served divey food, most of which was seafood, which is quite popular in my hometown. They made the best cream of crab soup on this planet! Believe it or not though, the most popular dish there was the chicken and liver. What the hell!? Gross. The old country folks loved it. It was located directly across from my mom's neighborhood, so it was super convenient. Something that I learned real quick was to NOT work in a restaurant where most of the customers are retired. They are sweet as can be (well, most of them), but they live on their fixed retirement incomes for the rest of their days, so whether their meal is five or five-hundred dollars, your tip will remain the same (a.k.a. three dollars or less, sometimes in the form of coins). No bueno! I did, however, really enjoy working in the restaurant industry. The other Servers and Hosts were also young and fun. We all knew our job sucked and it was only a temporary thing. We struggled with those annoying guests on the job together, and drank our sorrows away outside of work together. Most of the other employees were pretty good-looking, so flings were a common trend, which of course led to some fun conversations and awkward drama when polishing the silverware together in the coming days. We were all people-persons, so the job worked out well for us, unfortunately it didn't really resonate with the tips we received.

Due to the inconsistency of shitty tips, I decided to mix it up with something more steady and apply at local hotels for a Front Desk Agent position. If there was ever a time I wished I got struck by lightning, this would have been it. That sounds horrible, I know, but there is a reason that "Hate" is also in the title of this book. Anywayz, with this job, I figured I could get hired pretty easily with my education, personality, and nice appearance. I always had a love for hotels from growing up traveling and staying in pretty nice accommodations with my parents. And luckily for me, I grew up with two sets of parents because my parents got divorced when I was young, and remarried to different people. Needless to say, I traveled quite a bit between the two sets.

I mean, who doesn't love hotels right? Even if it is standard-ass hotel that you stayed at on a trip to a soccer tournament growing up, it was still great because it was a vacation away from home. You could use fancy soaps and shampoos, there were always fluffy and clean towels and pillows, and usually a heated pool, better yet....a fucking hot tub! A mother f-ing hot tub! Who doesn't love soaking in 105 degree bacteria infested water with bubbles. Heaven on earth. The hotels usually had some sort of 24-hour market for late night snacks that our mommies and daddies would pay for. Then you would wake up to some sort of an all-you-can-eat breakfast...say whattttt!? Unlimited chocolate milk cartons and Captain Crunch cereal!? GTFO! This was really my first experience with elevators, and likely every kids, unless they lived in an apartment complex with one. Not having to take the stairs and playing with the buttons on them was priceless. Giving that random guest that steps in the elevator the ole hitting all the floor buttons and bolting out prank. Classic! I remember using the long hallways to practice our soccer and floor hockey skills before getting yelled at by other guests, or the hotel staff from complaints. And how cool was it that you could pick up your room phone and have access to call all of your teammates and buddies rooms? Those were the days...pre-cell phone days at least. It's safe to say that we are brainwashed to love hotels as young children even though we may not have ever thought about it.

As you get older, your viewpoint of hotels changes a bit, but still in a good way. Instead, you are looking to see what amenities the hotels have. The second you or your buddies book the hotel for your vacation, you instantly get online and check it out! You see how awesome the pool looks, or the lobby bar, and maybe spa. Then investigate how close it is to attractions, whether it be local bars, sports venues, or even just the grocery store so you can load up on booze with ease. You then brag about those future accommodations with your friends, family, and whoever else cares to listen on every form of social media possible. Although, if you are cheap as fuck like most of us youngins, you may not brag about that crummy motel you booked, as you are crossing your fingers that you don't get eaten alive by bed bugs. But I would say that for the most part, a hotel/resort is something everything looks forward to on a trip.

Me particularly, I always loved the arrival experience at a hotel or resort. The friendly customer service hits you as soon as you pull through the Valet loop. The presence of entering a hotel's port-a-cacher (the big overhanging roof thing that covers the Valet loop) instantly makes you feel like a celebrity of sorts for that very moment. Then you have Bellmen rushing, sometimes fighting to get you out of your car and assist you with your luggage. Little did you know the first time that the reason was to collect a fat tip from you for their assistance. The lights were always super bright (Cue the song, "All of the Lights" by *Kanye West*) and all the employees had big smiles on their faces as you arrived. Damn, what did I do to get this treatment? Oh yeah, my parents were spending hundreds per night for us to stay there. I particularly remember my first time in Aruba at my parent's timeshare. As I walked through the front doors, I was greeted with an ice-cold sugary mixed cocktail with the cliché mini umbrella hanging out of it by a beautiful lady in a tropical shirt. Oh, helllllll yeahhhhh! Not only was I underage so I thought this was awesome, but I felt like a "somebody" even though i was just another Joe Schmo guest. It was one hell of a way to start the vacation out being treated like the king of the land. Look out ladies!

My love for hospitality in general probably dates back to staying with my grandmother in her mega-mansion of a house in Hockessin, Delaware. Naturally, you are already small as a kid, so when you enter a big, beautiful house it is jaw-dropping. You entered her house through a grand foyer where the staircases split in each direction to get to the top level. My sister and I would race up opposite sides to see who could make it to the top-center the quickest. My sister was a quick little booger for being a girl! At that center point, there were dual French doors to enter the master bedroom. The house was ridiculously huge. It stretched four stories high with a monster kitchen, monster multi-deck balcony, monster man-cave/game room, and of course monster pool and...you guessed it, an M f-ing hot tub! Without getting into too much detail, it was basically a house you would see on *MTV Cribs*. It was like heaven as a kid, and it gave me that same feeling of being in a hotel, but the only difference was we had the whole hotel to ourselves here. My Mommom was the sweetest grandmother on the planet, so she was always quick to greet us with drinks or snacks, very similar to that of the hotel employee in Aruba. Mommom was always whipping up some cheese and cracker dishes, dessert, or firing up the grill for a filet. It was like Texas De Brazil up in that bitch with around the clock food being shoved in your face. She was what people call a very good host. Her mini-resort and great southern hospitality kick-started my appreciation for luxury living and great hospitality.

Ok, so back to my job hunt. Believe it or not, the very first hotel I drove by had a "Now Hiring" displayed on the 1980's looking street sign with the black plastic lettering where you always see the guy on the ladder switching out daily with some corny saying. You know those signs that read "Free HBO" or "No Vacancy" or "Air

Conditioning." I walked in with my modern slim-fit H&M suit and skinny tie on, and dropped off my resume with the Front Desk Agent, as the Manager was not in. Sure enough, I drove off the lot and before I even busted a u-eey (slang for U-turn) to head home, I was receiving a call from an unknown 301 number. It was the hotel's Sales Manager who happened to be in the back office that day. She wanted me to come in for an interview that instant, so I busted another u-eey and went in for an impromptu interview. She was not the person hiring for the position, but the Assistant General Manager appreciated her word and opinions, so it simply took a quick follow-up interview with her to land the job as a Front Desk Agent. And little did I know on that very day, this would be the beginning of my long, fun, yet treacherous career in the hotel industry.

We have all done it…sat there at the Front Desk of a hotel waiting for the Agent to give us our keys so we can get vacationing ASAP. I am always thinking, "What in God's name is taking them so long to select my room and check my ass in?" Well, I learned the hard way by being on the other side of the desk. The computer systems used at this hotel, and come-to-find-out at most other hotels, look like they came straight from the Stone Age. Remember back in the day when we used the computers with the huge-ass TV-like monitors with the black background displays, green lettering, blinking box where the cursor was?…yeah, hotel software was STILL like that in 2009!? Don't even get me started as to how mind-boggling this was to me in the twenty-first century. Although, as much shit as I give hotels for being behind the power-curve, believe it or not, those ancient programs were pretty damn easy to operate. That is of course after you have to log in like fifty-nine times in a minute time frame because apparently your colleagues are the biggest thieves in the world. WTF!? You would run to the back office for half a minute to grab something and come back to the desk to be greeted by the "Please input your username and password" prompt. Ugh! Yeah, this was a pain in the royal ass, but it was all for good cause. The reasoning behind the constant logging in was so that other Agents, or even Managers (or in the super rare occasion, guests) don't come up behind you to refund someone hundreds of dollars under your log-in and you get blamed for it. It still happens, but the constant re-entry does help minimize this. Unfortunately, the guests pay the consequences waiting in line with the extra time it takes for the Agent to log in. Even longer if it happened to be the day you were forced to change your password and you kept typing in the freaking old one because you forgot. Time is money, especially when checking a guest in. And for those guests who travel frequently for work, their patience level is few and far between.

So not only were these programs ancient, but God forbid there just be one program that runs everything! That would just be too easy I guess. There was a program for literally everything: One for general checking-in-and-out and billing; another for logging guest requests; one to make room keys; one for in-room movies; and others for who knows what else. If there was one for blowing your nose, I am sure they would have that separate too. Absolutely ridiculous. Again, this being in the twenty-first freaking century. I learned real quick that the hotel business could use a technology mogul to come in and revamp everything. That will be the day! "Hello out there, where are you!?" I think hotels hesitate to do this because of the massive database that would have to be transferred over to any new system, but still. Either that, or they were locked into a contract with these program's companies. For being a multi-billion dollar industry, it truly is shocking. Dude, the movie system...this thing was a machine where someone would come in with actual VHS videos and swap them out occasionally so guests had the newest movies to order from their guest room TV's. Fucking VHS! Hilarious. The best part had to be our excitement when the latest HBO TV Guides would be delivered and we got to see what great movies, boxing matches, and series were playing that month. This became the alternative for guests instead of buying the movies through the hotel channel guides, because it was free. Hotels cleaned up some profit on those movie rentals. They were ridiculously expensive, although a lot of guests didn't care because they would expense it to their company, so a ten dollar rental didn't phase them.

Now checking guests in-and-out on these ancient programs came very natural to me. Just be friendly and polite and it's smooth sailing…or so I thought. What I didn't have any experience in was when guests would object or complain and expect refunds or freebies galore. Fuck me. I was very narrow minded (thanks Dad), so I would simply have the response in my head of, "Umm…no. Why in the hell would I give you a free upgrade or bottle of water? I don't know you." I came to learn the famous and very true motto in the hotel biz, "The guest is always right." For the most part, there is always some way you can bargain with a guest. You just have to find out what exactly will push their button and make them happy, but doing so without giving away the entire hotel. I learned the phrase, "My apologies Sir/Ma'am, well, here is what I CAN do for you." My sales skills were polished during my time at the desk.

Perhaps the best sales practice was selling the hotel's "Walk Away Rate." This was a rate that when people would walk in to get a room and it was too expensive, what we could drop the price down to before they "walked away." Just think of when you are leaving a used car lot and the Salesperson won't let you leave the lot. Instead, they bug the shit out of you to buy something, even if it isn't the car you initially came in for. It's tacky, but it works. This was basically the same idea. Throwing in the white surrender towel to drop the rate. There was an amount we couldn't drop below because at the end of the day, the hotel needs to clear a certain amount on a room night to make money. It's really easy to think, "Well, the room will just sit empty anyway, so why not give it away for next to nothing towards the end of the night?" Well, you have to take into account the time and money it takes to clean the room afterwards, the maintenance it could require, the electricity/water that would be used, etc. This whole flexible pricing thing was new to me because I was a very by-the-book person, so these discounts and deals I had to cut guests was a bit difficult for me to get used to. Negotiating was not my strong suit.

13

Along with the useful sales techniques I was soaking up at the desk, I was also learning about repeat groups and guests. We had one group in particular, an electric company that would come every Sunday night and stay through Thursday morning for a project their company had contracted in Southern Maryland. They would go back to the Carolina's where they lived for the weekends. Now that's a freaking commute! These were very blue-collared guys just looking to come, get their work done, drink some beers, get some sleep, and head back home. It didn't take much to impress them, but they did indeed take a liking to certain rooms in the hotel. Here, I became familiar with the lovely guest room requests, which is very commonly frowned upon in the biz. These ten guests requested the same five double/double rooms every time they stayed...ugh. At this property, a double/double room was one with two full size beds. You could technically fit two people on each, but it was a tad tight, thus convincing people to purchase another room. Shady AF! All for the money! It was up to us as Front Desk Agents to make sure these guests were booked in those requested rooms or else we would not have happy guests for that week, and unhappy repeat guests at that. The tough part was that if we had a guest check-in the day before or even a few days before, we had to be careful not to put them in these rooms for multiple nights because our loyal guests wouldn't be happy.

Now, let me tell you why hotels do not, or at least should not, take room requests. Let's say a one night stay guest checks in on a Thursday, and comes to the desk and requests to extend his stay by a week. Ok, we have availability, so why not? Uno problemo...the room that this guest is in is the room that Mr. Smith stays in upon special request every week, and checks in on Monday. Shit. You only knew this because you see him week after week. This particular hotel's computer system had no sort of calendar alert system to notify that a particular room was being held for a guest. The only way I would see this request was if I went into Mr. Smith's reservation and saw the note that he requested room #303. So had I not known this from him being a familiar guest, some Agent would have been in for a nice scolding from Mr. Smith when he checked in Monday. There are some systems that allow you to block out a room ahead of time, and a pop-up would appear on the computer notifying you when you go to extend the current guest. So we would flip into the lying, manipulating Front Desk Agents that we were, and lie to that extending guest, telling him his room is scheduled for mandatory maintenance so we have to move him for the remainder of his stay. Sometimes it worked like a charm, but most of the time, you'd get the death stare, or straight laughed at. You certainly wouldn't want to let that guest know that Mr. Smith is scheduled to check-in to that room, because first, giving other guests names is illegal (ask Erin Andrews about that), and second, you don't want that guest to feel like they are less important than the incoming guest. Who would have thought so much went into simply extending a stay, right?

We would prep goody bags to give to the electrical guys upon arrival, with water, their favorite snacks, and even stock their favorite beer in their "requested" guest room mini-fridges before arrival—-FOR FREE to the guest! This is how you get repeat guests! Treat them like a damn member of the family. We would normally do some sort of amenity for all of the loyalty members. Most were pretty boring, with apples, bag of chips, and water...but again, it was free, so I'm sure they weren't complaining. It was shocking to me that we gave anything away for free simply for the guest giving us an email at some point to sign up to become a loyalty member. I have always been more of a pay-for-what-you-get person, so freebies were never an option in my book. This was a totally new concept for me. I had never seen that side of sales or bribery/brown-nosing to keep business, but that's the nature of the game. At the end of the day, what I assume is us giving away free things, the guest in-turn pays for at some point during their multiple stays with the brand.

The hours and days off in this job straight sucked ass! No better way to put it. Going from real estate, which was make-your-own-hours and holidays, to the restaurant which was pretty much dinnertime to close, and flexible holidays. At the hotel, there were three main shifts: 7 a.m. to 3 p.m.; 3 p.m. to 11 p.m.; or 11 p.m. to 7 a.m., which they called Night Audit. Occasionally, based on the occupancy of the hotel, it would require an Agent to come in for a midday shift that would be like 10 a.m. to 6 p.m., or 12 p.m. to 8 p.m. We would have random days off and not always two in a row, or even two off in the whole week. Sometimes you would get Monday/Wednesday off, sometimes Thursday/Saturday, maybe a Sunday/Monday...you get the point. Holidays...wait, what holidays? Hotels are open 24/7/365, so there is no such thing as holidays off. However, the hotel did do something cool instead. You would get the option to choose another day to have off because you would be working the holiday. Maybe one or two Agents would get the actual holiday off, while the others worked the desk. The rest of us would request other days off which could sometimes work out better for you. Then you would likely get the next major holiday off because you worked that one. For example, if you worked on Christmas Day, for New Year's Day you would have off. Not always, but most of the time it would work out fairly.

That being said, guess what my shift came to be at this hotel after just a few weeks in? Mother f-ing Monday to Friday from 7 a.m. to 3 p.m. Say whattttt!????? This just came to show how bad this particular hotel needed help. I was promoted to Lead Front Desk Agent with those lovely bankers hours. The most bogus job title on the planet because the "Lead" portion provides absolutely zero benefits. They just want to make you feel special. Regardless, I lucked out big-freakin-time with that time-slot. If you have ever worked in hotels (and I am not talking about Sales or upper management), you know this is impossible, unless maybe if you have worked there for like twenty-plus years and earned that schedule. So you could put this on the list as to how I fell in love with working in the hotel industry from the get-go, but little did I know the rarity of this occurrence at the time, and should have milked it to the grave. Naturally, I just assumed like most jobs, sports, or anything, that if you were the best, you would be rewarded.

Man, oh man, did this hotel have its issues. Let me tell you what! I felt it was my mission in life to do whatever it took to correct these issues..."Tony for President!" I will explain later. This hotel was an older property that had changed names and gotten a facelift inside-and-out with new ownership. It used to be a run-of-the-mill, cheap brand hotel, but it became a young, up-and-comer brand that still had some climbing to do to get a name and compete with the big boys. It was by no means much better than the brand it used to be, just more of an unknown, so I assumed the new owners thought that it would still change the crappy reputation it had. Now you would think changing the brand of a hotel is no big deal, right? Well in this particular case, it was indeed. The ever-lovely *TripAdvisor.com*, which is one of the main resources for hotel guests to go to for honest guest reviews, decided to stick a giant pinecone up our ass. Great site, but in our case, it was enemy #1. I am sure it was not their intentions, because I am sure scumbag hotel owners try to work the system on a regular basis.

TripAdvisor, for the love of God, would not let us clear out the reviews from when the property carried the previous hotel name, even though it was a completely different hotel, remodeled inside and out, and a new company running it, they considered it the same place because of its physical address. Bullshit! To compare, let's pretend that you took your old ass car, replaced all the interior engine parts, put on new tires and rims, stripped and re-did the interior, and gave it a new paint job. It's like a brand new car right? Well, kind of. I called, emailed, and wrote letters to *TripAdvisor* weekly trying to build a case to remove these old hotel reviews. If they could put a restraining order on someone, it would have been me because I was not letting this go. The reviews were BADDDD. I mean bed bugs (two words you don't want within miles of your hotel), cockroaches, undergarments left in rooms, mildew, homeless roaming the halls, hookers, you name it! Every possible red-flag hotel word that you don't want on your reviews were there, and we had to take the blame for it simply because it carried the same address. We would forever be a 1-1.5 star hotel on *TripAdvisor* because of this. The only way to fix it sounded quite easy...just get good reviews. But this was not a simple task because it took like nine good reviews to void out any one bad review. I gave it my all on this mission to help the hotel, but was unsuccessful. Of course now-a-days, *TripAdvisor* has a feature where it will say the hotel name, with an "UPDATED" next to it. It seems that *TripAdvisor* cleared out our hotels bad reviews at some point, but of course I was gone by then. I will go ahead and pretend that it was my annoyance that made them finally say, "Fuck it," and remove them. You're welcome!

Another problem with the hotel was the restaurant and bar that was situated right next to it. Originally, I was thinking this would be great that we had a restaurant and bar beside our hotel because it saves us from dealing with the pain of having food and beverage on property. Instead, we could point guests in their direction, and even have their menus in the guest rooms and it became "Room Service." Fucking genius idea if you ask me! The big problem...this bar did not draw the nicest crowd in the area. It was a mix between biker, urban, hooker, hillbilly, and who the hell knows what else could fit in that place. So naturally, it being next to the hotel, it gave us that trashy stereotype that went along with the bar, and a lot of times that trash would make its way over to the hotel. Although, this was great because we were putting *Heads in Beds* (read the book by Jacob Tomsky if you haven't). These trashy guests that spilled over were really the least of our problems.

The big problem was the noise and the lack of parking that we shared with this shithole. There were barely enough spots for all of the guests at the hotel even when the bar was closed. This caused for an absolute nightmare come Friday and Saturday night when guests were paying money to stay at our hotel and got stuck having to park at the sketchy pizza shop next door. Just lovely. The bar produced quite a bit of noise from their shitty sound system, blasting white-trash music all night. Can you tell I loved the place? As you could assume, this made for some lovely guest complaints, especially on the side of the building that ran snug to the bar. We had to get crafty with what guests to put in those rooms. I'm glad I only worked the night shift a few times on weekends. It took a strong soul to put up with those guests and late-night bar crawlers trying to get some ass in a cheap room at our hotel. So I learned pretty early on in my illustrious hotel career that there will most likely always be some problems that you will face at any hotel that will be out of your hands, and you do your best to work around them in creative ways. Whether it was a crummy surrounding area, a defect in the hotel, loud planes flying overhead, or even basement rooms (I'll get to that later), there will ALWAYS be something. You learn to love this challenge and any future funny stories that come from it, but hate it during the immediate moments.

Beyond the craziness of the hotel itself, there was something to be said about working the Front Desk and being the only punching bag for guests, and controlling the hotel from day-to-day. All of the guests had to go through me, and only me to get anything accomplished. For example, extra cleaning service in their room, maintenance, items brought to their rooms, corrections with their billing, etc. The Front Desk Agents are Managers in their own sense, without the title or the pay, or in normal cases, consistent hours. I took on some tasks on my own to better organize the hotel processes, and freaking loved it! You could call it the OCD in me. I created training and process manuals (also know as SOP's or Standard Operating Procedures) as this hotel was lacking them. I dressed overly dressy, as I have always been known to do. I always tried to looked sharp and I would always getting made fun of for it in Southern Maryland, where style doesn't exactly thrive, or even exist. The one thing I have always been good at, is people. I got along with everyone in every department at the hotel. I can get along with the rich, the poor, the smart, the stupid, etc., and let me tell you…this hotel had it all!

One of these characters happened to be the Houseman at our hotel. A Houseman or Housewoman for those of you unfamiliar with hotels, is the person that assists Housekeeping with any needs, normally running ragged through the hotel, stocking Housekeeping supplies, folding linens, cleaning common areas, etc. The roll can vary from hotel to hotel. Our Houseman was one piece of work! He was a big gay black man with a bit of a lazy eye. Growing up in a small town like Southern Maryland, there weren't too many gay people in general (or at least out), but I would have never been able to tell if this dude was gay if someone hadn't told me. He was real chill, cool, polite, deep voice, and very blue collar. As I came to find out, working in the hotel industry, you come across quite a bit of gay people, mainly because they tend to be naturally social and hospitable (well, most). Some of my best memories and friends are from this crowd of goofballs I worked with! This Houseman was my first taste, and he certainly didn't disappoint.

This guy would get caught on the reg (regular) by Housekeepers or the Engineer just straight kicked-back in a guest room chair with one foot up on the ottoman with his shoe kicked off, just passed the hell out! Apparently, he had an old injury on his foot so he would always be walking around with half of his shoe hanging off of that foot, with his pant leg dragging along the floor getting torn to bits. I was simply a Front Desk Agent, so it wasn't really my place to say anything to him, instead I just made fun of him. I will never forget him always responding with a "Shut-up Tony," and us both laughing. Although he wasn't the most professional looking, it really didn't matter because this guy had one of the most important traits you need to succeed in the industry…a big personality! I don't even think guests thought twice about that foot or lazy eye because of his great attitude. If anything, it added to his goofy and friendly personality that people loved. Nardy, yes that was his name, short for Ernarde, would also get caught on his flip cell phone more than I think was humanly possible. I'm pretty sure he went over his minutes daily on the job. SMH! He had a huge heart and a huge passion for making the guests happy. He may have slacked off on his job duties at times, but at the end of the day it is a customer service industry, and this guy had it nailed down, and had plenty of good *TripAdvisor* reviews to back it up!

I remember one day in particular, I told Narde I could drop him off at his place on my way home from work. Come to find out, Narde lived in Section 8 housing (government funded). I am pretty sure he lived with an entire family...like, multiple generations of a family. I didn't judge, because I was living with my parents, free of charge, at the time. It really made me think because I was making a measly $8.25 an hour at the desk, and he was at the minimum wage, which was near $7 an hour at that time. It was just eye-opening because he was an adult, and I was still a young buck. It gave me some super low expectations for my future in the industry and further encouraged me to succeed and move as high up as I could and make as much as I could. I always remember (well, and still do) complaining about my low pay, so this made me complain even more, but on behalf of those like Narde, in the hotel industry.

This hotel came pre-stocked with another gem, named Peaches. Peaches was our Executive Housekeeper. She was the besssssttttt! She didn't put up with ANY of the Housekeepers shit. My kind of Manager! No letting people bend the rules, including Narde! She had worked there for a century, even when it was run by the old ownership company, so she had the system down pat, and could tell you every nook and cranny of the hotel, blindfolded! She would come into the hotel, dissect the numbers for the day, and immediately call our on-call Housekeepers, if needed. The Housekeeping schedule is more unpredictable than that of the Front Desk. Housekeepers normally have a few days that they are scheduled to work the entire day, and then the rest of the week, they are on-call based on how busy the hotel was the night before. They would clean all the rooms necessary, and then the next day, the only rooms needing cleaning were the overnight guests, and those rooms that were checked out of. It was great working the desk with Peaches in-charge because I would never hear complaints from the guests concerning unclean rooms (unlike other hotels I eventually worked at). This is HUGE for Front Desk Agents because being the punching bag for guests, when one common problem is eliminated, it makes our job a lot easier, and makes us less likely to want to punch the guests right back.

One of my most fond Front Desk memories involved Peaches. I had a guest come down to the desk to check-out with a large clear trash bag full of his clothes. Interesting. Time for a luggage upgrade buddy. Quite resourceful I must say, but this was normally not a good sign. Just gonna go out on a limb and assume this was a cash-paying guest. Just a hunch. Yup, he was. As with any check-in, guests must put down a security deposit, also known as an incidental deposit (each hotel requires different amounts). If someone wants to pay all cash, it gets a bit tricky because we would hold that cash deposit until their room is cleared by a hotel associate after they leave the room. This could be the Executive Housekeeping, Engineer, Houseman, or even another Front Desk Agent running up to check the room. They are checking for damage, smoking odor, missing furniture, etc. in the room. Believe it or not, there are still a lot of people that prefer to pay in cash. Not to stereotype, but typically when a guest pays all cash at a hotel, there is usually some sketchiness associated with it. If it takes a while to get a response from the person checking the room, that's usually not a good sign. When they do eventually call you back at the desk or even come down, and inform you of some bad news, you as the Front Desk Agent, or acting Manager, have to tell the guest they will not be getting their deposit back. Oh boy. This never goes well. Usually, there is a lot of yelling, denial, and a lot of blame placed on another individual (or made-up individual) that was in the room as well. But this still won't change the fact that they aren't getting their deposit back. So if you decide to pay with cash at a hotel, you better make damn sure that none of your buddies, or hookers, are smoking or damaging that room.

I kindly explained to the gentleman that he would not be receiving his deposit back as he smoked in the room. As expected, he freaked, and proceeded to tell me that his girlfriend must have smoked in there. Riiiggghhhhtttt! Let's just say he would not have been nominated for an Oscar with his acting skills. He insisted me to give his money back multiple times, and even threatened to call the Police. I told him politely to hang tight and went to check the room with the Peaches for a second opinion, and to give the guest the courtesy of doing so. She opened the door, and my God, I think I caught lung cancer immediately! The smoke smell was mixed with some cheap fragrance, which was most likely sprayed to try and cover up the smoke smell. Didn't work. So we did the normal checks just for extra proof: Checked the windowsills (as guests will try and puff out of the windows and ash will fall on the sill); checked the trash cans (easy place to find cig box, wrapper, or even used cigs); and the toilet and sinks (to check for more ash as they think the bathroom fan with soak up the smell if they smoke in there). In this case, there was ash in ALL THREE places! #RookieMistake. And to our surprise, he left a lovely gift right beside the desk immediately when you walk in the room, a nice little dime bag with some white powder inside. Classic! Peaches and I looked at each other and her jaw literally dropped as she didn't see it the first time she checked the room. She went to pick it up, and I shouted, "Don't touch that! You don't want your fingerprints on that shit!" So now we had even more of an issue on our hands. The guest had already told us to call the Police, so guess what we were going to do next?

We returned to the desk downstairs and the gentleman proceeds to drive us bananas, demanding for his money and how he's calling the Police...blah blah blah...making a huge scene in the lobby. He did indeed call them before we even got the chance to. The Officer arrived and came to the back office where we explained the situation and what we found. He was cool, calm, and collected. The Officer had myself and Peaches go with him to the gentleman's guestroom. He saw the evidence he needed, and explained to us how we would go about this with the guest. We returned to the desk to get the guest and all of us went back up to the room. We stood outside of the room and the Officer made the guest verbally admit that it was indeed the room he stayed in. After repeatedly saying that it was his girlfriend's perfume that made the smell, he finally admitted it was his room. We opened the smoke-filled room, and once we all entered the room, the Officer had the guest again verbally admit that it was indeed his room, and he agreed.

Immediately after, the guest noticed the lovely little mystery white powder bag and immediately positioned himself to cover with his foot while we stood there and continued to talk. The Police Officer asked him repeatedly to step aside, and the guy tried to drag the bag with his foot with him as he moved. Unfortunate for him, that didn't work too well, and the bag ripped open, dragging the white powder across the floor. Haha! The Officer asked the guest what it was, and of course the guy denied it was even his. Lawwwddddd!

Then, the Officer had us all head back downstairs. When we all finally made it back downstairs after that awkward elevator ride, he explained to Peaches and me in private what we could do for the guest: Give him the deposit back, and hope he never comes back; or keep it, and file a no-trespassing. Fuck yeah we were getting our money back! That was our protocol, and we will follow it. This room would have to be out of inventory for a few days while Housekeeping and Engineering worked to get the smoke smell out, so we were definitely taking that damn deposit money. Come to find out, the Police Officer had a drug test kit in his car and apparently that white powder in the bag was not one-hundred percent cocaine. It had some ingredients found in cocaine, but it was not pure, so the Officer believed the guy was selling it to people and ripping them off. Classy move. Go figure, our General Manager wasn't present for this lovely event. In fact, I don't think he even found out about it. A few weeks later, we ended up seeing the guy on the counties go-to drama website, *TheBaynet.com*, as he was arrested for drug possession. Karma is one biatch. Fucking cash paying guests. SMH.

Someone who I learned to work very close with, but tell very little to (gossip queen), was the Sales Manager on property. She was the one that initially brought me in for the interview, so I loved her for this. She seemed to really like me. I think it was because they didn't get many clean cut, preppy, well-dressed, well-mannered gentleman coming in for jobs there. Those people had more legit jobs. FML. She was responsible for the pro-active selling of the hotel. She would do whatever it took to bring business to the hotel, mainly giving people or entire companies a special corporate rate, and who knows what else with some of the outfits she would wear to her company visits. Let's just say they were questionably appropriate for work, but hey, whatever works! The hotel was located outside of a naval base and surrounded by government contractors…a goldmine for hotel business! These companies would fly people in all of the time and they would need a bed to lay their heads on. Our hotel's fresh remodel and dirt cheap rates (normally at the government per diem) helped gather this business. Government per diem rates are the max rates that government employees are allowed to spend on their sleeping arrangements in order to get reimbursed. If they get a room over their daily per diem, it would come out of their pocket. So a lot of government employees would try and find a hotel cheaper than their per diem limits so that they could bank the leftovers. They would do this for their meals as well. Must be nice. Although, I have heard the government has cracked down on this since then.

The Sales Manager's pretty face certainly helped her sell. She was flirty, and as I said earlier, wasn't afraid to show a little skin for a sale. She was an ex-Bartender with a raspy New York accent, nicely placed tattoos, and a nice figure. She was a great resource for me when I started, as far as general hotel knowledge, sales secrets, and hotel gossip. We ended up butting heads in the end because I found out she was feeding things I would tell her in private to the GM and Owner. Not cool! Rumor on the street (or should I say, hotel hallways) was that she may have had more than just a working relationship with the GM. Heyooooo! Whatever it takes to climb the company ladder, right? She had a big personality and brought people into the hotel, and that's all we could ask for. At the end of the day, I could talk smack about every single person I've worked with, but if they get their jobs done successfully, that's really all that matters in the end. No one ever said we have to be BFF's with our coworkers, but it is fun to talk shit and complain. It's human nature…so screw her!

Our Chief Engineer and I became very close. He was around the age of my father and was a real cool cat. Like typical guys, we would shoot-the-shit about sexy girls or cracking beers when we got home, the usual. He had been there a few years too many, and I could tell he was frustrated with the way things were run around the hotel. Ray loved to hear that I was trying to change things to make them better. He had been trying to change shit in his department forever. It was evident that the things he needed in order to fix things around the hotel were not being provided by upper management. It's hard to get perfect survey scores and keep *TripAdvisor* scores high when you have a leaky sink, malfunctioning door lock, or toilet lid sliding off as you're taking a crap. I simply became the middle-man between him and upper management to get things accomplished. For some reason, upper management valued my opinion and would listen and take my suggestions much more than they would his. Ray loved me for this, and saw that I was God's gift to the hotel. He would vent to me about other employees or our crappy pay, and how he was looking for other jobs. I was right there with him. We knew we were both on the same page and could keep each other's secrets safe, unlike other coworkers. He actually warned me about the snitching tendencies of the Sales Manager.

Along with mastering being the middleman between the staff and the General Manager, I did master quite a few other things at the desk. First and foremost, I became the master of checking guests in/out and handling a long line with ease. You learn quite quickly that the desk is and ALWAYS will be short-staffed. At times, the desk would be so ungodly slow that you realized why you didn't have help at the desk, but in the snap of a finger, this could change to getting slammed at the desk, and wanting to kill yourself and your Managers for leaving you stranded by yourself. You are forced to learn little tricks of the trade to survive these death traps. For example, if you are getting clobbered in the morning when guests are trying to check-out, you can politely shout out, "If anyone is trying to check-out and doesn't need a printed copy of their bill, you can leave your keys with me and I will email you a receipt (and likely forget to). This would normally cut the line in half because guests literally don't need to do anything when checking-out. You can just roll out. It only benefits the Housekeepers because by the guest letting the desk know, the Agent can check-out the guest in the system and that room can be cleaned earlier. Worst case, the Housekeeper gets to their room later after check-out time and will see the guest has checked out. If they haven't, then that's a whole other issue. I always laughed when guests would freak out because they "forgot to check-out." I would have guests come back to the hotel to drop off their room keys as they were afraid the hotel monster would come after them. But very nice of them to do so! Although, from my understanding, some hotels will charge guests for not returning the keys. Not sure if that is actually true, or just a rumor, or just a method hotels use to keep and reuse keys to save money and "the environment" (eye roll). Sounds like a farce to me.

Let me tell you what, patience will be your best learned trait after working the Front Desk. I was far from a patient person, but you really become accustomed to it at the desk. It is the only way to keep sane. For example, when that line for check-outs is building, you just have to learn to handle them one-by-one. At the end of the day, if the guest didn't prepare enough time in advance to assume someone would take a moment before them in line at the desk, than that was their issue and not yours. If they decide to make a complete ass about it in line, then be polite about it and let them know you will be right with them. Here, you get a mixed bag of results: 1. The guest shrugs it off and waits his/her turn; 2. The guest you are currently handling at the desk says, "No worries," and lets the other guest in front of them (best case scenario); or, 3. The guest throws a complete conniption fit, huffing and puffing waiting in line, then gets to the front of the line, asks for a Manager (because they were in such a rush), complains about how long it took and that we weren't staffed well enough, then explain how they are late to an important meeting or flight, then asks for some sort of discount, then when denied of a discount, threatens to write a horrible review. The list goes on. That's when I happen to misplace my nametag so they cannot see it. Whoops. That is also when I slide to the other computer at the desk and continue to work the line of check-outs and back myself away from that virus guest and let my Supervisor handle. The only major problem here is when there is no Supervisor on Duty, and it is just you to take the beating and do the best you can to handle the situation and move onto the next. Like I said, mastering patience, one guest at a time.

I also became the master of rekeying guest room cards. What a pain in the ass! For whatever reason, hotel key cards and magnets along with pretty much fucking anything else you put in your pocket do not get along. Back in the day, cell phones must have had some sort of magnet or something in them because if your key card was in the same pocket with the phone, forget about it! That bastard wouldn't work anymore in your door. Also, because we had a lot of government employees staying at this hotel, they would often go through security to get into the building they were working in. Guess what, that bitch deactivated the key cards too. Christ almighty! It was extremely frustrating to the guest after a long day of work, going up the elevator, and down the hall to their room just for their card not to work, and then have to come all the way back to the desk. That is one thing I really felt bad for the guests for. It was out of their control, and ours. This would not only happen for non-working keys, but also dying door locks. Those particular door locks were battery operated, so they do indeed die eventually, although at this cheap-ass owned hotel, it seemed they always bought the refurbished ones, because we had dying locks on the reg! Come to find out, those replacement locks are expensive as shitttt, and take forever to order, and receive! Who would have known? Certainly not me.

Money handling also became an acquired skill of mine. I dabbled with it at my previous Server job, but here it was more strict. We had a locked drawer at the desk that each Agent had to count at the beginning of their shift, and at the end. This was surprisingly important because you didn't want the idiot on the shift before you leaving you with a hundred dollars short in the drawer and you be held responsible for it. We would have to take the cash that we took in from cash-paying guests and put in a money envelope with details on what was in the envelope, such as how many pennies, nickels, bills, etc. Even my OCD-ass thought this was a bit excessive. Then we would have to have someone else double check and sign off before we dropped it in the safe to never see again. The GM would come at the end of the week and empty the safe. We would also write down the details of what was left in the drawer so that it would be at the correct amount for the start of every shift. Annoying as shit! I got in the habit of starting to count the drawer about fifteen minutes prior to my replacement at the desk showed up. This way when they rolled in, I could roll out and not fuck around at the desk. After eight hours of standing up and dealing with guests bullshit, I was ready to bounce. The only problem with this little shortcut was when a guest came to the desk within that fifteen minutes to make a cash transaction. Those little fuckers! You could always pull an "Oh, my cash drawer is messed up, would you mind paying with debit or credit?" Sometimes it worked, most of the time it didn't. Errrr!

Another odd skill I mastered was the art of getting good reviews for the hotel (to offset the shitty ones previously mentioned). This hotel chain, along with many others, automatically sends out a survey after a guest checks out. The obvious solution to get good reviews is to simply give good service throughout their stay, and keep the hotel clean. Some of these things we can control, but some are out of our control. For example, if they happened to check-in when the line at the desk was a mile long, they are not going to be happy from the get-go. If their key card was having issues throughout their stay, this could warrant a four out of five stars. They could have had a loud and obnoxious guest in the room next to them, or had TV issues, or a squeaky bed. What we can control is our recovery from those issues. Sometimes, a good recovery can earn you an even better review than the one from a guest with no issues at all. But some things and/or some people are unrecoverable. In these special cases, we would use a simple little trick that is wrong and unethical in so many ways. We would simply remove the email address we had on file before they checked-out so that the guest would never get the survey to begin with. No survey equals no bad review. Simple. Hehe. Although, a lot of hotels send surveys upon the guest checking-in or during the middle of their stay, so deleting it right before check-out doesn't do shit. Those bastards. They figured us out! Also, anyone can go on *TripAdvisor* or other review sites and leave reviews whenever they want.

There are lots of little tricks to gain and keep guest loyalty. Along with the little techniques and goodies that the Sales Manager would provide to guests to bring them back that I mentioned earlier, there were things the company did that helped with guests returning. The company made themselves known through commercials, web ads, room key card graphics, and banners/memorabilia at the hotel itself. If a promotion was being run, we would receive boxes with new pens or cards to hand out, or big banners we were to display in the lobby. We would have to be knowledgeable at the desk with whatever new campaign was going on. It was pretty cool because it made you feel in a sense, proud to work there. I think no matter what your job is, there is nothing cooler than seeing commercials or ads of your place of work. It reminds you that you work for a legit-ass company and makes you feel a little more secure with that company. It also makes guests recognize and respect the brand more. The goal is for them to enter those hotel doors and already know what they are getting into, because of the national representation.

This hotel chain had a great rewards program as well. Guests could earn free nights in no time! At the time, if you stayed five nights, you would get a sixth night free in the amount of points that you had accumulated. Of course, each hotel in the chain had different point values associated with them. For example, a waterfront hotel or one located downtown in a major city would both required more points to redeem and use there. This is a pretty impressive incentive if you stay at hotels quite a bit throughout the year. Those guys from the electrical company I spoke of earlier would load up on some rewards points. This opened me up to how important hotel rewards were and how some people were obsessed with them, as they should be! At the desk, we were trained to promote the rewards program at every check-in because it was a great way for the company to gather information about a certain traveler and do whatever we could to keep them loyal to our brand, just by getting their email. It boggled my mind as to how many people wouldn't even bother hearing about the rewards program just because they wanted to speed through their check-in. Don't get me wrong, when you're tired AF from traveling, the last thing you probably want to do is listen to a spiel or sign up for some shit and get bombarded with spam emails. Little did they know though, they could be redeeming points they earned for all sorts of free stuff, such as hotels, flights, rental cars, and more. And for God's sake, it's free! No brainer!

It seemed that upper management noticed my drive to succeed and the great job I was doing at the desk. They heard it from not only my coworkers, but guests as well. I bonded well with everyone and they respected my strong work ethic and how I handled situations at the desk. The GM and Owner actually came to me one afternoon at the end of my shift and asked me out of the blue if I would be willing to step into the Front Desk Manager/Assistant General Manager role overnight if they decided to let go our current one go. Umm…awkward. But, fuck yeah! Duh! What else do you say to that? Super weird though because I liked my current Front Desk Manager/AGM. Yeah, she may have been very shy and easily stepped on by guests and some of her staff, but she was a nice lady, meant well, and taught me a lot. Oddly enough, before upper management even got the chance to let her go, she quit overnight. Duammmmnnn! So, guess who was promoted within just three months into starting in the hotel industry? This guy! Not exactly the way I would have scripted it, but sometimes you have to take what you can get. This would come to be the true moment that sucked me into the industry. Remember, I only started this job to make money while I was getting my feet wet in the real estate game.

So there I was, not even a half a year out of college, and had already cycled through three jobs. I officially dropped the Real Estate Agent and Server jobs. Hotel management was built for me. I was already good buddies with everyone at the hotel in all departments, so they were just as excited as I was that I was now the one making decisions. They knew that I would come in with fresh, young ideas, and make shit happen…which this place needed badly! Fortunately, I had already gotten a lot done without even being in this new role. There was one little set-back…my management training was non-existent. I had my puny Business Management degree from college, but let's be honest, it doesn't exactly prepare you to manage immediately, especially in the crazy-ass hospitality industry. The hotel's solution...have the General Manager sit with me for a total of about five minutes to show me how to do payroll and fix time issues with the pay clock, and that was a wrap. Five minutes!? WTF? He said he would handle billing, and just have me put the bills in his mailbox. Umm...ok, seemed easy enough. Little did I know, as much as I complain now-a-days about how long job training takes, I learned to be very thankful for it, because here I was being fed to the wolves for a mere $12.50 a goddamn hour. A solid $26,000 a year before taxes. That was the same cost of only one year of my college. Yikes.

I had already been dealing with complaining hotel guest issues as an Agent, so that was nothing new to handle. The only difference now was that I could override rate discounts, and not have to reach out to my Manager to better resolve issues. I was now able to hold meetings with different department heads to get updates on supplies needed, employee issues, etc. I was now able to order things and fix issues that had been in limbo for years prior. Instead of just bringing it up to management and hoping it was ordered, I simply did it myself. Well, for the most part. I implemented a bonus plan based on our Guest Service Satisfaction (GSS) scores and got upper management on board. This stuff I was accomplishing was not rocket science. It all needed to be done, it had just lingered. I could only assume because the GM and Owner were very cheap. The previous Manager likely got to the point where she tried to get shit done got denied multiple times, and just gave up. Not to brag, but I was the best thing that ever happened to that hotel, and pretty much ran that bitch by myself. On my resume it reads: "Front Desk Manager/AGM," but in reality, it should read "Hotel Manager/Director of Operations/Director of Front Office/Human Resources/Fucking Boss!"

I experienced a few new things while being a Manager. The first of which was employee spot checks. I would have a checklist that came from corporate dedicated to each position at our hotel to make sure we were staying up to par with the brand standards. At first, I thought this was stupid and a complete waste of time, but it was pretty impressive what I discovered when going through these detailed checklists. For example, for our Houseman's checklist, there were items such as dirt on the public stairwell guard rails, and dirt in between lobby floor tiles. To check, it would be as simple as rubbing my hand along the guardrail to see if there was dirt. And the tiles, if there was discoloration, out came the toothbrush to scrub it out. It was more of a deep-cleaning checklist, but nonetheless, it kept the hotel spotless in areas that we may not have thought to check, but the guests might. At any time, someone from corporate could drop by the hotel and do a spot check. If you scored badly time-and-time again, the brand could actually give you the boot, and ownership would be left to find a new brand, so it was imperative we do these checklists.

Another new process to me was handling the hiring and firing at the property. I was pretty excited about this task as we needed some higher quality individuals, at the desk in particular. I quickly learned that hiring is not as easy as one may think. You get about a thousand responses to your job postings, and have to comb through the good ones, and take time out of your already busy day to interview them. Keep in mind, this was before the days of all of the job board websites. Thank goodness this hotel did not have a specific interview guideline I had to follow (or I hope they didn't, because I didn't follow it). I would just ask the usual: "Why do you want this job?; What experience do you have?; Do you have reliable means of transportation to/from?; Are you willing to work crazy-ass hours and deal with crazy-ass guests by yourself?; Why should we hire you for the job?", etc. Of course, you forget about half of the questions you probably should have asked after the interview is over, similar to a first date. You have to be careful not to ask questions that will get you sued. The workplace has become very PC (politically correct). The interview process forces you become very open minded because you gather so many stereotypes based on the resumes you read, and also during the phone interviews before ever meeting the candidates in person. You will get this super experienced person and their references all check-out, but when you meet the person, they are dressed poorly, or smell, or are super rude. Not everyone is built for hotels, so if they aren't polite and presentable to the person they are trying to get the job with, you could assume they won't be with guests either. Let's face it, there aren't many positions in the hotel besides upper management (even that is debatable) that requires anything that couldn't be trained in less than a week's time frame, so if you have manners, and present yourself well, you are likely a good fit.

I remember my first hire was a girl, whom I found out, had worked at the hotel years ago when it was under the different brand and owner. She had quite a bit of hotel experience, so I was a little concerned as to why she was applying for only a Front Desk Agent position. Apparently, she had a rough go at her previous gig. It happens. I honestly didn't even question what went wrong because I needed an Agent ASAP, and one that already had experience in not only the position, but the computer systems we used as well. This would take any training time off of my plate. She could pretty much start from Day 1. It gave me a glimpse of hope in the interview process that I was beginning to lose faith in. Occasionally some great ones come through. She was hired. Bad idea.

This little-miss-perfect turned out to be a huge know-it-all. I don't mind that as long as you don't act like that in front of the guests, and more importantly, your coworkers and boss. Well, this girl not only came equipped with hotel knowledge, but a big set of balls as well (not literally). She would specifically call me out on certain things that I was doing incorrect, or not as efficient as her. As you may recall, I was technically still newish at the hotel, so was indeed still learning. I don't mind advice, in fact, I am welcome to it, but sure as hell didn't need someone I just hired trying to talk down to me. There is a difference between dropping some advice or a tip to someone, but another to come across like an ass and make someone look stupid. Not cool. I brushed it off, mostly because I am nice and most things are not worth the argument. She was late on the regular, and would come in hungover (maybe even drunk) quite often. As I said, I was a very play-by-the-rules kind of guy, so I could care less if someone is two minutes late or thirty...you're still late. The person working the shift before you had to stay that extra time because of it, so don't even apologize to me that you were late, apologize to your coworker. I remember playing soccer in this adult league with a bunch of old high school buddies, and get calls from the Front Desk Agents all pissed off because this girl hadn't shown up for her shift. Ugh! This meant my tired and sweaty ass would have to go cover the desk until this chick showed up, if she even did. You best believe I wrote her ass up every time she was late, or slipped up.

One night drew the final straw with this bimbo. I was covering the night shift for one of our Agents, and guess who comes around the corner from the direction of the guest rooms, and stumbles up to the desk, completely hammered? You guessed it, this chick. Wow. I am going to assume that she thought the original Agent would be working the desk that night, instead of me. Come to find out, she had been drinking with our most frequent guests, the guys from that electric company. I knew she was friendly with these guys from noticing their interactions at the desk, but didn't realize how friendly! SMH. I likely would have brushed it off had she saw me and continued about her business, but instead, she took that moment of drunk courage to unleash her true feelings on me. She ripped on me for being a shitty Manager; that I didn't know what I was doing; how I dressed "too nice"; and pretty much anything else she could think of. I'm not sure what kind of alcohol she had been drinking in that room, but it sure wasn't a happy mood drink, like tequila! I didn't even know how to react. I just kept quiet and responded, "Ok," because I knew we would address this the next time we spoke (sober), when I would show her the front door. Well, let me tell you, that was one awkward ass convo the next day. She threw out an apology, but not a convincing one. Almost like a "Yeah, sorry about last night." My reaction...as the famous Jesse you will meet later in this book would say, "See yaaaaaaaaa!" I should have done my research a little more as to why she left (or was forced to leave) her previous hotel job. Lesson learned.

There was another ray of hope when we had that girl's potential replacement come in for an interview. This girl had a solid customer service background, but not in hotels. She was polite, well-mannered, and very easy on the eyes. It never hurts to have good eye-candy at the Front Desk at a mainly male clientele hotel, similar to the Sales Manager. In fact, The Sales Manager happened to be a big promoter of this girl being hired. I had my doubts with her because she was very girly-girly, with a possible prissy attitude. Most girls like this can't hang at the desk (or so I thought), because let's face it, it's boring as shit, you normally have to wear ugly-ass uniforms, and you have to stand all goddamn day. Heels and standing for long periods of time don't mesh well. Nonetheless, I gave her the benefit of the doubt and hired her. As it turned out, she handled herself well, and actually made suggestions to me of what we could do better, but not in a demeaning way like the last girl. She turned out to be my best agent. Again, those damn stereotypes! The hardest part with managing her was telling her to get off the damn stool that sat behind the desk and be attentive. The obvious fix would be to get rid of the stool, but I couldn't knock her too much because standing for eight hours is brutal, and I definitely leaned on that bad boy when I was working the desk. I could only imagine with heels on, although she could have worn flats. Like I said, girly-girl.

The hotel really started to take shape when we had good staffing at the Front Desk and in the back-of-the-house. The only major downfall to the hotel being in full working order was that upper management would neglect to come to the property even more so than previously. This resulted in issues beyond my control. I learned really quick that management would lie to me on a daily basis. It was second nature to them. The GM would swing in so quickly on his one-day-a-week visits that when I mentioned something to him, I felt it was being ignored completely. I would tell him something and get the "Uh huh, yeah," or simply a head nod...a.k.a. not paying attention to anything I was saying. One of those moments when you can slip in a "Fuck you," and the person wouldn't even blink because they weren't listening from the start. The times when I did manage to grab his attention, I was able to get some things through, or so I thought. I would ask if he ordered a part for me, or paid the so-and-so bill that I kept getting called about, and I would get a "Yes" answer. Well, wouldn't you know, a few weeks later, I wouldn't see the part or kept getting the same damn bill collector calling. I knew nothing was really getting done like he said. Honesty is all I ask for. If we were behind on bills and he wanted me to delay the collectors, then I would. No worries. If we couldn't order a part that month and have to wait until the next, then just tell me that. I can live with that, but what I can't live with is lying to my face, and giving me the work around. I am the most honest person I know, and maybe because of the military family I was raised by, or the Boy Scouts, or learning good sportsmanship from playing so many sports. I don't know, but I think this world would be much better off if everyone were honest. Although, the hotel industry is probably not the best one to be in for honesty, because you are constantly putting on a fake smile, pretending like you like people, and lying, or bending the truth consistently. The industry was indirectly training me to lie and become just like this Manager. Not good.

The breaking point with this shitty management and hotel was when I was blatantly lied to twice in a row on pretty big issues. As I said I earlier, I was able to order new things for the property that had been needed for years. Well, one thing that was desperately needed was pool furniture, and that was beyond my ordering allowance. Pool furniture is insanely overpriced, in case you didn't know. Literally a hunk of plastic lounge chair with spray paint on it is over three hundred bucks. Insane. It was getting to be summer in Southern Maryland and we had to make sure we were ready for it. After my suggestion, upper management ordered someone to come in and fill in the cracks on the pool deck cement, as we had weeds coming out of them all over. It looked like we just went through an earthquake. It reminded me of the pool in the motel from the movie, *Grind*. Well, go figure, they hired the cheapest guy out there to do the job, and you could tell! I'm pretty sure a fifth grader could have done a better job repairing it. I mean it's not hard. Put the putty in the cracks, wait until it dries, sand smooth, and paint. Well, these goons not only did a piss poor job of that, but they didn't even paint over top of it! Ghetttooooooo! So just imagine a pool deck with a ton of different colored patches of cement all over it.

I attempted to look past this and concentrate on things that were in my control. I reminded the GM that we had to get someone certified on our property to run the tests and put the proper chemicals in the pool to keep it up to code. This is required by anyone and everyone that operates a public pool. Having the incorrect chemical mix-up can really hurt, even kill someone. That would be all we needed at this damn place! So, after reminding him multiple times, he decided to have the only trained person be from one of his other properties that was forty-five minutes away. Oh yeah, and the dudes certificate would be there as well, which is required to physically be at the premises with the pool. So, both the man, and the certificate were not on property, but instead forty-five minutes away. A.k.a., if the inspector came, the hotel would fail inspection, and the pool would be shut down immediately. Idiots. I tried to turn a blind shoulder, yet again.

I showed the GM which pool furniture I thought would look good out of this pool supply magazine we would always get in the mail. We only had about two chairs and one lounge chair that weren't missing straps, and the ones that remained were nasty and discolored. There was no way of repairing these chairs! The GM seemed to acknowledge my suggestion, and said, "Ok" and took the magazine with him to his office. I asked, "So does that mean you're ordering them?" And he said "Yeah" as he walked away. Schweeeeeeetttt!!!! My designer dreams were coming together with a poolside redesign in the works, kind of. About two weeks later, I began to worry. I'm very impatient. I'm an Aries through and through. I knew it would probably take a while to be delivered as it was going to be a pretty large order, but thought I would follow up. I asked the GM where the furniture was, and he said they were on the way! Great! A few more weeks passed by and I got another one of those pool supply magazines, and still no pool chairs. More than a month seemed a bit excessive for delivery time. So, I asked the GM again in person when he came in on his usual Friday-only visits what was going on with them. I let him know that I got another magazine, so it reminded me about them (even though I thought about it daily). He asked to see the magazine, flipped through it, and then asked, "What happened to our old furniture?" My face had to have been as red as a damn tomato in anger when he asked this question ever so calmly, as it was obvious that he had never ordered the new ones in the first place. Are you fucking kidding me? Like seriously? I literally had to take a few laps outside to cool down before getting our Chief Engineer, Ray, to walk with me to the shed to grab the few shitty-ass pieces of pool furniture to prove to the GM what we had, which we already told him over a freaking month ago when he was supposed be ordering the fucking new chairs!!! Unreal! The pool was supposed to open like the next day! I hope the guests remembered to pack their own pool chairs!

The second lie was THE deal breaker. You could say it was the straw that broke the camel's back. Shortly after I took over as AGM, as I mentioned earlier, I convinced the GM to instate an incentive program for all of our staff. It would be based on survey scores as we were not only trying to increase them, but also show our staff that we cared about them financially. The GM agreed that if all departments hit over ninety percent, then everyone would receive $100 bonus for that month. This was not as easy as one may think, especially since we were not one of the major big-dawg hotel chains, and not having the best product in the land. I suggested to the GM that we write something up and everyone sign to agree to it (both him and each individual employee). This way, we knew it was official and would be taken seriously. He didn't find it necessary. Ok then. Everyone busted their asses to hit these numbers, even Narde's goofy ass! Also, the new girl at the desk because she was all about an extra hundy spot on her check, because remember, Front Desk Agents were at a whopping $8.25 an hour. Wouldn't you believe it, as the first month completed and I received the final scores, each department actually hit above that ninety percent! Holy shit. It worked!

So me, being the payroll man, I smiled as I input the extra hundred bucks on everyone's paychecks, as I felt that I truly played a part in bettering the lives of my employees. I shot the Owner an email just to give him a heads up that this would be on everyone's checks, as the GM was out of the country at that moment. The Owner replied to my email with, "Are you sure he [the GM] approved this?" Well no shit, Sherlock! I'm not just going to throw an extra hundred dollars on everyone's paycheck for the hell of it. I confirmed with him that this is what we all agreed on, and he could ask the Executive Housekeeper, the Sales Manager, and every other freaking employee there that stood in front of the GM as he announced it to the team, of course without giving me credit for the idea. Sure enough, I get an email from the GM overseas, saying that we actually didn't make the bonus because each department had to not only be over ninety percent, BUT ALSO this separate category, "Total Hotel" score had to be above ninety percent. What in the fuck!? We were in the high eighties in that category. This was never ever discussed and was complete and utter bull shit from the king of bull shitters. Unreal.

That did it for me. I was not going to work for someone that lied straight to my face on a daily basis, especially when it started to impact my money, and every other employees. That is the sole purpose as to why we work, at least the majority of us. I went home, wrote a multiple page resignation, put it in an envelope with my company-issued phone and keys, dropped it in the GM's little plastic mail collector outside of his dusty, unused office, and called it quits. I believe in integrity, and if my two bosses didn't, then I'm out. And let me tell you, I did not hold back on my letter, telling upper management EVERYTHING they were doing wrong, and what needed to be done to correct that mess of a place. And guess what I have still in all of its glory? Enjoy, and don't judge my poor grammar from then, but I wanted to keep it authentic:

[General Manager],

I appreciate having the opportunity to be the Assistant GM of the hotel. I learned quite a bit during the short time period I held the position. Unfortunately, it was not quite what I was looking for, and because of this, I am formally stepping down from the position.

At this point, I am sure there is not much you may want to hear, but if you do indeed want to know my reasoning, continue reading. First of all, I felt that I was disrespected from the start, being offered an outrageously low salary, and being lied to about the previous AGM making less than that amount. Not to mention, I was working three days on the desk and saving you thousands of dollars. What I thought would have been a good bonus structure turned out to be nonsense because the goals are set too high, and the Front Desk bonus structure requirements would changed as soon as the bonus was met.

Aside from the salary and bonuses, I felt that my training was completely brushed off. Whereas I could have easily been trained in a week, or even a few days, instead it was a last minute, quick temporary show me how to do something. This is not a good way to train anyone in an Assistant GM position. If you had simply taken the time to sit down with me, we could have covered the majority of things needed to properly manage the hotel. And when I did indeed

41

have questions, I felt that you were not willing to give me the time of day because you were constantly rushing to get out of the hotel. I feel that this hotel is on your back burner and it was not fair to me, any other employee at the hotel, or any of our guests.

From Day 1, I felt that I could not trust you at all. When I would simply ask if you were ordering this or that, it was clear to me that these items were being put off and I was just told they were ordered to shut me up. I would rather have been told you were waiting for this check, or until after this date, not a blatant lie to my face. Necessary items, such as paint for Ray [The Engineer] to touch-up spots throughout the hotel, name-tags, pool furniture, business cards - the list goes on. It is not a good way to manage a hotel by putting off taking care of important items. And it is none of my business if the funds weren't available to purchase these things, but I would have preferred to not be treated like someone that didn't matter.

Along these same lines, it was very frustrating when we had a problem in the hotel that I told you about, not being notified when someone has come to look at the problem. I should have been notified as to the status of the situation (ex: ice machine & doors). Not only was I not made aware of what was going on, but Ray, "the maintenance guy" was never updated. So our hotel staff was left out of the loop. Awareness of what was going on in the hotel would have been great, considering I was there everyday running the place.

I found it ridiculous that I found out you were leaving for a week-long trip minutes before you left the hotel. I was given no time to ask you anything that may have been pressing before you left. I also found it crazy that I had never received [his cousin, an Engineer at another property] information until then, considering he should have been the person I had been contacting for supplies from Day 1. Bottom line, I should have been given a list of important names and numbers the first week I took this new position.

The accruals on my and multiple employees paychecks took from the first couple of months I worked here until now to get fixed, and they are still incorrect. That is uncalled for. What is also uncalled for is the fact that if employees get over 80 hours, you expect me to only put 80 hours on their paycheck. Not only is this completely unethical, but this could easily be reported. It is a miracle none of the past employees have done this. I know there were multiple times on my paychecks before I was AGM where my paycheck was oddly enough exactly at 80.00 hours.

The whole wedding group was another issue. I asked you from the beginning about that because I was having problems with it. I had never handled billing with a group before and simply asked for some help. You gave me about 3 seconds of help. However, when I gave them your number and they called you, you immediately got upset. Had you have given me the time of day when I originally asked; it would have never been a problem. The fact that you refuse to give out your number to guests or even employees as the General Manager, strikes me as odd given the position title.

The pool: again I was left out of the loop. I had no idea when the pool openers were coming, and what we were going to do about certification, chlorine, etc. That pool would have failed opening if it were not for me going to WVU and the inspector as well. We do not have certifications from anyone on the property. Someone needs to take the REAL complete course at the hotel (not just [the cousin] up in Waldorf). Not the 30-minute run through. The certificates need to be present at the hotel. The pool will most likely be shut down during the next inspection because of this. This was something you brushed off, like a lot of other things, and it is going to come back to cause issues.

Lastly, I feel that you need to learn to trust your employees. Constantly thinking that everyone is out to get you and your money is ridiculous. Everyone at that hotel works very hard and you have no right to be paranoid about everyone there not working, especially since you are only in the hotel one, maybe two, hours a week. And *saying that our hotel is not "TownePlace" caliber is pathetic. I do not know if you even looked at the scores from last month, but our staff is kicking butt. I believe employee turnover happens like it does at this hotel because the wages are so low, as well as because of faulty bonus structures. I don't know if you have ever calculated what an average person's monthly bills are, and then calculate a months pay at $8.25 an hour. They're lucky to have any money left over. And with our Housekeepers $7.25 an hour, forget it. Housekeepers should be making the same as Front Desk, if not more, because without them, customers would not return.*

It is a shame because I was 100% for the hotel and promoted it to its fullest until I begun realizing what goes on beneath the surface. I commend [The Owner] for stepping in and helping when he came down, and I did my best not to bring him into any of these issues simply because I thought it would change. Not to mention, I did not want to play tattle-tale and be frowned upon later simply because I wanted something resolved, and the only way it would happen was by going to [The Owner].

This is all just some food for thought, but I recommend making a lot of changes before hiring a new Assistant GM and do not take advantage of them in the way that you did me.
Good luck with everything and thank you for this opportunity.
—Tony

….drop the mic!

Believe it or not, I received multiple calls from the Owner trying to get me to have a chat with him. I gave him the time and heard him out. He claimed he wanted me to stay and he was going to put me on the fast track to become the GM, as apparently the current GM was looking to get out of the hotel business. I spoke with my parents about it, and my dad happened to have worked with the Owner when he did the masonry work for one of his hotels. He gave me the advice to lay out what I wanted/needed in order to stay, and if they can't match, then move on. I took his fatherly advice and I proposed a pretty high salary. A high salary for not only someone new in the industry, but a first time GM, and the property being a smaller limited service hotel. Fuck it! I threw in some hefty benefits too. Shockingly, at first, the Owner was on-board. Damn Dad, killer advice! Whelp, later, I received a call and he said he couldn't do it. He used the phrase, "You are too green" in his reasoning why. Green, meaning new/young/fresh. Made sense, because I was. This was probably for the best, because regardless of the new pay and benefits, the dishonesty would likely not change. Time to move on to bigger and better things.

So you wouldn't believe it if I told you, but about a month later, I get a call from Ray, who was still the Chief Engineer there, and he says in a laughing, yet excited manor, "You will never fucking believe what happened at the hotel!?" About a hundred thoughts ran through my head: Did it burn down?; Did it get bought out?; Did everyone get raises and promotions!? Well, close. First off, the county pool inspector dropped by and SHUT DOWN the pool because they didn't have the certification OR a person who was trained on property! LOL! Karma is a bitch! And second, the Owner decided to give every employee the bonus' they earned and deserved, along with individual raises. I guess they did read part of my resignation letter. The General Manager decided to step down and pursue his passion in IT, because clearly hotels was not his strong suit, instead a family tradition. You're welcome! "Tony for President!" The motha fuckin hotel industry!

CHAPTER 2 - LIFE'S A BEACH

All the meanwhile, I had been in contact with an old high school pal, Adam, whose family moved down to Naples, Florida towards the end of our high school days. I was in dire need of a vacation. Adam was living with his sister in a nearby town called Estero, which is where Florida Gulf Coast University is (a.k.a. Dunk City). He told me to "Come on down," in his country twang, Clayton Bigsby (*Chappelle's Show*) accent. Since I had just quit, and had time to spare before starting to work part-time for my dad's masonry company, I figured I would take a little vacation and relieve some much needed stress. And just maybe, I would bring a few crisp resumes and a suit with me. I was feeling quite confident after quitting and hearing about the hotel instating some of my suggestions.

I walked out of the doors of the Southwest Florida International Airport in Fort Myers, and was met with the glorious warm Gulf Coast breeze. I got the same chill in my veins that I get when I land in Aruba on family vacation. When people always ask me why I hate the cold so much, I try to describe this exact chill or feeling. The best way to describe this feeling is that it is the same feeling that you get on those days where you're a little chilly and you hop in your car that has been sitting in the sun for a while and you just sit there, lay your head back, and soak in the heat for a minute. It's like my body telling me, this is where I need to be permanently. Adam arrives in his sweet little black BMW M3. Adam was always a major car buff, so no surprise he was driving a quick little stick-shift roadster. However, I was a bit disappointed that it wasn't a convertible. He did, however, have the windows cranked down because apparently his A/C was not working, which isn't ideal for Florida summers. Although, at the time, I didn't care how hot it was because I absolutely loved it! We cruised to his apartment, warm breeze blowing through our early stages of receding and thinning hair. I was in shock because the roads were all new, crisp, clean, and the grass, bushes, and palm trees perfectly manicured lined the streets. It was like straight out of a movie. Before I even got to

Adam's neighborhood, which happened to be in a gated community right on a golf course, I'm pretty sure my mind was made up that Southwest Florida was going to be my next home.

We actually ended up going to stay at Adam's parents' house in Naples for my visit, which is just south of Estero. Growing up, his and his parents' house was in the same neighborhood as mine. It was just a standard single family home in a cul-de-sac, with the community pool, tennis courts, and whatnot. Nothing too fancy, although they did have a pretty killer man-cave basement where all of us guys would chill at when we were in high school. A lot of video games, *Chappelle's Show*, and gossip about who saw what girls' boobies took place there. Ya know, "locker room talk." His dad was a Dentist and ended up retiring, and his mom was his Dental Assistant, so she did as well. They decided to sell that home and retire in sunny South Florida. A lot of people do this just to soak up the sun year round and sit on the beach. People also do this because there is no state income tax in Florida. In Maryland, there was, and this could set you back a few thousand bucks plus every year. Also, the value of homes in Maryland, and most other places in general, were wayyyyyy pricier than that of Florida. Florida homes are dirt cheap! Adam's parents were able to sell their home in Maryland for $600k plus, and buy a Florida home for just over $200k. Not only was this new home a third the price, but it was your typical Florida-style home with stucco siding, orange terra cotta roofing, equipped with a pool and Jacuzzi. The ceilings were huge...hence the term Florida ceilings, and counters, crown moldings, and other furnishings were super high-end. This house was in a super ritzy, gated neighborhood, with a members-only golf course, pool, spa, you name it! What the fuck? Ridiculous right!? An upgrade for a downgraded price. They were able to take the money they made off the house up North and bank it for retirement, and then soak up the sun and lounge on the beach. Living the life!

Adam was kind enough to show me around Southwest Florida. We biked to the beaches, hit some fancy restaurants, shopped on Fifth Avenue, and went to a couple of the local college bars. We lounged by his parents' pool and Jacuzzi and watched some movies in their movie room without any care in the world of life going on around us. It truly was great and I was ready to move in. His parents, who like I said I had already known, were super hospitable, offering constant food and beer and offering rides to pick our drunk asses up from bars. I couldn't escape hospitality if I tried! Aside from all the fun and R&R, as I mentioned earlier, it jussssst so happened that I strategically packed resumes and a nice H&M suit to apply for hotel jobs in the area, and Adam was kind enough to drive me around to a few Naples beaches and up to Fort Myers Beach that were flooded with hotels. Fucking right!

Florida is relatively the same all over the state. You have the Ocean or Gulf, then the beach, maybe a jogging path or boardwalk alongside, and then condominiums and hotels stretched for miles and miles. You look one way and don't see the end of beaches and buildings in sight, and then look the other way, and it's the same. This made it pretty easy just to drive along the beach and drop off the twenty or so resumes I had printed out with me, and I could have (and should have) brought plenty more. I needed a change of pace in my life, so why not go for a new life in the Sunshine State. I was born and raised in Southern Maryland, and rolled out for college to get the hell out of there, and then for some genius idea decided to go back there after college. It was time to go. I could write an entire different book on the love/hate relationships we all have with our hometowns. Maybe I will. *Love Hate Hometowns.*

I had been to Florida a few times before, but mainly Disney (in Orlando) when I was too young to remember, and then a little trip with an ex-girlfriend's family early in my college years to Destin, Florida. It is impossible not to fall in love with Florida beaches when you visit them, and this trip brought it to my attention again. Maryland beaches were great fun, but we only have three-to-four months of warm beach weather, and it seemed to be getting shorter. The Ocean up there is not clear, or warm, and the sand isn't exactly soft and white. Florida has beach weather YEAR-ROUND, the crystal-clear blue water is warm and swimmable YEAR-ROUND, and you have mostly white baby-powder soft sand (depending which part). As I always say, it is the closest you will get to the Caribbean without actually being in the Caribbean. Having grown up traveling around the Caribbean, it made Florida feel like home. Yeah, there is some humidity and afternoon rain in the summer, but this is expected in a tropical climate. We get the same up North too. Not to mention, the Florida breezes on the coasts make you forget about the humidity. So as long as you are near the beach, you are set. If you are in the middle of the state, that's a different story. The atmosphere on Florida beaches are amazing year-round too because people are normally there vacationing, or have relocated there and love their new life there compared to the one back home. People living in Hawaii or Southern California tend to have this similar vibe. Did I mention the women down there? Holy moly! It helps that being on the beach year-round encourages the women to stay in peak shape, keep a nice golden tan, and can always show off their hidden tattoos or piercings in their swimsuits. Not to mention, these women are much more outgoing, social, and far from prude. Ok, I will stop rambling about Florida. You get the point. When you moving?

I eventually flew back home after picking my jaw off of the floor from all of the beautiful women I saw on my late night ventures with Adam in-and-around the FGCU campus. Wouldn't you believe it, I received a call that next week from a little quaint hotel situated on the north end of Fort Myers Beach that I dropped my resume off at. I remembered this place in particular because it was yellow in color and when I walked into the front door, I was staring right at the pool, overlooking the Gulf of Mexico's calm, gorgeous, clear turquoise waters. Pretty impressive entry! For being a little, quaint, almost motel-looking place, with all outdoor entry doors, it had the location and views nailed! On the phone, the Manager asked if I could come in for an interview the following Monday. Oh shit. Remember, I was back in Maryland. He sounded so interested, that it seemed like the in-person interview would just be a formality. So what did I do? I packed up my little SUV and prepped myself for a Florida move that Sunday.

I broke the news to my parents and siblings, and they weren't too happy. They didn't see why I had to move. They had all lived in Southern Maryland, and ONLY Southern Maryland all their lives (besides my sister who was only a few hours away on the Eastern Shore). I wasn't like most in the fact that I was and still am very independent, and I guess you would say Gen-Y, ready to explore the rest of the country and world. I wanted to experience different scenery and cultures, mainly in warm climate areas though, obvi! My style was always different, my views on design, and overall ambition to succeed and do bigger and better things beyond my hometown were known, so I don't think they were all too surprised. Luckily, my mom was hosting a college graduation party for my sister, so most of the family was in town for it, and I was able to say majority of my goodbyes all at once. The plan was to leave straight from there to begin the long drive to the Sunshine State. My car was packed to the brim ready to roll.

Adam was gracious enough to let me crash at him and his sister's place for a few weeks until I found a spot on my own and secured a job. Luckily, I nailed the interview at the hotel, and was able to quickly secure a little one-bedroom apartment right down the lone beach road from the hotel. It was a stone's throw away from the Gulf beaches in one direction, and the Intercostal in the other direction. Needless to say, if a hurricane hit, I'm pretty sure my apartment would be under water. I found this little slice of paradise for a whopping six hundred bucks a month! This was unheard of for a one-bedroom I am pretty sure anywhere in the entire state of Maryland, and this was freaking walking distance to the beach!!! Electric bills were basically nonexistent because you don't need heat at all throughout the year, and rarely use air conditioning during the summer. Instead, just open up your windows and doors and enjoy the Gulf breezes. Freaking heaven!

I made it. I had my own place, had a new job, and a new life in Florida. The dream growing up in Southern Maryland (as with many hometowns) are to get the hell out, which strangely enough, is a great metaphor for working in the hotel industry. The common saying in the field if you find a non-hotel job is, "You made it out!" I was very excited to get decorating the apartment to my own liking, as I was living with roommates prior and didn't really have the freedom to do so. No, I'm not gay. Although with my love for design, one would think so. In my apartment living room, I painted an entire wall lime green, hung a huge bamboo piece, got an all-white futon, and a jet black leather love-seat. I stripped the kitchen cabinet doors and painted the insides and outsides with a clean, modern white. I was able to display my colorful dishes and mugs against the white backdrop. I had a mini palm tree, modern glass coffee table, and a big Ikea shag rug. My bedroom kept the contemporary/modern theme going with a platform bed and slate grey color walls. The bathroom was equipped with a modern cloth designer shower curtain and nice rugs and wash rags to match. Bachelor pad ready! Oddly enough, my design strikingly resembled that of a hotel. Hmm.

My first day of work at this little quaint beachfront hotel on Fort Myers Beach was an interesting one. For starters, my sanctuary, the Front Desk, was about six feet wide, maybe three feet deep, and only one entrance in-and-out of it. This area housed two people and the occasional Manager sliding in and out. There was a large handmade sailboat behind our Front Desk area, which to this day, I am not sure of the significance other than to look nautical, because sailboats were not a common thing in that particular part of Florida. There were a few shelves and messy drawers behind the desk that needed some serious "Tony OCD Love." There was also this disarrayed stack of metal money boxes where each Agent would keep their money, as opposed to one master drawer like my previous hotel. And then, my absolute favorite part about this little condo-hotel was that we had two tall comfy computer chairs to sit on behind the dual computers! Forget about the guests bitching at you non-stop, just give me a goddamn chair and I'll be happy! Some hotels like my last one, had these little black rubber mats to put behind the desks for Agents to stand on to supposedly help when standing all day, but they flatten out so quickly and don't seem to do jack shit. So, I was in heaven here to start, regardless of the lack of the desk organization and tiny back desk area. The lobby was more like a clubhouse that was located in a separate building from the outdoor-entry guest rooms. It carried the exterior yellow paint color inside, as well as Tommy Bahama-looking wicker furniture, apparently called West Indie style. There was also one big tube TV (I know…) in a closed-in wicker cabinet, with a wicker table and chairs in front of it. This came to be the popular gathering spot for our Midwestern guests to watch the *Green Bay Packer* games.

I thought my previous hotel was behind the times in its processes, until I stepped into this gem! It likely lacked this because it was not a chain hotel like my last. Pretty much everything that should be tracked at a hotel, was not at this one. For example, a Call Log for arrival guests, where us Agents call them a few minutes after they check-in to see if everything was good with their accommodations. They lacked a Housekeeping Room Status Sheet that showed if a room was clean, dirty, vacant clean, or vacant dirty. There was also no Maintenance Issue Log to track issues with rooms or around the facilities, nor a Room Request Log for guest requests that showed if/when they were completed. At this property, it was all being tracked by memory, or maybe the occasional sticky note. SMH! There was no training manual what-so-ever, so my training was on the spot, learn as I went. I immediately started to realize why the AGM wanted me on his team so badly. It needed some serious reorganizing and needed someone from a more structured hotel chain to come in and teach them the proper way to do things. This hotel was owned by a large property management company, but was known for managing mom and pop no-name hotels, rather than huge, reputable chains. I was hired as a Front Desk Agent, but with the intent to be the acting "Lead Agent'", as they didn't really have the budget for a Front Desk Manager at the time. Here we go again with this "Lead Agent" shit!

I was ok with that because I was so ready to take a job on the beach, even if it was to mop the damn floors. My mind to move there was made up. You could say this job move was a mistake in my career path by downgrading my title, and I totally agree, but oh well. It made me who I am today, and part of what inspired me to bring you this story.

I got paired with two polar opposites as my trainers at the desk. One was a hardcore fisherman, named Jesse, who was very set in his ways. He was a perfect example of a Fort Myers Beach local. He fished, smoked, had no car, no cell phone, and no bank account. WTF!? He lived check-by-check, and would cash it, and that would be his money for bills and spending. Sometimes he wouldn't even cash his check and sit on it for a few weeks to a month so he wouldn't spend it. Interesting way to save if you ask me. To put it nicely, he was behind times from living on the beach all his life. All of this being said, he was a cool-ass dude, and came to become my best bud in this laid back beach town. He was super chill, loved drinking, loved the ladies, beach volleyball, and lighting up a little extra-curricular ganja. He was very straight forward with the guests, sometimes a tad harsh, yet still managed to be very hospitable. He had a deeper voice, and was very proud to be a "man." To this day, I haven't met anyone more proud to be able to grow a solid beard in my life. Cracks me up! This dude would tell girls straight to their face within five minutes of meeting them that he would be the best fuck of their lives. Classic! I hadn't seen anything like that being from conservative-ass Maryland. I was a little more shy than that, but definitely learned that I needed to step my confidence level up after hanging with him. Credit Jesse because that pick-up attempt worked more often than not, which to this day, blows my mind. We were definitely complete opposites when it came to style of life. He would rock the Costa sunglasses (the fisherman special) with Croakies (the things that attach to the ends of your sunglasses so you can hang them around your neck), long-sleeve Salt Life shirt, fisherman khakis, and leather flip-flops. Me, on the other hand, would be in John Lennon looking Ray-Ban's, a polo or button-up, above the knee pastel colored shorts, and laced up boat shoes, Van's, or loafers. You could say more of the Miami Chic/preppy look. Jesse rocked what I came to call the typical Florida fisherman beach bum look. You can peg it from a mile away, but I never gave into it! Although, I did end up rocking a long-sleeve beach tee from time-to-time, mainly for night volleyball matches.

The other Front Desk Agent that trained me was absolutely one-of-a-kind. Rodney was the sweetest, skinniest, gayest, youngest-looking older guy you will ever me. Confused? Me too. Very hard to describe Rodney in words without meeting him. Freckled ginger with a bowl cut, glasses, tall socks, and hunched over posture. He also became a really good friend of mine, but not one that I would stroll the town with chasing skirts. Rodney preferred to live his ventures through Jesse and I, as he was happily married to a real nice guy. Rodney was far behind in the technology sector, but not as far as Jesse, who didn't even have a freaking cell phone! When I showed Rodney my Android phone, I think he literally shit his pants with shock. He was still rocking a flip phone. He had been at the hotel for forever, and I think this was the reasoning behind all of the paperwork and lack of computerized checklist and documents. However, where Rodney lacked in technical skills, he made up for with his interactions with guests. The guests absolutely LOVED Rodney, even more so than guests loved Narde at my first hotel. He was the walking definition of great hospitality. He would be hugging guests and conversing with them about their kids and grandkids, and catching up from the last winter when they stayed at the hotel. I think he was on every single *TripAdvisor* review possible. "I can't remember his name, but that red-head kid at the desk was a doll!" Good ole Rodney! He would disappear from the desk quite often because he was off catching up with guests. Yes, he was one of those. I learned to hate that as I got stuck answering all the calls and getting slammed at the desk with guests checking-in. We took all reservations for the hotel at the desk, so needless to say, the phone was always ringing with people from up North trying to book for the warm Florida winter months.

As I mentioned, the hotel was actually a condo-hotel. This meant that each unit was individually owned by someone, and we were just the company who managed them. The owners had access to them for two weeks during busy season, and four weeks during slow season, but many opted not to stay at all, but instead rent it out and turn a profit. When guests weren't there, it rented per night like a hotel. This was very interesting and new to me, coming from a normal hotel. We couldn't just throw guests in any room and call it a day. We had to instead look at the revenue of the units available and place them in one of the lower earning units so it was spread evenly amongst the owners. We had partial ocean view rooms that were on the first floor with walk-out balconies to the courtyard, and then second floor units with balconies that overlooked the courtyard and had that same partial ocean view. Then we had three floors of oceanfront rooms with the first floor balconies being about twice the size of the upper two floors. This made it quite interesting to sell because the unit types were priced the same: Tier 1 - Courtyard Partial Ocean View; Tier 2 - Building 2, which was Ocean View, but set back from the beach; versus the Tier 3 - Oceanfront units that were right on the sand. The problem with this was that for example, a corner, first floor Oceanfront was the same price as a third floor center unit which had a smaller balcony and neighbors on either side. So we would commonly have guests that would come year-after-year and want the exact same unit, because they had stayed there enough times to know which were better than the others. Management wasn't that strict about allowing room requests when I first started there, but it eventually became a requirement and we could no longer guarantee certain units to guests. This was because some owners were getting way more revenue than others because their unit was more desirable. We had owners dropping by the property like hawks while we checked-in guests, and would jump in and ask, "Is my unit open, they can stay in there!?" How freaking awkward is that!? You're already trying to do your damn thing at the desk and put that fake smile on and tell the guests all the amenities and what not, and likely already had a room assigned for them with all of their keys made and welcome packets labeled, and then this bitch-ass owner goes and does this. Then, they would try and sell the guest as to why their unit was better than the others, even though it was likely not, and that's why they were in there begging guests to stay there in the first place. I just had to stand there, try to remain quiet, keep a straight face, and try not to roll my eyes. Something we learn to master working at hotels.

Being the type of property it was, it truly gave guests the home-away-from-home feel. Me personally, I am more of a fan of visiting new locations year after year. Others prefer going back to the same place where they feel comfortable, and employees working there remember them by name. My parents love that shit with their Aruba and Saint Kitts timeshares. I remember in particular, there was one older guest at this property who was the sweetest, yet slightly crazy lady that we all knew and loved, named Nancy. She would stay in her unit for like a month every year. A month. Can you imagine a guest for an entire month? A guest coming to get coffee and a paper and keeping you occupied at the desk for a month. Thank Christ she was the nice and kooky kind of crazy, and not annoying as shit, "please leave me alone" type of crazy. Rodney was on a hug-a-day basis with her. I grew to that level with her eventually, but have never been a huge affectionate guy just from the way I was raised, at least with strangers. Because Nancy was older, we would oftentimes have to check on her for her children that would call us to make sure she was alright. Initially, you would think this would be annoying, but this property was such a small and chill vibe, it was pretty common practice to leave the office and venture around, so it was a good change of pace to go check on Nancy. Just not too much...cough, cough, Rodney!

The layout of this hotel was very interesting, as I mentioned before. All the units had outside entries and seemed very motel-ish. As I would learn, this was pretty common for the beach, especially being in sunny South Florida where the weather was always nice enough to enter a room from the outside (minus those thirty minute rain downpours in the summer afternoons). In other words, it wasn't seen as trashy, but instead, just old-school beachy. The property was actually on the ritzy end of the beach, with celebrities' mansions right up the street in Bonita Beach. The location of the hotel's units made it real tough on Housekeeping. The property was made up of five separate buildings, and four of them had three separate floors, with NO elevators! This made servicing the second and third floors quite difficult as the tiny, fragile, female Housekeepers couldn't bring their supply carts up the stairs. Instead, there were storage closets on each level in each building that the Houseman would keep stocked on a regular basis. That poor guy got some exercise stocking those bad boys on a hot Florida day. The Houseman, Grant, was the man! He played the dual role of the Houseman and Engineer. There really wasn't much to fix besides the old malfunctioning key locks (sound familiar), your usual light bulb replacements, and those damn wall A/C units. Try lugging those M F'ers up two flights of stairs! Yours truly helped with that when he needed. Grant was an older, skinny black man who was clumsy as hell, had a bit of a lisp, and rocked a hat and glasses at all times, with a t-shirt tucked into his shorts. He could walk to and from work from his house, but occasionally rode his scooter in, which he actually let me borrow a few times. That thing was freaking awesome! I always dreamt of owning a scooter on the beach, and only having that as my means of transportation. About ninety percent of the people on that beach were car-less, and either walked, biked, took public transportation, or took their scooter. Bad-fuckin-ass! Florida doesn't require you to wear a helmet on motorized vehicles, so it was so cool/scary AF to be able to ride around with your hair blowing in the wind. It was similar to riding in a convertible, but on steroids. You would just have to throw on some glasses because of possible bugs flying into your eyes.

Did I mention how casual this place was!? Huge plus! I was able to wear khaki shorts with sneakers and our assigned polo. This was amazing coming from my skin tight H&M suits and skinny ties. Pardon my French, but a man's nuts need to breath a bit, so being able to wear loose shorts was beyond amazing. The casual attire went well with the chill beach vibe of the hotel. Our Managers were also casual when it came to the way they managed. This was great, but also a negative at the same time. I compare it to the "cool parents" as a kid. Their kids always seem to end up in jail or fucked up somehow. Our Assistant GM was originally from Vegas, so you already knew he must be either a huge party animal, a complete nut-job, or both. He was my first taste of a Cuban-American. Man, did he love women! Too much! And he really loved their feet. Yeah, feet. Very weird, I know, but it is a fetish to some. This guy would straight-up stand on his tiptoes from behind the desk to look at some of our prettier guests' feet. He would nudge my arm to grab my attention, to point out that the guest had great feet. Awkward AF, but I just laughed and brushed it off. It was like working with my dad, except my dad isn't weird about feet. It was all guys working the desk, so for the most part we all laughed it off and even teased him about it, but after a while it got really old. Rodney was not a big fan of it one bit. Our General Manager was also a pretty casual and cool guy. He drove a Harley into work daily and thought he was a real stud for it. He was an older guy, Florida born-and-raised, and liked to let people know that he was a Harley guy and Florida native. Fuckin loser! He rocked a handlebar mustache and leather jacket over top of his button-up that had one too many buttons open. We don't need to see your chest hair bro. He was the one that handled the billing, and was the liaison between the owners and their units. For the most part, he kept to himself in an office at the bottom of one of our buildings.

In that same building where his office was, our hotel laundry was as well. We had the same basic washer/dryer combo that people have in their households. With the limited number of units and most guests staying for over a week, we didn't need much because their linens weren't cleaned daily like a regular hotel. Most of the washing was actually that of the pool towels. Our night Security Guard, Mike, didn't care that I would do my own personal laundry there during my shifts at night. #Winning. I would put the "Be back in five minutes" sign on the Front Desk counter and run over to that building and toss in a load, and do the same to switch the load. It was great, and free! Mike was the Security Guard for our hotel and the one next door. Double pay for one night's worth of work...can't beat that! His number was posted on our lobby door and guests would call him if they needed anything after our closing hours. The lobby building was only open until 8 p.m. every night, except on Sundays and Wednesdays it was 6 p.m. for some reason. This worked out great for us as Front Desk Agents because that was the latest we would ever have to work on any given day. Our shifts were either 8 a.m. – 4 p.m., 10 a.m. – 6 p.m., or 12 p.m. – 8 p.m. The latter two being great for partying the night before. If we had any guests that needed to check-in after we left, we would simply put their last name on an envelope with their room keys and a sheet of paper with a welcome spiel and instructions to come to the desk in the morning to put down a card for incidentals. We would put these envelopes in a metal mailbox that was on the back of the building, tucked in the little coffee station area (yes, we served our coffee outside…welcome to Florida). So, in essence, anyone could come grab an envelope and have a lovely night's sleep for free. It wasn't that easy though because of Mike being on duty. They would simply call the number on the door if they couldn't find the mailbox, or if for some reason their envelope wasn't left out, and Mike would assist them. Mike had very basic knowledge of Front Desk operations, so he would call Jesse, Rodney, or myself when any issues arose. It was such a crazy way of doing things, as I came from a very secure military family where even leaving a door unlocked anywhere was a sin.

All of Fort Myers Beach pretty much lived by this chill, laid-back lifestyle. There wasn't a care in the world of national issues, politics, sports, weather (unless a hurricane was coming), or anything that didn't affect the beach directly. I remember the biggest news when I lived there was that they were painting the bridge to the beach a seafoam green color. I'm not kidding, look it up. People went to the beach, drank, smoked, played volleyball or other beach activities, and just lived their happy, careless lives. Jesse and myself took part in beach volleyball and would play every chance we could get. We were in a winter Sunday night league that took place on a court at this bar right on the Bay. Yes, I said WINTER outdoor beach volleyball. Again, I love Florida. It was a league of men and women of all ages that played on teams of four. Luckily, we paired up with two older guys that were tall and awesome at volleyball. I was quick and could get to almost any ball, but not tall, and could not spike by any means. Jesse was pretty quick and tall, so could hang with the big boys. Sure enough, we came in second place in the league. I particularly remember the championship games being a bit chilly. When I say chilly in Florida, I mean it was in the sixties, yet we were frozen solid! We were playing in sweatpants, sweatshirts, and socks because the sand was cold on our spoiled Florida toes. Jesse and I would run to my SUV between games and put the heat on full blast to keep warm. Pretty pathetic right?

Jesse and myself would run the town quite often, probably too often. I traded in my paid-off SUV from college for an Audi A4 convertible and we thought we were the shiiiit rolling up to bars in that thing. I eventually traded that car in for a little yellow Audi TT Coupe, so even more so with that little bad boy. We would hit all the typical Fort Myers Beach trashy spring breaker spots, mainly the Lani Kai, The Cottage, and The Beached Whale. The Lani Kai was the definition of Spring Break. The entire hotel/bar/club/arcade/shop was painted in that beachy seafoam green with murals all over. It looked trashy as hell, but they provided live music on the beach during the day, along with tasty slushy drinks, and of course DJ's at night. What more could you ask for? Andddd the bar had a hotel right upstairs. Perfect for Spring Break hookups, and pre and post-game drinking. The Cottage was right next door, and was more of a local, less trashy spot we frequented. The Beached Whale though was OUR bar. This place was a super chill, judgement free zone. Downstairs, it had an interior bar with seating that was cleared out later at night and turned into a dance floor, and a rooftop with a big bar and tons of TV's. It was a very beachy place and you could always count on a solid cheap meal here. We knew all the workers by name, and they knew ours and loved us, as we probably paid half of their rents between Jesse and I. I think we both unsuccessfully tried to get with every cute Server and Bartender that worked there, as well as every visiting beach-goer. If this failed, there was only one place we could count on to drink our losses away…the infamous "Panty-Fleas."

Our favorite spot on all of the beach came to be Fantasies at the Beach, or as we called it, "Panty-Fleas." You can probably guess by the name that this was a high-class gentlemen's club…not! This was the trashiest of the trash strip joints out there. But you know what, they had $5 pitchers of beer. What kind of beer it was is still a mystery. This doesn't sound like too great of a bargain, but in a tourist driven vacation town, drink specials are few and far between. And keep in mind, Jesse and I worked in the shit-paying hotel industry. We would normally go here and just sit at the bar to enjoy the cheap spirits, and watch from afar because we were too cheap to sit at the stage nightly and toss singles. From time-to-time we would go toss some bills to our favorite dancers. We became good buds, even *Facebook* friends, with most of them there. They would come sit with us at the bar to catch up on life. They knew not to bother us with begging for dances. There was only one that I got dances from occasionally, because her body was out of this world. She was a little ratchet for my liking, but I wasn't planning to marry her, although after a few of those mystery pitchers, I am sure I wouldn't have ruled it out. Funny how I mention that, because Jesse actually came pretty damn close to marrying one! He dated and moved in with one! You can take a wild guess how that ended up...short-lived.

Ok, back to the hotel, as nightlife and pretty women tend to distract me. That AGM I spoke of with the foot obsession ended up getting caught with his hand in the cookie jar. Other than the fact that he was your typical Vegas nutcase, but like I said an overall good guy, he tended to not think straight at times. I think he had marital problems at home and sometimes it would carry to the workplace. He would be very grumpy at times for no particular reason. He very well could have been an alcoholic, or hooked on some meds. You remember earlier I said we had our individual money boxes? Well, the AGM had keys to all of them to check up on our money and make sure we had the proper amount in there.

We were actually allowed to use that money to pay for lunch or anything else for ourselves as long as we paid it back. He was pretty lenient in that sense. I never fucked with that because credit cards taught me the lessons on debt already. We were supposed to document everything we took, but we all know how well this property was at documentation. Rodney would frequently pay for his pizza with money from his box, and I never once saw him keep track of it. Sure enough, there came a day where Rodney went to count his box and it was way off. He said he was missing over $150 from it. We had all witnessed the AGM going in there multiple times and taking money from it, but we assumed for hotel supplies, so never really questioned it. My immediate reaction when Rodney told me about his bank being short was, that's what you get for never tracking the money you borrowed from it. Duh! How would we know it wasn't just all his lunches finally catching up to him? He swore up-and-down that he would put in what he owed the next day. He was a trustworthy guy and wasn't hurting with money as I knew his husband did pretty well, so I really didn't doubt him when he argued that he wasn't the reason it was so short. So one would assume, it must have been the AGM. Eventually, the money borrowing from our boxes, the awkward/inappropriate jokes to us, and the obsession with guest's feet added up, and as a collective unit, us three Front Desk Agents had to say something.

The corporate bigwigs, that we didn't even know existed, were scheduled to come to check up on their four Fort Myers Beach properties, and we decided that this would be the perfect time to mention it. We decided not to even mention it to the GM because we knew him and the AGM were buddies, and assumed he would just laugh it off and not do anything about it. So sure enough, after our little meeting with corporate, we shut the door and asked for them to stay a few minutes for us to voice some concerns. We laid it ALL out: The feet, the inappropriate jokes, the missing money, and the overall unprofessionalism. They heard us out, and judging by their reactions, it seemed as if they already weren't too pleased with him. My guess was that our property's numbers were down and that was the whole reason they were there to begin with. Either that, or someone had already complained previously. Chatter had already begun at the property where we were having the meeting, and before we could even get back to our hotel, the Manager's seemed to know something was up, but didn't ask us what. I have a feeling one of the girls working at that property mentioned to them that we closed the door and had a private meeting with corporate. Damn snitches! Although, that's exactly what we were doing.

The timing of all this drama was impeccable because that same week, I received a call from another beach hotel that I had on a whim applied for a Sales position there. And coincidentally, I got a letter of recommendation from the AGM before all of this mess. He reluctantly signed it as he didn't want me to leave, but I think he knew I was ready for bigger and better things, and the hotel that I had applied to was the best one on the beach. He couldn't argue with that. The lady that called me told me that the exact position I applied for was no longer available, but they wanted me to come in for their Valet/Bellman/Concierge role. My initial reaction was hell-to-the-no! But upon further thought, I considered it because if I was truly going to make a lifelong career in the hotel industry, it wouldn't hurt to get experience in all positions under my belt, and possibly move up the ranks in that awesome property. That, and to get the hell away from all the drama going on at my current hotel.

So here I was, an Assistant General Manager, back to Front Desk Agent, and now I am interviewing for a Valet/Bellman/Concierge. What in the fuck!? All of this with a goddamn college degree. I was so dedicated to living on the beach in sunny South Florida, let me tell you what. During the interview, I sat with two ladies. One being the lady that called me, who was the Guest Services Manager. The other, the Guest Services Supervisor, who just so happened to be a young, Hispanic beauty. She had naturally tan skin, curly dark hair, and quite the nice figure. Not someone you would see in my hometown. My mind should have been focused on the interview, but she was a slight distraction that I wasn't expecting. However, she was very serious and professional. It kind of threw me for a loop. She seemed like the type that doesn't allow party boys to get in the way of her career. I can respect that. Kind of hot. As I was told prior to the interview, the pay would be a whopping $8.25 an hour, but the majority of my money would be coming from tips. So being able to get to at least $10 an hour like I was getting at my current job didn't seem far fetched. I would need to make just $14 total in tips in an eight hour shift to average $10 an hour in this new role. Easy. So even though the title itself might have seemed like a downgrade, the pay would not be. I could average anywhere from $50 to $200 in a day, depending on how busy the hotel was. Well, I must have worked the charm enough on these ladies because I got the job offer, and started two weeks after putting in my notice at the other gig. I was sad to leave my boys Jesse and Rodney, but it was time.

This new "Resort & Spa" as they called it, was literally only two blocks from my apartment. This definitely played a factor in me taking the job too. This hotel was a BEAST compared to the others on the beach. It had a pool with a cabana bar and grill, and a spa, which most did not. It was also technically a timeshare hotel that we rented out by the night like a regular hotel. It was twelve stories tall, which stood well above the rest on the beach, as I believe there was a height restriction that this hotel was grandfathered into somehow. My sanctuary at the hotel was actually on the ground level. Guests would pull up with their vehicles, and I would offer to valet it and bring their luggage up to their eventual room. Most decided not to have their vehicles valeted and simply parked it themselves, but I would grab their luggage with a smile and meet them upstairs in the lobby for their check-in. It was a pretty awesome system because the guests would either tell me their names or I would see it on their luggage when I greeted them as they arrived, and I would discretely radio upstairs to the Front Desk Agents to inform them that the so-and-so family was checking-in. The smiling Agents would then greet them BY NAME when they stepped out of the elevator on the lobby level, which was directly above the ground level. Most of the time, they could even have the keys ready for a speedy check-in for the guests. Look at that service! I would normally follow right behind them with their luggage, and escort the guests to their room.

I would show them the main features of their room, and let them know they could reach me by dialing zero on their room phones. I would remind them that me, being the Concierge as well, carried all the discounts and connects at the local spots. This would normally lead them to then try and become my best friend, and hopefully hand me a lovely tip. Then, I would head back down for the next arriving guest, and repeat. Now that's what I call a smooth-ass, customer focused check-in experience!

This was exactly why I came to this hotel. It was an upgrade whether I was working at the Front Desk or the position I took. At the end of the day, I could not only put that I gained experience as a Valet Attendant, Bellman, and Concierge on my resume, but also that I learned the ins-and-outs of how timeshare hotels operate. So my hotel resume now entailed working at a run-of-the-mill chain hotel, a condo-hotel, and a timeshare hotel. This hotel was actually equipped with an on-site Timeshare Rep who would try and sell the dream to guests who weren't already members. She would try and get guests to sign up for a little tour and spiel about the property and how you could pay X amount and get a week or two there in paradise every single year. And if you wanted to go to other places around the globe, you could simply trade in your week(s). I was pretty familiar with timeshares already, as my parents had three of them with a major hotel chain. My parents loved them because we were able to take a week or two long vacation, and then trade the timeshare week(s) we weren't using to pay for our flights. This lady's position was actually that Sales position I initially applied for at this property. She seemed pretty miserable ninety percent of the time, so I don't know if she wasn't hitting her goals, or was just a miserable person. Either way, I was half glad I wasn't given the chance to take that position. I absolutely loved my new job! I was always in a good mood, and I got to sit outside under the shade, with the breeze coming off of the Gulf in my khaki shorts, sneakers, polo, visor, and sunglasses hanging around my neck. I was literally "living the dream!" I got to meet and make the first impression for all of the guests at the hotel, so it kept me in a super good mood all the time, unless they were grumpy (which sometimes happens after a long day of traveling). I got to meet people from all over the world, and learn which countries tipped well, and which didn't. German guests, I'm talking to you! But in all fairness, in a lot of other countries it isn't customary to tip, so I couldn't really blame them. I was given my new minimum wage hourly pay and my earnings relied mainly on these tips. A few three, five, and ten dollar tips would add up quite quickly, and I had no problem bringing in over a hundred a day in cash tips. Also, I would always get the occasional rich old guy that would throw me a fifty or hundred dollar bill at once to make me his bitch for the week. And I would gladly take on that role for a hundy spot!

I was able to drive some awesome cars that I never dreamed of, except for the stick shift ones, as I still to this day do not know how to drive stick. Don't ask how I was a Valet Attendant and didn't know how to. I guess I always lucked out, or we had someone else on duty that could assist when a manual rolled up. Majority of rental cars that tourists get are automatics. I learned the tricks of the trade, like blasting the A/C in the car before pulling up guests cars before their departure, or on a beautiful day, having all of the windows cranked open. I never did take any cars for joy rides as I always feared people were watching from the high-rising hotel, and also because that beach was way too small not to get caught. As I mentioned, I also acted as our hotel Concierge, which was hilarious because I had only lived on the Island for half a year, and was by no means a local expert. But I sure pulled it off! The guests would ask me about a restaurant, and my response would be, "Oh yeahhhhhh, I love that restaurant!" Yup, never been. The Front Desk Agents or Engineers would send guests to me if the guests had questions about the area, wanted to dine somewhere, or to set up a tour. I was the king of coupon books, so guests gravitated towards me. This worked out great for me because restaurants, taxis, and attractions would keep track of who I sent to them simply by me writing my name and hotel on their coupons, and then they would receive them when the guest used them. I got more free rides, meals, drinks, and boat rides that I could keep count of because of these referrals. Most of which, I didn't even get the chance to take advantage of. Eventually, I got a part-time job driving for a luxury transportation company that our hotel recommended (pre-*Uber* and *Lyft*), and I would double-dip by recommending the car service, and then end up driving them myself. I learned the Concierge hustle for sure.

My counterparts at the Valet/Concierge desk were two older gentlemen that had been at the resort for yearssss. One guy by the name of Dave was really cool and spunky, and the returning guests loved him. Dave was your typical Florida boy with a little twang, and you could tell he did nothing but fish, smoke, and drink when he got off. It was funny because our uniforms consisted of a polo, shorts, sneaks, and visor that I legit think was the exact same thing Dave wore off the clock. Maybe swap out the polo for a Guy Harvey long sleeve tee. He rocked the Croakies and Costa sunglasses too, just like Jesse. Dave was on quite a few *TripAdvisor* reviews, and really knew how to work a guest. I think it was just his natural southern hospitality. He did, however, seem like he was checked out mentally from the role since the day I started there. Like, "Thank God this dude is coming in so I can retire," kind of vibe. Sure enough, soon after I started, Dave told me he was retiring and that he was going to groom me to be the head guy. What the hell!? This would be the second hotel (remember my first one) where I timed my start date perfectly without knowing. I was all about it, and I had heard there was a pay increase for his role, like a legitimate salary, not minimum wage plus tips. He ran me through all the daily routines and told me the ins and outs of the resort, and who to trust and who not to. Each property has those snitches that you don't want to vent about certain shit to (like the Sales Manager at my first hotel). He showed me how to sweep the parking lot for trash (yeah, that sucked), change the wording on the billboard with a ladder (yeah, that sucked too), check the arrivals and departures for the day, and check the shift log to make sure there wasn't any imperative information from the shifts prior. All shit that a third grader could do. But after working two different hotels at the desk and even being in charge of the desk (arguable an entire hotel), I was in a chill beach-mode, and this was perfectly fine with me.

My other coworker seemed to be pretty close to retirement too, but didn't quite have the savings to retire yet, so he always seemed a tad grumpy. I don't think he liked that I was half his age coming into the same job as him either. Regardless, he was an alright dude and we became pretty good buds and shot the shit together quite a few times. He and I seemed to work together a lot based on our schedules. Dave would normally work the veteran, morning-glory shift, the other guy worked the mid-shift, and myself, the P.M. shift. This was great because that's when the majority of the check-ins took place, a.k.a. the good tips shift. He likely seemed grumpy because I was catching him towards the end of his shift. We've all been there. Another reason I loved this new role so much was because we didn't have to count a fucking bank at the end of our shifts, so what was there for him to be depressed about!? He kind of looked like a skinnier Santa Claus, but without the beard. He had jolly ole cheeks, white hair, and cute old man giggle. Shopping mall Santa should have been his retirement plan, and very well may have been.

We literally had an old school black and white composition book, like from elementary school, to write our shift notes in. I mean, are you kidding me? In 2013!? Christ, here we go again with this lack of technology. What would happen if someone were to misplace the book, or it was stolen, or even got wet? We would be screwed. I ended up doing what I did best, and organized and digitized our shift notes to a file on our computer at the Concierge desk. This way, we could even email out our shift notes to the rest of the Guest Services Team so they would know what was going on as well. This seemed like common sense to me, but as I found out at the previous property, this little beach town was not known for the use of technology. The grumpster did not like this too much. He didn't like much change period. Regardless, I did it, and management loved it. Gotta look out for number one, and honestly, I was looking out for everyone because it was always my ultimate goal to make everyone's life easier, especially in the hotel biz! The Guest Services Department at this hotel was made up of our Front

Desk Team, the Concierge/Bellman/Valet, and our Recreation Department. I also took the time to reorganize our brochure rack, which was much needed, and came up with a more organized layout for our dirty-ass desk. The desk was indeed outside, so even though it was undercover from the floor above it, it would collect dust, dirt, and dead bugs. Neither of these guys cared as they were the old blue-collar type. They were the type that would brush the dust off a brochure before handing it to a guest and think that would be perfectly normal. Me, on the other hand, continued my typical "Tony OCD fixing" and made this desk area sparkle.

In my down time at the Concierge desk, I would oftentimes venture over to the Engineering room, which was also on the ground level across the parking lot. I would bull shit with the guys over there, or I would head upstairs to the Front Desk and bull shit with the girls in the back office. I always had my radio at my hip, so was always reachable if a guest was downstairs looking for assistance. Also, the desk downstairs was equipped with a phone that guests could pick up and be directed to the Front Desk, and the girls would inform me. I'm telling you, this job was a cakewalk! I miss it.

I met a pretty awesome dude named Chris who was one of the Engineers at the hotel. We were king bull-shitters. We would kick back in the comfy wheeled computer chairs in their office, twirling around, rocking back and forth. You know, the exact thing you do when you're killing time, bored. We would chat about life, great business ideas, and our future careers outside of the hotel industry. He was looking to tap into real estate, which I already knew that shit wasn't for me. As for myself, who the hell knew my future plans. Chris was blonde, blue eyed, just like someone else I knew...myself. The girls at the desk joked that Chris was my long-lost older brother. We would always fill each other in on our beach sexcipades, or lack thereof. The girls at the desk were pretty awesome too, and quite easy on the eyes. We were equipped with a pretty good-looking team I must say, as most hotels are, especially in the Guest Services Department. This seems to go hand-in-hand with the common term in the service industry, "customer-facing" employees. Nothing makes people feel more welcome than being greeted and taken care of by friendly, yet beautiful people. I know that sounds shallow, but think about it. I didn't come up with it. So this made it pretty easy for me to kill time/flirt with the Front Desk girls on the daily, especially my favorite curly-haired Manager that interviewed me for this position. Believe it or not though, we were all just buds…well, maybe more for some of us...

Let me take you back a few months to before I started working at this hotel. I was out with my buddy Jay on our normal late-night shenanigans through the town. I'm not sure what Jesse was doing that night because it was rare that I would be out raging without him, but he was absent. Jay and I went to this super divey Irish bar that was at the end of my street that I had passed a thousand times, but never actually stopped in. It was normally an older, rougher crowd with a bunch of Harley's lining the entrance outside, so it wasn't exactly my usual scene. We wanted to mix it up, and didn't want to spend a lot of money. We heard this place was super cheap. We went in and we planted at the bar right by the entrance. I sat snug to the wall, and Jay towards the corner where there were seats on the other side of the bar beside him. We pounded a few cheap pitchers, and for some reason Jay bounced early. I believe he worked early the next morning. I decided to stay and drink solo.

I ended up meeting an older Swedish lady who was originally seated next to Jay, and she became quite flirty with me after he left. She had a nice accent, and a nice shape for a forty-to-fifty year old woman. As the pitchers continued to flow, so did my liking to this random Swede. Next thing I knew, I was waking up on my apartment's white futon. Weird. I looked in the bedroom to see a blonde head peeking out of my comforter. Oh boy. I am not one to snuggle with a one-night stand, so it didn't surprise me at that point that I was on the futon. I waited until she left to make any moves because I sure as hell wasn't trying to make or take her to an awkward morning after breakfast. Come to find out in the next few days, she actually lived on the same street as me! I didn't get her number or keep in touch with her, and never really ran into her where we would have to have that post-hookup awkward convo. I would just see her on my street from afar and would only assume she saw me a few times too.

You may be asking yourself, why am I telling you this story? Whelp, guess who was one of the Front Desk Agents at my new hotel? Yup, that Swedish hook-up! Too freaking funny! People always say the hotel world is a small one. Well, let me tell you what! When we first re-acquainted at the hotel, I honestly wasn't even sure if she remembered me, or she did, and wondered if I was wondering the same. As it turns out, she ended up being super cool, and believe it or not, we never discussed it. But, I do think she knew. She was pretty hilarious and a really good Agent. Guests loved her with her constant laughter, Swedish accent, and ditzy blonde attitude. I guess we were just both mature adults and knew it was a harmless, fun night out. Yolo! And wouldn't you know it, I actually ended up falling for another girl working at the hotel, and hard. One that you may have already seen coming. Shit.

You remember the dreamy Latina Manager that interviewed me for the position? Well, let's just say it turned out that I wasn't the only one with an attraction. One day I was pulling out of work and received a text from an unknown number, saying "Was that you in your new truck?" Between my two Audi's, I rocked a little white Ford Ranger pickup for a very short period of time. I had a feeling the mysterious number was her because I pulled out right behind her car when leaving the hotel. This was after a long, slow shift of hanging out with the Front Desk girls, including her. The follow-up text from her read, "You're really smooth, Mr. Matthews." I remember thinking, was this flirting? And how the hell was I supposed to respond to that being that she was technically my boss? It was hard to read this girl because as I said earlier, she was strictly business. No play with her, or not that she led on to. I threw a few safe tester texts out and then the next thing I knew, it was indeed full-fledged flirting…and it was freaking on!

The next day at work, the flirting continued, and I would have to look around to see if anyone else saw or heard. No one reacted as it if was anything out of the ordinary. We would text each other while I was at the Concierge desk downstairs, and she was right upstairs managing the Front Desk. I remember telling my Engineer buddy, Chris, about the recent developments, as I knew I could trust him one-hundred percent. His reaction was, "No way!" He found it hilarious, and didn't really believe me at first because she was such a serious person, like I said. He then started to pay attention to our interactions, and caught on to her flirty nature with me. She made it way more obvious than me. As it turned out, she was still "kind of" in a relationship, on a "break" or whatever. I never brought it up as I figured it was none of my business, but I was growing to like her a lot, so it eventually came up.

One of the nights soon after the flirting began, I innocently invited her over to watch a movie with me and my new roommate, as I had relocated to another apartment with a friend of mine, named Josh. Josh had set up a projector in his room to watch movies the size of the entire wall above his bed. His room must have been an addition to the building at some point because there were two levels to it. He had his bed set-up in the lower level, and in the upper level, had a loveseat and a few chairs to watch the movies overtop of the bed in the lower level. It was a funky layout for a bedroom, but he made the most of it. It was more of a man-cave really. By asking her to watch the movie with the both of us, versus a one-on-one thing, I felt she wouldn't be pressured into thinking it was a hookup attempt, as it honestly was not my intention. This was mainly because she was still my boss, and she had that "break" thing with the BF going on. That, and I don't look for a quick hookup with girls I genuinely like. To me, it's more meaningful if you wait a little bit. I mean, not too long, but at least a few dates. Naturally, my Manager (weird to say, right?) and I sat on the loveseat in the back of the room, and Josh laid on his bed in the lower level in front of the screen. The movie began and I was very hesitant to make any moves because of the obvious work relationship, and because she was hot AF and made me nervous like a high school boy. She, of course, was wearing a skirt of some sort, so her nice, smooth, tan legs were just lying there next to me. Ahhhh! Killing me! She would make these little teasing comments and I would just laugh and keep to myself on my side of the small loveseat. I didn't want to snuggle with her off the bat because I didn't know what was going on in her mind yet. Then, she says to me, "You know, you can put your hand on my leg." Say whatttttt!? From then on, I knew she meant a different kind of business, and I am not talking about work related, I am talking about "Da bidness," as Jesse would say!

Post movie, we made it over to my bedroom, and let's just say there wasn't too much talking involved. Next thing I knew we were rolling around, making out, and doing other adult things that I will leave to your imagination. It was like a fantasy all of us guys dream about...to hook up with your hot boss. The problem was that she was amazing in every way, so it was more than that to me. I actually liked her. Not that this was a bad thing, but it would just be difficult because she was my Supervisor and not technically fully broken-up from the BF from my understanding. We would slip away during lunches at work "coincidentally" at the same time, and go to the nearby Subway. Super stealth! Actually, not really, as the Subway was like a block away, and a lot of work people would go there, but she never seemed to mind. The texts at work were taken to the next level, and let's just say it was a good thing there was a floor that separated us, and no one could see my facial reactions to some of her texts. I would blush like hell! Even in person, she would continue to make obvious flirty comments that would make me blush and feel super awkward because I was thinking everyone would figure it out. The weird part is, no one did. No one had any clue we had anything going on, so I guess they didn't think to look or listen to anything out of the ordinary. Crazy. She even came over to my apartment to stay with me when my brother was in town visiting and he was able to meet her. I was glad because I wanted someone else close to me to meet her and see how great she was. Like I said, I liked her more than just a hookup buddy, and pretty sure she did too. We went to the beach and she brought her little brother too. It was a good ole day of fun in the sun. My brother gave me the thumbs up because he thought she was super-hot too! He also thought she was a great person, and called her a "keeper" and "wife-material."

The best memory I had with her was one day when we both ended up having the same day off (I wonder how that happened), and decided to go to the beach together. We listened to some live music at the Lani Kai, had some of their fruity frozen drinks, and were just living in fantasyland, enjoying life. After, on our way back to my truck, I received a phone call from the Manager on Duty at the hotel, asking where I was at. I thought for sure we were busted, as we were only a few blocks away, and someone must have seen us. I didn't sell us out, but did say I was on the beach enjoying my day off, and asked, "Why, what's up?" The Manager on Duty informed me that I was scheduled to be at work and was late. WTF!? As they are telling me this, and my face is turning red as I was scared of getting fired, I mouth to my Manager with me that I was supposed to be working. She starts giggling in the background, practically getting us busted! I apologized to the MOD, and told her there was no way I would make it in, as I thought I was off, and had already been drinking. Luckily, I didn't get written up, for obvious reasons. Engineering could easily fill in for me and assist guests if needed. I'm sure they wouldn't mind some extra tips. Too funny. We made it back to my apartment, had some drunken fun, and passed out for the remainder of the day/night. Awesome day, and one I will never forget.

Oddly enough, after that awesome day of beach, tunes, laughter, and some love-making, I never got to hang with my Manager outside of work ever again. Not what you were expecting right? Neither was I. Talk about being blind-sided! As it turned out, she was more religious than I thought, and she didn't do much partying or love-making (actually none at all), and came to see me as a bad influence on her...the devil! My guess is she was badly hungover after that day at the beach and she took it all out on me. I do remember her getting sick at some point during the day. You know we have all been there, where we wake up and say, "I am never drinking again!" Well, she took it to the next level. It really made me depressed for a while, as she ended up getting back with her boyfriend too, and went back to her super religious, celibate, and non-partying ways. To each their own, but I really liked her, and even told her I would be willing to wait to have intimate relations with her again until she was ready, or even until marriage…yeah, she had me like that! For Pete's sake, I even took salsa dancing lessons with this girl! I'm gringo as hell…I don't dance! I guess she just wasn't the one for me, and little hotelier babies would have to wait.

At this point, it was time to focus on my career. I now had the motivation I needed, so I asked upper management about being able to shadow some of the girls at the Front Desk and learn the system. Permission granted. This system was modern as hell compared to the others I had worked with, and even the key-maker machines were fancy as fuck. All of the others that I had worked with ran completely separate from the computers. You just punch in the number and swipe the card in, then out. Shout out to Onity! This hotel's machine would allow you to pull up a program and it would notify you to insert the card and it would tell you when it was ready. Slide it in, and it spit it out. It had some other features too, but way too high-tech than it needed to be if you asked me. In fact, I believe it is because of these very key machines that enabled people to steal guests personal information because it was linked to the computer system, whereas the old ass ones were actually hacker proof. What's that saying, "Technology will be the death of us?" It figured that this was my third hotel, and all fucking three had different systems! Christ! As I was learning the ins-and-outs of their check-in/out systems and procedures, I found out that the Agents had opportunities to earn extra money by simply getting guests to upgrade. What the hell!? That's awesome! How easy is that!? As guests are checking-in, simply inform them that you have a "Whatever-View" room available for only $XX more a night. A lot of times it was only $20-$50 more a night, and a lot of times that upgrade was to a sick Ocean-View room. That's an easy sell! The Agents would get a percentage of those upgrade earnings on their paychecks every month. Where was this at my last two hotels!? Great incentive for the Agents, and a great opportunity for the hotel to earn more revenue. I was thinking about all of the possible money I could have made in my last two roles with all the upgrades I gave without even having an incentive. Ugh, that sucks.

Along with my love interest depression, I started getting a little homesick. I wouldn't even as much say homesick, but city-sick. I was ready for the fast-paced environment that I had back in the Northeast. Not that where I was from in Southern Maryland was super-fast paced, but anything was faster than this Key West vibe beach town life. I loved it for the year and a half I had been there, but it was time to go and make some career/life moves. "E.T., phone home." --- *E.T. the Extra-Terrestrial.* I began perusing jobs at the Concierge desk computer in my down time, which there was a lot of, as off-season in Florida is truly a ghost town. The guests disappear, so the tips disappear as well. So go figure, I actually got busted by our Guest Services Manager searching for jobs, as apparently our IT guy was spying on my search history and notified her. I knew I didn't like that little prick. He had the hots for my girl at the hotel, but little did he know, I had the girl...well almost did. Nothing came of the GSM catching me, except for the fact that it prompted our conversation that I was looking to go back home. She totally understood, as she was a Florida transplant herself, and had contemplated going back home multiple times. She just asked that I put in my two weeks' notice when it came time, so she could find my replacement. Luckily, I had good relationships with everyone at that hotel, including her. I never did find a job up North, but put in my two weeks anyway. My dad said he would let me work as a Laborer for his masonry company for a while until I found a new job. I rolled out about as quickly as I rolled into Florida, packed up my little Audi TT, and left the rest of my shit in the apartment. I ended up giving most of it to Jesse, as he eventually moved into my spot in the apartment with Josh. I was surprisingly, incredibly happy to be going back home, giving up the sunshine, beaches, and beautiful women…what in the F was i thinking!?

CHAPTER 3 - CITY LIFE

I had actually received a call before I put in my two weeks' notice for a Front Desk Agent position at a boutique hotel in Washington, DC. I told the gentleman that I would have to put in my notice still at my current job. Unfortunately, they were looking to fill the position ASAP, so it wouldn't work. Although, I wasn't too upset because I was debating getting out of the hotel industry anyway, and getting a better paying, more steady, Monday to Friday type gig. Not so fast! The Hotel Gods weren't going to let me escape that quickly! As fate would have it, a few weeks settled back in at home, I was sitting on the couch by the fire, just watching TV, speaking with my dad and stepmom, and I saw a posting for another Front Desk Agent position at that same hotel. Hmm. I applied and reached out to the same gentleman that called me while I was in Florida. I got an interview, threw on a slim fit H&M suit, and nailed it! He's backkkkkk! This saved me from working out in the field laboring for my dad's company. No more waking up at 4 a.m. to go tote brick and block, and mix mortar in the brisk Maryland mornings. No better way to appreciate an indoor job than working in freezing temperatures and days over hundred degrees in the soaking wet summer humidity.

This hotel was awesommmme! From the outside, it looked like one of the DC museums. In fact, it was actually a registered historic building. It was the original United States Post Office that had the famous Pony Express going through it daily. Pretty cool stuff! It was made up of that white marble that all the DC statues and monuments have. In front, it had huge column pillars with beautiful steps leading up to the huge, all-wood front doors. Possibly my favorite part about the hotel was the fact that it was situated right across from the [then] Verizon Center, which was where my favorite hockey team in the world played, and the local basketball team as well. When you made it through the lobby doors, you were greeted with super tall ceilings, even more so than the Florida ceilings. It was breathtaking! Then you were hit with these hot green-colored walls, with funky colored and shaped furniture and sculptures all over. It was one of those hotels that you would always remember stepping into. Not typical in the least. The Front Desk area was huge, with an all antique glass backdrop behind the desk, making the lobby look even bigger. The actual check-in counter itself was an incredibly long, wooden piece of beauty, with marble tops. Let's just say it was a step up from the last Front Desk I worked behind. There were like four people behind this desk, and one of which was specifically the Concierge. It was very intimidating walking into this lobby knowing that I would be in command of this place at the desk. I was also very intimidated because the staff was wearing fitted suits and stylish city attire. This was far from the cargo shorts and polos I was wearing down South. I loved it, but it was a feeling I had never felt going into a new role. Me, with my little Southern Maryland accent, coming from Florida, and knowing nothing about DC other than the fact that it was our nation's capital, and I visited the museums on elementary school field trips. Regardless, this was the exact kind of hotel I aspired to work in, somewhere I could brag about. I had been dressing like this for years, so it was time to put it to use. I think I finally found my work match.

I met with the Front Desk Manager on my first day, and he set me up with a few brown double-breasted suits, cream colored dress shirts, and a brown diagonally striped skinny tie. Uglier than sin if you ask me. Who in their right mind decided on shit-stain brown for our uniform colors? I guess maybe one could argue that it was a conservative offset to the crazy ass colors going on in that lobby. Although, I probably would have voted for all-black. I had to get the suits fitted prior to starting, which was a first for me. In the past, growing up, my mom would handle that for me with her little sewing table at home. One of the Concierge's at the hotel informed me that the hotel would reimburse me for the hemming, so that was good to know as my ass was broke as hell. I donated all my money to the Fort Myers Beach Stripper Foundation. Ha! I took the suits to my nearby laundromat that also did adjustments. They did a lovely job for the small price of $400! Just think of the emoji with the big eyes and hands beside its mouth...that was my reaction. I guess I should have taken a glance at the pricing before simply dropping the suits with them after they measured me. And of course, in the name of the Hotel Gods taking a shit on me, it turned out I was misinformed by the Concierge, and the hotel would not reimburse this cost. Motherfucker! The Front Desk Manager told me that the Housekeepers would hem the suits for us for free. Goddammit. Lesson #1, don't listen to the Concierge. Great start...in the hole before I even got my first paycheck!

Speaking of the Concierge, I loved that at this hotel the Concierge was truly just the Concierge, and that was it! It was not part-Concierge, part-Valet, and part-Front Desk Agent. The Concierge Agents at this hotel did not know how to check guests in-and-out, but simply be the right hand person for guests (well, the younger Concierge did actually know how to because he was previously a Front Desk Agent). They gave suggestions, made reservations, offered discounts, gave out amenities, etc. They knew the ins-and-outs of the city, and truly knew anyone and everyone in the city. We had two at this hotel. The morning shift Concierge, Luis, was an older, shorter, gay Nicaraguan man that could come off as very harsh, but just didn't like playing games with employees or guests. He loved giving tips and suggestions, but if people shrugged them off, he didn't like that. He was very sweet and caring and would give you his left nut if you were on his good side. He was the President of the DC Concierge Association, and proudly wore the little membership pin above his name tag to show that off. He was very serious about his job and his position in the community. He was not, however, too keen on the hotel, or the management, as I found out most employees there weren't. This seemed to be a common trend at all of the hotels I worked at. Luis was kind enough to take me on a little neighborhood tour and show me the hot dining spots, drink spots, and attractions so that I could give guests simple recommendations and direct them to him for details, discounts, etc. I assumed he just wanted to get the fuck out of the hotel and enjoy the nice DC weather that day. It can get quite stuffy and claustrophobic behind any Front Desk, even at hotels with bigger ones. They tend to seem smaller and smaller the longer you work there.

The afternoon Concierge was also named Tony. He was a young, trendy, Hispanic, bisexual guy (although you would never know), and was born and raised in the DC area. Besides myself, I don't think I've met anyone else who poured their heart and soul into the hotel they worked at like this Tony. Tony absolutely loved being a part of a trendy DC hotel, and made it well known. He also dressed very trendy outside of work and enjoyed the social scene. Think Drake 2.0. We instantly made a connection in that way. He was the one that would pitch in and help check-in/out guests if needed. I think he did it more-so to hopefully gain some potential customers of his own and later received some cash tips throughout their stay for helping them out with recommendations. Tony really knew how to play the Concierge game. I loved it because that is what I had been doing for the last eight months or so. I quickly wondered why the hell I went back to being a Front Desk Agent when I had that freedom that most Concierge's have. They tend to not be managed closely like the Front Desk Agents are. In a sense, it is its own little department. How often do you see a bad complaint on *TripAdvisor* about the hotel Concierge? Never. It is more of an extra feature that hotels have that majority of guests don't ever take advantage of, especially with all of the websites and mobile apps available.

The Front Desk Manager seemed like a total cheese ball. He reminded me of the stereotypical Used Car Salesman, pitching you a great deal of benefits, but doesn't back them up. Don't get me wrong, he was a super nice and cool guy from New Orleans, but I think in the end, he equally didn't want to be there working like the rest of us. He was an oddball for sure, but I have heard that's pretty normal for New Orleans natives, kind of like that previous Front Desk Manager from Vegas. He was, however, super attentive to details at the desk, which I actually really liked. He would let you know if you were missing your name tag or if your tie was crooked, but did so in a real dick-ish way. Instead of just letting you know that you needed to fix it, he would make it a damn trivia game and you would have to guess what was wrong about your look. Me being blond, it took me ages to figure out, and it would just piss me off. Don't ask me what my name is five times so that I have to realize my name tag isn't on, or upside down. Ass! This guy tried to be best buds with us guys at the desk. He would give us daps (fist bumps) on the regular, and commonly referred to us as "bro's." Ugh! He had a little hop in his step like he owned the joint, and this clown would wear the earpiece with the little curly wire behind his ear tied to his hotel radio, as if he was a damn Secret Service Agent. To this day, I am convinced that is what he aspired to be.

He was well-known for taking advantage of the great Front Desk staff he had. What I mean by this, is that he was constantly late or would constantly be absent from the desk, as he knew we could handle our own, or assumed we could. I guess you could say this should be an honor to an Agent because he hired you knowing that you could manage the desk solo. I am all for this, because I am not a fan of management breathing down my neck, but he took advantage entirely too much during the busiest shifts possible, when we actually needed backup. I wanted to strangle him for leaving me at the desk solo at times. He would simply bribe me by ordering the amazing eggs benedict that the restaurant served up, which I must say, was a great bribe. As I later found out, he would charge these to a random guest room, and simply void them out when the guest checking-out would say, "I never ordered breakfast!" What a skeeze move, but pretty slick! I guess you have to create some of your own benefits working at a hotel when you can, to make up for the low pay, shitty hours, and dealing with guests' bullshit.

I do, however, remember two good bonding moments I had with my Front Desk Manager. First, he invited me to a stand-up comedy show because he got free tickets to see the famous Comedian, Eddie Griffin, who was staying at our hotel. This was a common occurrence for comedy shows, as the venue was right next-door and the Comedians and their Agents would often stay with us. You might have seen Eddie in the movie *Undercover*

Brother, or other comedy films or stand-ups. Eddie ended up having one, or three too many beverages, and his comedy skit turned into non-stop racist and political rants. It was quite awkward. So much so that my boss walked out right in the middle of the show. I stayed and stuck out the awkward "comedy" act. We reunited the next morning at the desk and he couldn't believe I sat through the rest of the show. I don't know how I did either. True bro bonding moment.

The other bonding moment I had with him was when an older, pretty, established-looking blonde lady came to check-out at the desk. She seemed like your typical driven, hard-nosed DC businesswoman. My Manager was at the terminal beside me and handled the check-out. He asked the usual check-out questions: "How was your stay?"; "Would you like a bottle of water to go?"; "Would you like your incidental charges to stay on the card we have on file that you gave us at check-in?". The last question was very important because a lot of people traveling on their company dime preferred to switch their method of payment for their incidental charges. She quickly and assertively responded, "There shouldn't be any incidental charges!" He apologized, and went ahead and reversed the charges without hesitation from her bill. I figured it was one of his famous breakfast charges and she just so happened to be the recipient of the bribery meal. I was trying to mind my own business at the computer beside him, so didn't think much of it. It just seemed like your average check-out with a charge sent to the wrong guest room. Wellllll, little did I know, there was more going on behind the scenes here.

The guest walked away and went about her day, and my Manager gave me a grin, almost as if he had seen something he shouldn't have. The first thing that crossed my mind was, did he hook up with her previously? Or did I miss an episode that happened with her during her stay, or were her honkers hanging out? I had no idea because I really wasn't paying attention. He points to the monitor on the computer that he was on. I lean over to look and it was a movie charge that was close to twenty bucks. I wasn't sure what point he was trying to make here. Ok, she watched two insanely overpriced hotel movies? I didn't know. He escorted me to the back to the ancient in-room movie tracking machine (yes, the same one that was at my first hotel). Here, he pulled up her room history and what movie(s) she was watching. Apparently, the only movies that ring up at that exact price are the "special" movies, a.k.a. naughty flicks! Say whatttttttt!!!???? That Sharon Stone look-alike was watching spanktravision in her room!? Awesome! This gave me a whole new view of cougars, and a good ass laugh with my Manager that I wasn't so fond of. I guess you could say we had a few good "bro" moments.

The three Supervisors under my Manager were pretty freaking awesome. One was actually in a Manager-In-Training program that most good hotel chains offer. She was a very pretty, always smiling, goody-two-shoe Southern California girl who thought her shit didn't stink like the rest of the girls from there. Yeah, I said it. I'm not sure if it was from her being from SoCal, or the fact that she graduated from Penn State University. That college is known to breed graduates with this high-class entitlement. I love him to death, but my stepbrother is living proof. Not sure why this school's grads think this because it's not an Ivy League school. I mean, yeah, they have a killer football stadium, but so what, so do a lot of other colleges. I don't get it. She was one of a few coworkers I had that went there. Anyways, this Supervisor was a good chick. She was pretty down to earth and fun, and was part of the Front Desk gang. She became my main trainer at the desk, and God she would get on my last nerve. I think it was just that we were both very hard-headed and opinionated, so we constantly butted heads. It was like fighting, laughing, and flirting all at the same time. Weird. Eventually, she and I took our love-hate relationship to the next level, and had some relations outside of work. We were young, single, decent-looking, and a bit tipsy, so why not!? Yolo. It only happened once, but I think we both needed to get that pent-up aggression out of our systems, and we knew we weren't trying to date or get serious. Just a good old-fashioned quickie. #HotelierLife

Another Supervisor, Ted, was yet another gay guy who was extremely hospitable. I really looked up to Ted as he had this way of dealing with guests that was so calming, but serious and friendly at the same time. He would then talk complete shit about the guests after they walked away. Hilarious! Ted always dressed super sharp with his hair perfectly groomed and always clean shaven. Well, we all were clean shaven as that was just one of the lovely requirements of working at most desks in hotels. The Supervisors could wear their own suits instead of that ugly brown shit us Agents had to wear. Those lucky bastards! Ted was the son of a COO of another big hotel management company, so needless to say, he knew a thing or two about the industry. He graduated from a big hospitality school and was determined to make it on his own without the name of his dad. I loved this, as I had chosen to take my own path rather than taking over my dad's masonry company. Ted and I often worked the 3-11 p.m. shift together, as we were both newer to the hotel, and that was considered the shittier of the shifts. We actually kind of enjoyed it, as we were able to snag some drinks post-work at the nearby DC dive-bars. Get off at eleven, get some drinks, sleep in, head into work, and do it all over again. #NightShiftLife

Probably the best story I have with Ted occurred during one of these post-shift ventures. Ted and I decided to go to this bar across the street that we frequented, as it was severely needed because we had a huge Jewish conference in town, with guests that demanded a lot, and tipped nothing. The Bartender didn't even have to ask us why we were needing a drink, as he was experiencing the conference guests' lack of tips as well. We were finishing up a beer and Ted was looking to venture elsewhere after. A lot of times, the agreement was that he would go to a straight bar with me if I would go with him to a gay bar after. Ugh! I was comfortable with my sexuality so I didn't mind it too much, and there were usually single straight girls there too. My odds tended to be good. Before we completely finished our beer, two girls popped a squat to the right of me at the bar. They seemed a little tipsy. The one beside me started getting chatty with me, asking about the beer menu and such, clearly just trying to strike up conversation. She asked me if Bud Light was any good, and she was American. Hmm. Meanwhile, Ted downed the rest of his draft and said, "Let's go." I told him to hold on a second and let's get another one, as I was working on some game to my right. He sighed and got another. The other girl eventually made her way over to sit next to Ted, as I think she assumed he was straight as well. Next thing I know, I look over at Ted and the girl is massaging his legs. I look up at Ted's face and his expression was priceless! He rolled his eyes and chugged his second beer. Wingman of the year! Meanwhile, my girl was ready to get it at the bar! She guided my hand up and down her shirt and pants, and was making out with my entire head. I specifically remember as she was molesting me, looking at the other people at the bar behind her, along with the Bartender, and they were all staring at us like WTF!? I'm glad we provided some entertainment for the bar that evening. Finally, I said, "Let's get out of here" to the girl, and grabbed some cash for a cab, and rolled out. I told Ted we were headed to the Grand Hyatt where she was staying, and I would see him at work the next day. I wasn't sure where his night was headed with a girl whom he obviously wasn't interested in, but was curious to find out.

So the taxi ride was quite an interesting one. Let's just say the driver probably got a nice show in his rear-view mirror. It was a nice prep for what was to come at the Hyatt. The remainder of the clothes still on from the taxi ride quickly came off in the hotel room. She was quick to brag about her big fake boobies and asked if I liked them, as apparently she had them done recently. It sounded almost as if she had someone back at home who underappreciated them. Oh boy. We did our thing and I was ready to bounce, as I was getting the vibe this girl was a tad clingy. Likely, because I was respectful and nice. I didn't need anyone falling in love with me from out of town at that point in my life, especially if she truly had baggage back home like it seemed. She did not want me to leave and wanted to go all night. As I mentioned before with the Fort Myers Beach girl, if I'm dating a girl, I'm all about post-hookup snuggle and breakfast, but one I just met randomly at a bar, probably not. Sorry. I ended up lying to her and said I had to work the 7 a.m. shift, when I was actually scheduled for my normal 3 p.m. shift with the one-and-only Ted, who God knows how he escaped his girl.

I got up to take a pee in the hotel room, which was very lovely by the way (nicely done Hyatt), and she didn't even want me to go do that. She was holding onto me. I slithered my way out and made it to the bathroom. I remember so clearly that as I was standing there peeing and looking at my naked, sweaty self in the mirror, contemplating if this was one of my best life decisions, the bathroom door suddenly flies open. The girl kicked the door in, and I could see her in the mirror standing there, naked, with her hands holding the door frame as to not let me out of the bathroom. On one hand, super sexy, but on the other, straight psychotic! How the fuck was I going to escape this? It reminded me of the little red-head on the movie, *Wedding Crashers*, when she tells Vince Vaughn's character, "Don't ever leave me. Cause I'll find you!" Save me! Where was Ted when I needed him!? I had to first finish up peeing as I planned my escape. I had to calm her down with some kisses and made my way back to the bed to toss her on it and grab my phone. I asked for her number so I could text her the next day. All the meanwhile, she was trying to convince me to stay the night with her. Got her number, or so she thought, kept blaming my exit on work, gave her some goodbye kisses, and made a run for it, as I ripped my way out of her grips. I literally ran down the hall, and even took the steps down because I thought she was going to come chasing after me. I bolted out of the hotel entrance, and called a cab to get me the hell home. Good freaking times!

I somehow stumbled into work the next day, and met Ted at the desk with a big grin. He of course, made every smartass comment in the book about my late night ventures. I filled him in on the psychopathic activities, and he was dying laughing. Apparently, he managed to finish his beer at the bar, and roll out right after me solo. He told the girl he was gay so she would let him be, because otherwise Ted could have been in the room next door to us at the good ole Hyatt. We eventually got to checking-in guests, as the night shift is commonly known for because of that time of the day. Ted, coincidentally had a guest come up and ask where the Grand Hyatt was (of all places), as he had a conference there the next day. Immediately, my head dropped to my chest in disappointment because I still couldn't escape that damn girl. Ted, in the most excited, yet professional response ever, says to the guest, "We happen to have our resident expert of that hotel, Tony, right here, as he pats me on the back. Tony, can you explain to Mr. Smith how to get to the Grand Hyatt?" That bastard had the biggest grin ever on his face, and my face was probably redder than ketchup in embarrassment. I had to be quick on my toes with my reply, and try not to punch Ted. In a sense, it was a good Front Desk training exercise. That bitch!

God, there are too many stories to tell featuring Ted, but I will spare him for purposes of the future of his illustrious hotel career ahead of him. Ted was one of those leaders that you will miss to death as you grow in your hotel career. He knew how to handle things professionally, but in a fun manner. He really taught me that the hotel industry can be an enjoyable one. Get our shit done, treat the guests well, and we can all party after hours. The last true memory I had of Ted before he took a promotion at a nearby hotel was when we were in the back office bull-shitting, and he asked me if I had any dates recently. He found it amusing that I not only went out on quite a few too many dates, but also that I tended to gravitate towards ethnicities other than my own race, normally pretty exotic ones. He asked me where my date from the previous night was from, and I just shook my head, laughed, and replied, "Saudi Arabia." He cracked the F up, and grabbed a thumbtack on the desk, and put it right on Saudi Arabia on the world map beside the desk. He said, "From now on, we will keep track of all the girls Tony dates on this map." That bastard! Made me sound like a real hoe...fo sho.

Believe it or not, there was another gay Manager at this property, named Anthony. Anthony was a very proper, no bull-shit kind of Supervisor. He didn't tolerate people being late or people fooling around. He might have been a tad too serious for a hotel like this. You could say he and Ted had opposite management styles. As I've said, I won't reveal the name of my hotels, but this one certainly was not at the Ritz Carlton level of service, so there was no need to be overly stuffy there. Anthony always rocked a super well-fitted suit, perfectly groomed hair, and was super clean shaven. He was one of those guys that has that baby face even as he gets older. Anthony was a great guy and taught me a lot about how to manage. One story that sticks out in my head involving him was when we had guests come up to the desk and ask for a tour of the hotel. He took me with him to shadow his tour. Anthony was extremely hospitable, holding doors, walking completely upright, and very welcoming with his hands and body language. He was pouring out knowledge about the history of the hotel and stories that were blowing my mind, and really made me want to stay at the hotel myself, but also go do some research as I didn't know any of the shit he spoke of. I later asked him how he found out about all of those historic stories, and he told me he completely made them up. I was flabbergasted! This was hospitality at its finest! Do and say absolutely whatever you can to win the business. So naturally, when I had family come to visit the hotel, I had my main man Anthony give them the hotel tour. The dude should have been in sales! Sure enough, in some convos at the desk, he was looking to get into real estate sales, and I believe he did eventually leave to do so. Classic!

We technically had another Supervisor, but he oversaw the Night Audit shift. I only worked this shift once at this hotel for training, just in case I ever had to cover the shift. John was a cool ass dude! He was a super emo kid that liked similar music and similar bar scenes as me. Somehow, this dude had super energy for working overnight. He must have gotten some killer naps in during the day, or was throwing down some Red Bull's on the reg. We eventually made it out for drinks together after multiple failed attempts because of his weird work schedule. The night we did make it out, we made it out alright! We hit up this little place called The Red Derby that he had read about having one dollar drafts from the classified section of a newspaper. Who the hell reads that!? Apparently a Night Audit Supervisor. He literally shows me a little cut out from the paper. Haha! I guess he must have gotten super bored working that shift. The place sounded super sketch, but we were broke as shiz from living in DC and working in the hotel biz, so one dollar beers sounded amazing. What's the worst that could happen...get hammered, blackout, and crash a DC rental bike? Exactly that.

We stumbled up to this little dumpy-looking building, and walked in and grabbed some drinks at the bar. It was definitely a hole. There were board games everywhere, and little plastic red hats where I'm guessing the name came from. From looking at pictures around the place, it seemed that people came and got hammered off of the cheap beer, and played board games and wore those red hats. Could it get any more hipster? Fucking board games in a bar. This was when hipster was becoming a new thing in DC, so I guess it was pretty cool. Come to find out, this place had a killer rooftop bar! It instantly became one of my DC favorites once I found this out, because this was not common at all in DC at the time. This place not only had cheap-ass beers, but had bar food items that ranged from two-to-five bucks. My kind of bar! We could get a chicken wrap for three dollars, five one-dollar beers, and give a two dollar tip, and get hammered AND full for only ten bucks! This was literally impossible to do in DC, and any major city for that matter.

The bar ended up being located at the very end of a pretty happening street in DC that neither one of us had explored, only heard about. We decided to walk down it and stop at each bar to grab a beer in each. A little bar hop action! We went in some interestingggg places. At one point, us two scrawny straight white boys were in an all-black bar, and later, a lesbian bar. Fuck it, we were both social dudes and far from discriminatory. We were drinking on another rooftop we discovered and looking around only to see girls in pairs, with short haircuts and super trendy outfits. I pointed it out to John, and he was like, "Wow, you're right." We ventured downstairs and it was the same. We talked to one of the pairs and found out this was indeed a lesbian bar. They said it was a good thing we came that particular night because the night before was gay guy night, and people are all running around shirtless. Ted! I guess we would have figured that night's theme out pretty quick. Hilarious! John became a very wild drunk, wanting to sneak into clubs through side and back entrances and such. This one place we went to had a very long line, so John literally had us go to a convenience store, buy markers, and try to draw on the stamp from the bar so we could hop the line. Didn't work. I wasn't trying to get arrested that night, so we eventually went our separate ways to reunite at work the next night. You'll never run short of good people and good partiers in the hotel industry.

That night actually prompted a call to my personal cell phone the next day from an unknown number. Luckily, it wasn't the Police, not quite. It was the Capital Bikeshare "Police." This was a company that had bike stations located around the city where you would insert your little keychain membership card and it would release a bike that you could drive anywhere, and park it at another one of their bike stations around the city. This was actually how I got to and from work and around most of the city; restaurants, bars, coffee shops, dates, hockey games, you name it. It was cheap and convenient, although not so fun in the winter with the cold-ass weather and wind-chill hitting me in the face. Anyways, they called me because they had a damaged bike reported that showed me returning it to a station around 3 a.m. Whoops. I may have had a little accident with a tree root that was protruding out of a sidewalk on my way home from that wild night with John. I remembered flashes of having to walk my bike most of the ride home through some not-so nice DC neighborhoods because I somehow jacked up the tire and it put it out of whack. I also shattered my elbow and had scars in random places on my body. To this day, I don't have feeling in that damn elbow. I blame John. Luckily, they reimbursed me for the bike damage charges and asked that I was in good health. Pretty damn good customer service! I probably got lucky that I didn't get a BWI (Biking While Intoxicated) that evening/morning. God, Managers are the worst influences!

Besides the Manager and Supervisors, I met some great friends at this hotel. One of my best girl friends came from this hotel; an awesome girl named Jess, who could be Taylor Swift's twin. She was very sweet, polite, and down to earth. If it wasn't for her being taller and a little more hippy than me, I would have tried to date her. I actually brought her to my hometown one time, but strictly as friends. She loved working the desk with me because I would keep her in the loop on my sexual adventures. She cracked up at the fact that my weakness was exotic, mostly Latin women. Me, being a blonde haired, blue-eyed white dude, this was the complete opposite. She was also blonde and light-eyed, but had no taste for exotic men. Jess was actually an International Political Science major, so we shared the common goal to GTFO of hotels, or least front office. Doug was another Front Desk Agent that I became pretty cool with. He was also from New Orleans like the Front Desk Manager. The hotel job was a pit stop for him, as he was actually interested in becoming a Journalist. He was a super calm dude that had a way of handling guests that put them at ease. I tried to emulate this at times, but it becomes hard when you have guests straight yelling at you for an issue that is completely out of your hands. I don't know how he did it. I thought Doug was gonna become a super good friend, but he was near impossible to get ahold of outside of work because he had a girlfriend and when he wasn't working, he ran straight home to her. One of those. Oh well. We did manage to get Doug out with the gang every now and again.

There were three other Agents that I worked with for a brief time that were pretty damn cool too. One was a dude named David, who was actually doing an internship for his college hospitality program. This dude was loaded with energy! If I didn't get to know him, I would have thought he was straight coked out all day, every day. It turned out he just loved life to the fullest. So much so that he got up and moved to Hawaii when he got back to his hometown of Philly. Fuckin badass! I gained instant respect for him, as I did the same when I bounced to Florida. Jen, was another cool agent that had moved from Seattle to experience the DC lifestyle. She put the "hip" in hipster. It was funny because she hated wearing that stupid-ass shit-brown uniform at the desk more than anyone. It definitely held back from her emo style. She lived in a cool, up-and-coming neighborhood in DC called H-Street. We had a night of shenanigans there once, as I lived pretty close by and had never been.

Another cool coworker at this hotel was named Donnell. Donnell was the man! This M F'er would come into work blazed as hell every night. He worked the overnight shift. You could say he was the total opposite of energetic-ass John. Donnell was cut-and-dry. He wouldn't take any BS. He had that vibe like, "Bro, I don't have time for this shit. You either smoked in the damn room, or you didn't." Loved it! I guess this was a little easier to do at night when you don't always have a Manager on Duty breathing down your neck. I would normally only see Donnell for a few minutes at a time as he was either clocking-out in the morning as I arrived, or clocking-in in the evening as I was leaving. I remember when one of my best bud's, Erik, from the Jersey shore, was in town staying with me because Hurricane Sandy put him without power, I decided to show him where I worked and wanted to scope out the hotel's restaurant scene. We were walking past the Front Desk and said hello to Donnell in passing. We scoped out the restaurant, and it was dead, so we decided to turn around. As we headed back by the desk, Donnell grabbed our attention and nodded his head, as if pointing towards the guest checking-in. I didn't understand, as it just looked like a homeless man. At first, I thought he was trying to show us the shit he goes through during Night Audit. Then, upon further looking, I realized it was none other than Danny Glover's ass, looking for a room for the night. Talk about random! Both Erik and I were huge fans, mainly from the movie, *Angel's in the Outfield*. Classic! I ended up talking to Donnell a few days later about it and reminisced as to how old and rough Danny was looking. Then,

Donnell went on to tell me how he always took pictures with the celebrities that checked into the hotel. I was shocked, as we technically weren't supposed to be doing that with any guests, let alone celebrities, because of that whole thing called confidentiality, and paparazzi! Donnell didn't GAF! He was spitting out names of tons of celebrities he had pictures with. I didn't doubt him as this hotel had quite the selection of politicians, athletes, movie stars, etc. staying there. My man, Donnell! #NoFucksGiven!

Believe it or not, I did get some actual work done at this hotel. I did my usual shit, got on the good side of everyone at the hotel, and shared my wealth of knowledge from working in hotels for one too many years already. My OCD at the desk kicked in, and I fixed as much as I possibly could. This hotel was actually pretty damn good compared to my previous ones...actually the best! There wasn't much to even fix, or put in place. They had their shit together. Not sure I liked that actually. I think I preferred a project. I believe it was in such good shape because I worked with all Gen X'er's and they (me included) are keen on organization and making shit easier, not more complicated and harder, as some of the older generations do. And to think people talk so much shit on Millennials (eye-roll)! This hotel was equipped with all hotel professionals. They all went to school and planned to make this a legit career, at least for the time being, until they found something with higher pay and better hours. This was pretty refreshing coming from hotels that just had people working to pay the bills. This was one of the main reasons I had moved back to DC from Fort Myers Beach if you recall, because I didn't see any drive or determination with people in their careers, or life in general there. I saw my future life before my eyes in Concierge Santa Claus, and those older people I was smoking, chilling, and playing volleyball with. Don't get me wrong, it sounded like the perfect life, but to me, success was a tad more appetizing to me, at least at that stage in my life.

I strived to be the best at this hotel, but it was tough due to the competition working around me. Somehow, I was voted by my colleagues and management to be in charge of our hotel's rewards program, or as they called it, "Rewards Champion." I guess I made a good impression pretty quick amongst them. Here, I would be the sole representative for our hotel to sit through company-wide teleconferences and sometimes in-person meetings to share best practices with our other property reps around the country. I would also learn new initiatives that the company was doing so that I could share and reinforce them at our property. Things like little promotions the hotel was running, or new collateral we needed to share with guests. It was very similar to things that my very first hotel did, but instead gave a Front Desk Agent some added responsibility and something to add to their resume. This was pretty cool because I got to feel like a privileged Agent, and got to meet people from other properties across the country that I normally would not have. A killer networking opportunity!

Although we had a loyalty/rewards program like most other chains, this hotel was far from your typical chain hotel. It actually named all of their hotels something different, not just your typical brand of the hotel and the city it's in. This made it a little more exclusive. It kept with their boutique vibe. Guests could then say they stayed at the XX hotel and everyone knew what hotel and in what city they were talking about, unlike most chains were they stay at the XX hotel and there are fifty other ones in that same city. This exclusivity along with the luxurious boutique feel brought exclusive clientele, as I mentioned before. Never had I worked at a hotel with the line-up that this one had. Of course for the privacy of the celebrities, we could not reveal who stayed there (no one told Donnell that apparently), but obvi, that never stopped us from telling our closest friends and family members. Paparazzi was not welcome at our property. Since I am not mentioning the name of this hotel, fuck yeah I will tell you a few celebrities that I came across during my time there! We had Floyd Mayweather, Steven Spielberg, Adam Lambert, Tony Horton (*P90X*), John Legend, Danny Glover (mentioned earlier), Train (the band), Sean Hayes, every political figure you can name, every NBA and NHL player you can name (because of that arena across the way), multiple ex-athletes like Bernie Williams, Dan Marino, a variety of comedians (because of the comedy club beside us), and more. The arena across from us was also used as a venue for concerts, so quite a few musicians strolled through there too. Most of them I wouldn't even hear about until after they left because they would come through late at night and be escorted through a basement entrance to save from fans/paparazzi, and they would have a false name on their reservations. DC was just then starting to get on the map as far as celebrity sightings. At that point and time, TMZ was not even allowed in the city, but have since been allowed to set up a camp there. It was pretty awesome working at a cool enough place that these celebs would stay at. A hell of a lot of different than the first hotel I worked at.

Checking-in celebrities was a total mind-fuck, to say the least. First off, you have to treat them like they are just your ordinary, everyday guest and not necessarily give them the celebrity treatment. You can't freak out and have a third grade fanboy/girl spasm. You just have to be cool, calm, and collected. You can't go asking them for their autograph or for a picture with them (this was in the early stages of the selfie…thanks Paris Hilton). You have to remain professional. It's weird because you almost prefer to just be cool with them instead of acting starstruck. This way the celebrity grows a respect for you instantly for treating them like a normal human being. There is a reason a lot of celebs wear hats and glasses in public, it is because they want to blend in. So just imagine that, but at the desk. The difference was that we happened to see their names on the reservations and had to ask for identification and a credit card for incidentals, so they couldn't exactly blend in. It is a pretty crazy experience physically holding and looking at a celebrity's actual license, and swiping their American Express black card. That bad boy just feels expensive from the weight and material alone. It's like made of metal! WTF!? I knew it would be black, but had no clue it was a completely different material than your average credit card. It legit felt bulletproof! So if all of this build-up wasn't already screwing with your head, you had to continue to keep your composure and select a guest room to put them in that wouldn't piss them off. In a perfect situation, your Manager had already selected one for them with a "DNM" (Do Not Move) on the reservation.

One check-in in particular I had, did not have a room pre-assigned. Motherfuckers! Tony Horton, Mr. *P90X* himself, comes straight through the tall lobby doors with a hop in his step, full of energy, ready to check-in. He came up to the desk with some cheese ball way of saying hello, as he is well known for his cheesiness in his fitness videos. I was pretty starstruck as I had done the *P90X* videos twice in college, and was a big fan of what he does. He asked if he needed to show me his I.D., and I responded, "Nope, I did my ninety days...actually one-eighty." He quickly responded, "I thought you looked like you were busting out of that suit!" I LOL'd and talked about how I needed to get back on it, and he asked me if I used free weights or resistance bands (as the video shows both ways to do the workouts). I told him how I only had two sets of weights, twelve pounds and twenty pounds for the first ninety days, and then an entire set of dumbbells for the second go-round. He convincingly told me to try the resistant bands out next time, as he said it makes a huge difference, which surprised me. He was telling me how he was currently trying to cut sugars out completely from his diet, but chocolate covered almonds were his weakness. I laughed, and told him that I need to focus more on the dieting myself, and made a mental note of his tips.

Back to the check-in…as you could guess by the fact that his room was not pre-assigned, my team, nor did myself have any idea he was coming in. It was towards the start of my shift, and I hadn't even gotten a chance to quickly look over the guests arriving for the day. Normally, we are notified at little pre-shift meetings of any important guest arrivals and their rooms would be pre-checked into a suite of some sort. Mr. Horton, however, was not. As I looked through the available rooms, thank the Lords above, I had one corner suite left. One problem, it was in our infamous basement rooms. Yes, I said basement. Oh good Lord.

The basement rooms were the exact same rooms as the ones on our other floors, minus the floor-to-ceiling windows. Because the rooms were partially underground, the windows were only around two-to-three feet tall at the very top of the wall. The hotel did a good job of disguising them and making them appear to be floor-to-ceiling windows by keeping the floor-to-ceiling drapes that they had in the upper floor rooms. So in essence, if the guests never opened the drapes, they would have had no idea. But if they did, they were watching tourists feet walk through the city on the sidewalks above. Awkwardddd. I think it was more or less the thought process of getting in the elevator or stairs, and going DOWN a floor. Every hotel has its problematic rooms, and this hotel happened to have an entire floor of them. Ugh! Fuck us Front Desk Agents! I put on my sales cap and sold the shit out of the room to Mr. Horton, telling him how this was actually my favorite room type because it donned a huge, spa-like shower with dual shower heads, similar to the ones you see in the Koehler commercials. I had to work the angle of the building being historic, and how it's really a great suite because you are secluded down there, away from the "everyday guests" (a.k.a. non-celebrities), blah blah. Or, as I would commonly say to guests, we keep these rooms for our "exclusive guests," especially basketball players, because of the huge showers. Whatever worked to save me from an ass-chewing! Sell, sell, sell!

Tony, as he said to call him (yeah, we were tight like that), said he would take my word, and give the room a try. I let him know that we did indeed have an upper floor suite that I could move him into the next day, worst case scenario. Sure enough, we received a call at the desk soon after, and it was Tony, asking to speak with Tony. Oh here we go. As nice as he could be, he said he was not happy about the room, as it was in the basement, and he was looking at people's feet walking the streets outside of his windows. Yup, yup, I know. I notified him that I would have him moved seamlessly the next day to one of our premier suites on the third floor, which for whatever reason had the highest ceilings in the building. I told him to leave his things packed up when he heads out in the morning and we will move everything for him without a hassle. He was very appreciative of my going out of the way to make this work for him. I followed-up by sending an amenity to his room with bottles of water, some almonds (non-chocolate covered), fruit, and a note apologizing for the room, and that I would take care of him for the rest of his stay. He later came up (get it...because he was in the basement) to the desk and shook my hand, thanking me for the nice gesture, and actually invited me to a private workout he was hosting at a nearby historic building the next day. Say whattttt!? The man who had whipped me into the best shape of my life via DVD was now inviting me to a live, in-person, private workout. Not in my wildest dreams. Badass! One tiny problem...I hadn't hit the gym in a hot minute! So needless to say, my stamina, and stretching (which he loves to do) was far from stellar at this point in time. Fuck it. I had to go.

So I get up bright and early to go get my ass kicked by the king of muscle confusion. I hop on my little DC city bike and head over to this historic building. There were about fifty people in total, and most looked like they had been hitting *P90X* hard for the last few months/years. Greaaaatttttt! The room was not the largest in the world, and they had about a twenty-by-twenty-foot stage set up for Tony Horton to stand on and instruct. I don't think whoever planned that space thought about the amount of room his workouts entail. It was a little tight. I strategically picked my spot towards the back corner of the room close to the door, in case I was dying and needed to escape. Mr. Horton was actually advertising a new *P90X* video, so he had all kinds of new workouts planned for us. This was cool, yet not cool at the same time, because the coordination of the crowd was pretty ugly. Either way, his workout straight whooped my ass up and down. It's funny because in the videos, you always see him taking breaks to go around and check on the other people working out, so you assume he never does the full workouts. Well, let me tell you what, this dude was crushing these workouts, and only went around the room once. This man was in freakish shape for being in his 50's. When he made his way around the room, he started inching closer to where I was posted up, sweating profusely.

I was thinking, "Please don't come over here, please don't come over here." Well goddammit, there he came. And of course, his ass stops in his place when he sees me, and shouts, "Tony!" Of course he was mic'd up, so everyone was like, damn, who is this guy? I was literally the only one in the entire room that he called out. He continued to speak in his super loud and sarcastic tone, "Tone! You gonna hook me up with an awesome hotel room or what!?" I was turning red as shit in embarrassment. I just laughed and said I would try my best, as I was trying to retain my breath from the workout we were doing. He gave me a fist bump with a grin on his face, and went along to whoop our asses some more. Class act guy!

Another class act was a hockey player by the name of Joel Ward, whom also stayed with us. He was a player on my favorite sports team on the planet, the *Washington Capitals* hockey team. The *Cap's* were in the midst of a great playoff run and a lot of players would stay at the hotel instead of traveling through the city traffic to their houses that were usually located outside of the city. I was working the desk one morning and I see this big, buff, well-dressed black man heading my way with his bags. Sure enough, it was my main dude, Joel Ward. He always looked happier than hell on the ice, rocking a smile most of the time. I greeted him at the desk, "Good morning, Mr. Ward!" He actually looked pretty pumped that I recognized him, and he gave me that infamous smile. I gave him a handshake, and wished him luck for the game that night, as they were up three games to one in the series against the *New York Rangers*, and only needed that home win to move on to the next series. I checked him out of his room, and he went on his way. I kid you not, during the game that night, the *Capitals* had it won with a one-goal lead with about a minute left to play, until my guy, Joel Fucking Ward, decided to slash someone for absolutely no reason, and get a penalty called on him. The *Capitals* would then be short a player, and the *Rangers* took advantage and scored a game-tying goal, eventually winning the game in overtime. Then, they went on to win the ENTIRE SERIES! Are you kidding me? I truly have the Washington sports touch of bad luck. Actually, my whole family does. Sorry DC, we are the DC Sports Curse. I should have kicked Mr. Ward in the shin when I had the chance to injure him and change that outcome! Ugh! Sorry *Cap's*!

Someone who was the opposite of a class act was one more coworker of mine. I saved the best for last. This girl had some issues! Each hotel has that one crazy Desk Agent or employee. Think about it for a second...you know who I speak of! Well, this one, was a crystal meth addict. Uff! Yes, a crystal meth addict working the desk of an upscale luxury hotel that serviced millionaires, like the aforementioned celebrities. At first, I wasn't sure what the hell her deal was. She was just super hyper all the time, smelt nasty, and always seemed to have her mind somewhere else when you talked to her. She was nice as could be, just a little wacky, and got wackier as time went on. I had been warned by other Agents to not lend her money, but wasn't really told why. Weird. I tend not to lend people money in general anyway, so that was normal to me. I mean, maybe to split a pizza with friends or something. After working a few shifts with her, I quickly realized something else was going on there. She would consistently almost fall asleep while checking guests in beside me. How the fuck is that possible because you are literally speaking with them! I would look over at her at the desk and her head would be nodding off, eyes closed. My initial thought was that maybe she just partied hard and didn't get a lot of sleep the night before. Damn girl, get your shit together. I remember guests would look over at me with a reaction like, "WTF?" and I would either have to quickly look away or jump in and try and assist this girl. When I did, she would commonly shoo me off, and did not want the help. I remember a time in particular when she couldn't even get her key into the keyhole to get money out of the cash drawer. I would watch her attempt to for a full minute with no success. She was hunched over, eyes closed, and trying to open this bank drawer with zero success. It was quite sad to be honest. It was sad for two reasons: One, because of the obvious issues going on with her; and two, because she was still working at the hotel!

After working a few shifts with this girl, I specifically requested to be put on another shift, as she was notorious for disappearing for long periods of time, and it was quite uncomfortable the way she acted. Also, as I mentioned, she smelt super funky. I complained and submitted concerns to the Supervisors and eventually the Front Desk Manager. They pretty much told me they knew of the situation, and to hang tight. I think they were following the proper, legal steps through Human Resources. I assume they wanted proper documentation of write-ups, situations, and such. It got so bad that this girl was found passed out with needles in the bathroom OF THE HOTEL and STILL reported to work for her next shift, allowed to work. How on earth she would still have a job after that was beyond me? Around this same time period, she came to me for money a few times, and I would kindly decline. Her problem was so severe that I remember her requesting to leave during one of our shifts, leaving me and the Supervisor (I won't mention which one) to man the desk. The Supervisor and I stood there shoulder to shoulder at the desk, watching her walk out those giant wooden doors, and he says to me, "I'm pretty sure I just let her take a break to go get her drug fix, and unfortunately, I can't do anything about it." I remember that day in particular because she smelt more horrible than normal. I can't quite describe the smell, but it was nasty as shit. I can still smell it to this day. It was a scary situation, and not long after, she was finally let go. Sadly, I saw her a few weeks after, sitting outside of the nearby CVS asking people for money. Don't do drugs kids! I think this whole situation kind of introduced me to the HR process in the business world. Because of unemployment, and lawsuits involved with firing employees, employers have to take every step necessary to cover their ass. Document, document, document. This includes you as an employee because you want to cover your own ass too!

As you can see, this hotel was a career pit stop/filler for many, but for some, it was a serious career milestone. I was at the point, believe it or not, that I wanted it to be a step in the hotel career direction. I was crushing it in the hotel game and wanted to move up in the ranks. This particular hotel chain made it tough though because they only had around fifty or so hotels at the time. There wasn't much room for growth. I eventually decided that the inconsistent and non-normal working hours at the Front Desk would not work for me. There was an Accounting position open at our hotel that I became very interested in, but I didn't think I was qualified enough for. I studied Business Management in school, which entailed Accounting 101 and 102, but I didn't necessarily feel comfortable handling an entire hotel's numbers. I spoke with one of the Senior Accountants at the hotel, and he told me it was easy, and would shadow me on how to do the job. I'm glad I was always nice to him in the lunchroom! Don't underestimate break room networking! So it sounded like I would be a shoe-in for the position with my great reputation at the desk, and getting a recommendation from this Senior Accountant. It came time for me to be able to post for the position, but of course, just when it was looking up, here came the Hotel Gods again to screw me over.

Most hotel chains require that you work in a position for at least six or twelve months before being eligible to apply for another one within the company and/or hotel. Typically, it is six months for an hourly position, and a year for management/salaried positions. This prevents employees from moving around constantly. And believe me, in the hotel world, as soon as someone can post for a new position, they will. You get paid far too low, and work way too shitty hours not to want to advance and get away from that ASAP! This requirement also ensures that the employee won't screw up in that role, because if you do, you can get written up, and your posting eligibility date could be reset. So, for example, in an hourly role, if you were written up at three months, your posting date would be reset to Day 1 and you would now have to wait another six months to post because of that write-up. If you were written up at five months and three weeks, it would still be reset. Didn't matter. This was never an issue for me because I was always on time and never really screwed up. It also helped that I was always cool with my Supervisors and Managers, or so I thought.

I woke up one morning, and was getting ready to go to work like a normal day. I had my eggs going on the stovetop, and was about to iron my shirt, then I received a call from my douche of a Front Desk Manager. I thought this was a tad odd, but thought that maybe he wanted me to grab something for him or a guest on the way in. This wasn't too uncommon as I was taking care of the rewards program for the hotel. I would occasionally run out to the local CVS or sweets shop to grab stuff for one of our loyalty guests. I answered my phone and asked, "What's up?" I got a really slow response from the Manager, asking, "What are you doing?" I explained to him that I was getting ready to come in. He slowly asks, "When are you supposed to come in?" I responded, "Noon, like I was scheduled. Why, what's up? Do you need me to grab something on the way in?" Noon to eight was one of our mid-shift times that I would do from time to time on busy check-out and check-in days because it covered both time frames to help the other A.M. and P.M. agents. He then proceeds to tell me that I was scheduled for 10 a.m. It was about 10:45 a.m. at this point. Of course, I questioned if he was looking at the wrong week's schedule, as our scheduling was a cluster to begin with. Apparently not. I apologized, and told him I would rush in. I somehow bicycled my ass off to make it there by 11:15 a.m.

He greeted me with his smartass-ness, asking, "What are we going to do about you being late?" I told him to do what he had to do, as clearly there was a misunderstanding. This was literally the first time I had ever been late (although I still think I was told a different time), so I don't know why the hell he was being so weird. So per usual, his shady-self asks me to come downstairs with him so he can smoke outside by the trash-shoot just to tell me he was writing me up for being late. Seriously, bro!? I was literally ready to post for that Accounting position that he KNEW I was interested in. That little fuck! Here, I thought we were "boys" with that whole comedy show shit we went through, and our porno watching cougar! Guess not.

The write-up was a "verbal" written warning, whatever the hell that means! Just a typical BS hotel work-around. I was hoping that this would still make it ok to post for a new position. I applied for the Accounting position anyway, because fuck staying at the desk with that prick of a Front Desk Manager after that shady move. I was even able to get the General Manager's signature on the sign-off to be able to apply. I was cool with him because we were both big *Washington Capitals* fans. Although, I think he was a bandwagon fan because I don't think he could name a single player on the team, except maybe Alexander Ovechkin. He just liked to load his office with free giveaways from all the games that he got free tickets to because the Sales Department had four tickets for each game to use for clients. Then, guess what followed? I was asked to join the Front Desk Manager againnnnn at that stupid dumpster smoke spot. He proceeded to tell me that he spoke with the GM and I would not be able to interview for the position because of that "verbal" write-up. Clearly, this guy wanted me to stay at the desk and continue to save his ass because I was good enough to do the job of two Agents at once, or even an Agent and a Supervisor. Are you fucking kidding me!? I told the Front Desk Manager immediately in response that I would begin my search for other jobs as I am not waiting in that same goddamn position for another six months. I think he was taken back a bit, and quickly tried to recover from it by making up this bogus-ass "Manager Training Program" he would run me through. No thanks. I'm good bro. Bye Felicia!

Sure enough, about a week after applying for a few new positions on my fav, *HCareers.com*, I landed an interview for a Front Desk Supervisor at a hotel whose management company's COO was actually my Supervisor Ted's father. Unfortunately, I didn't find this out until after my initial interview, so I couldn't even name drop. I was almost out of that damn hotel! It was crazy that I already cursed that hotel, and I was only there around six and a half months. Those basement rooms, snooty guests, the a-hole Front Desk Manager, and the fact that there wasn't much room to grow within the company, really got the best of me. I interviewed with the new hotel's General Manager, who just so happened to have been employed with the company I was leaving for over twenty years. He left the company because there wasn't much room for growth. Perfect, there was my in! He was a real genuine, nice guy, and he had actually just taken the job as GM a few weeks prior to my interview. He really liked my progressive attitude and the fact that I would come in with experience from multiple chains, and share my knowledge with our other Supervisors and Desk Agents. He said the current Front Desk staff at the hotel had been there for entirely too long, and were set in their ways, so he wanted a fresh face and attitude to whip them in shape. Sign me the fuck up! That's my jam.

I spoke with Ted about taking the position if I was offered it because he was a good mentor for career advice. This is when I found out about his dad being the COO of the management company of that hotel. He congratulated me, even though nothing was set in stone, but told me to be careful because that was a super old hotel. He joked about the parking garage caving in overnight in the near future. Typical Ted, always joking. He was also looking to make a move out of our current hotel (as he later did, like I mentioned), so of course he suggested I take it. Plus, it was higher pay and a higher position. Sure enough, I got offered the job soon after our discussion. I gladly accepted it. The new hotel's management company was much larger, and managed a variety of different hotel chains, so if I ever did move from that hotel, I could gain experience with a variety of different brands, yet remain within the same company. It sounded like a pretty solid deal! This hotel was situated in Georgetown, so it would be a cool new neighborhood for me to check out in our nation's capital. A part of town that I had only visited once or twice, but knew it had a great, yet ritzy reputation. I couldn't wait to see the look on my Front Desk Managers face when I submitted my written two weeks' notice at his favorite place, down by those fucking dumpsters! BOOM! Outta dis bitch!

Ever since the early days at my lovely starter hotel, I finally made it back to a leadership role. It took entirely too long to get back to this point, but I had my fun and experienced a completely different state (well, kind of two if you count DC), different lifestyles, and different types of hotels. I had already accumulated experience with a basic chain hotel, condo-hotel, timeshare hotel, and luxury boutique hotel. I had gained experience as a Valet Attendant, Bellman, Concierge, Front Desk Agent, "Lead" Front Desk Agent (eye roll), Loyalty Rewards Champion, Front Desk Manager/Assistant General Manager, and now a Front Desk Supervisor. Not too shabby. This new hotel management company actually managed a combination of hotels, condos, and timeshares, so I had this in the bag! In fact, it was the largest third-party management company in the world at the time. Upgrade!

This hotel had a very classy, luxurious feel to it. You drove up to the Valet loop on the cobblestone streets of Georgetown's famous M Street and were greeted with a lavish, burgundy colored awning with the American flag hanging proudly next to the hotel flag that had the name of the hotel elegantly written in gold cursive lettering on a black background. It was quite the historic looking and feeling hotel, even more-so than the last hotel I was at in an actual registered historic building. This building was all brick with antique light fixtures, as most buildings in Georgetown were. Guests were greeted at their car doors by Bellman with white gloves, burgundy colored suits with gold trim, and the typical Bellman-style hats you see in classic movies. Upon entering the lobby, it was covered in gold furnishings, with beige-colored marble floors and countertops. I'm pretty sure this was "the original" boutique hotel design, before boutique became trendy with bright ass colors and funky pieces of art.

The hotel happened to have a top-three restaurant in the city attached to it. It was an amazing Italian restaurant with a world-renowned chef. It donned a huge private chef's table, and outdoor seating with string lighting that was ever-so romantic. This was before every restaurant was doing that, so at the time it was pretty fancy-pants. So just imagine sitting outside on the cobblestone sidewalks with quiet (sometimes live) music playing, as people are passing by all dressed up to go eat or shop in Georgetown, or walking down to the Waterfront to enjoy a glass of wine and watch the boats pass by in front of the Jefferson Memorial. Cue the Marvin Gaye music. When I told people what hotel I was now working at, no one had a clue where it was, but when I mentioned this restaurant, everyone would react, "Ohhhhh, I love that place!" So whereas most hotels are known for the hotel itself, and the restaurants are secondary (if not unknown completely), it was opposite here.

So it was that time again...time to dust off the good ole H&M slim fit suits. With my little bump in pay, I was able to snag a few more from the H&M off of M Street. Any excuse to play the part of a successful hotel guy to my Front Desk Team, I would do it. Although, these suits became extremely difficult to wear to work as I had a new and longer route to get to the hotel. At least those shit brown suits from the previous hotel had some nut-room to be able to move in, and even bike comfortably to and from the hotel. The new commute was around fifteen minutes longer, but on one of the city's public transportation buses. The A/C in those things aren't the most reliable, so in the muggy hot DC summer months, this wasn't too pleasant in the slim fits. This was just one of the many reasons I hated the Winter's up North. It would be freezing outside, so the busses or interiors of buildings would crank the heat. Then you would sweat your ass off and pray to get back outside in the cold. At that point, you are just a hot, dried-up, sweaty mess. Anyways, I would get off the bus to walk through the quaint streets of Georgetown to enter through those elegant gold trimmed doors to be greeted with possibly the friendliest person I had ever met, and yes, even more so than Rodney. Is that humanly possible? Yup. And this friendly soul had a much cooler name, motherfuckin' Duskett!

Duskett was from the island of St. Maarten, so he spoke both English and French fluently. He had worked in hospitality on the island and at this hotel totaling some crazy thirty or so years at the desk. My man had it mastered! He had the directional open palm point that they teach us nailed! I would hope so after thirty damn years! He had this very friendly demeanor about him that made it seem like the world was such a perfect place when you stepped through those doors. The kind of person you always want around. Duskett was on every *TripAdvisor* review much like Rodney was. Although, as great as Duskett was, I got the vibe that he wasn't too keen on me coming in as the new Supervisor. I'm not exactly sure why because he had been in his role so long, I doubt he would even have an interest in my position, or maybe he just didn't like that I came in young and progressive, or maybe he just wasn't a fan of authority at all. I didn't know. After a few days of working with him and getting to know his background, and him learning mine, I think he came to like and respect me a lot.

Duskett became a huge help to me because there was a lot of training I needed at this hotel before I could even start "supervising." I thought the computer systems at my previous hotels were ancient...well, this one took the crown by miles! Luckily, Dusk-Diesel could operate it blindfolded! Majority of hotel reservation inquiries came from third-party websites, like *Expedia*, *Travelocity*, etc. Every hotel, or so I thought, had it set up to link automatically into the hotel reservation system. It would then usually say somewhere on the reservation that it was booked through one of these sites so that the Front Desk knew to fix some of the errors that came across in the system. Because it came through automatically, it would normally show "Direct Bill" or "Cash" as the payment method, instead of "Credit Card" to hold the reservation. This would make it even more imperative to get all of the information at check-in. Also, the names would normally come through spelled incorrectly. This made it one mother f'er trying to find third party reservations in the systems. The room types that they booked according to the third-party sites wouldn't come through correctly either and would cause some major issues, but that's an entire other freaking book!

I remember one of my first days at this hotel, I walked to the back area of the Front Desk and saw the summer Intern sitting at the computer with a stack of papers beside him, and asked him what the hell they were? It reminded me of movies and shows when the boss would go into the persons office and just slam a stack of files on his/her desk to input into the computer. That's what the massive pile next to him looked like. Our Intern proceeded to tell me that this stack was all of the reservations from third-party sites that needed to be input from scratch into our system. You have got to be kidding me! The amount of time that this took was insane! Here I thought I was taking a step in the right direction with this hotel. I was slowly starting to see shreds of evidence that it was well behind the times. I noticed the hotel collateral, advertising, uniforms, etc. was lacking. I got the vibe that because this hotel wasn't part of a run-of-the-mill chain, and instead, only managed by a large hotel management company, that it was not given one-hundred percent attention. It reminded me of my first Fort Myers Beach hotel. They didn't seem to have standards in place that other hotels I had worked at previously had. It was that naughty word in the hotel industry, a "franchise."

This hotel still had smoking rooms. Yes, smoking rooms. I know I seem old by some of the stories in this book, but not that old! What in the hell!? A luxury boutique hotel with smoking rooms...weird. It kind of worked for this hotel though because it had a rooftop pool (the only one in Georgetown at the time) and there were a few rooms that were entered from the outside on that pool deck. Smoker's paradise! And I guess you could say it was a niche for the hotel because you rarely found hotels with smoking rooms, let alone in a ritzy part of town like Georgetown. A lot of Europeans tended to smoke, and that was a large base of the tourists in Georgetown. So all-in-all, a good idea, especially if it didn't affect other non-smoking guests. This hotel also showed its age when we got a pretty severe rain storm. I remember coming into work for the evening shift and there were multiple trash cans placed under leaks coming from the ceiling in the back office area. Yes, multiple. I've seen a ceiling leak every now and again with a small bucket catching drops, but multiple large trash bins in one general area...scary. These leaks were coming through the white square typical ceiling squares you see in office complexes, and also through the receding light sockets. It seemed very odd. Come to find out, a few guest rooms were leaking like crazy too. This was pretty safe to assume because the Front Desk was on the main level, and that bitch was flooding! This monstrosity of a storm actually became classified as a derecho, which in layman's terms, means a shit-ton of rain for an overly extended period of time. I am talking about a week, plus. Just search *Google* for "Northeast Derecho 2012." 68,000 households were without power in DC alone, and resulted in twenty-four deaths in the Northeast region. This would explain the hotel flooding. This natural disaster resulted in a quick chain of crazy events at the hotel. Oh boy, here we go again. Can I just get a normal hotel with normal stuff that goes on? Not possible.

One day shortly after this storm, during one of my shifts, I saw a few suited gentlemen in the hotel, which we were told were Structural Engineers assessing the damages from the massive amounts of water. From what I assumed, this was for insurance purposes to get it fixed up and paid for. No big deal. Made sense. Then, a few days later, I came into my evening shift about an hour early, as I normally would to take advantage of the free employee meals the hotel offered...one before my shift, and one during my shift. Two free meals! #Winning! It seemed like just an ordinary day at the hotel until I was told that we would be having an entire hotel stand-up meeting at 4 p.m. Weird. We normally had stand-ups with only the heads of each department and Supervisors, as the rest of the employees were running the hotel, and we would know well in advance when all-team meetings would be. Whelp, we soon found out why this was the case. Our Human Resources Manager led the meeting, and let us know that there was severe water damage to the hotel because of the derecho...okkk, we knew that. Then, she informed us of some oh so lovely news...the hotel would be shut down immediately! Wait, what!? I probably took the biggest gulp I have ever taken in my life. Every thought possible was running through my head at this point. Mainly, that I was screweddddd! I had only been at the property and with the company for about three weeks, so there was no way my job was secure. Just great! The HR Manager then informed us that we would all be compensated for the next three months, and they would assist us in finding new jobs within the company. Well ok, now we're talking! Three months of free pay! Regardless of how great that sounded, there were still two big problems here: 1. I had to go on the job hunt again; and 2. I was still the Supervisor for the evening shift, so would have to shut this entire bitch down today! Those motherfucking Hotel Gods!

There are a few things (well, maybe more than a few) when working in hotels that are nightmarish. Most involve getting yelled at by guests for something that was out of your hands, or notifying a guest that they have to be walked to another hotel because your hotel was overbooked that night. Well, try having to walk all 120-plus guests that were already staying in the hotel, and an additional sixty arriving that day to check-in, and then getting yelled at by all of them. Fuck me! The employees were told in the meeting that they could either stay and finish their shift; or go home, and either way they would be getting paid. WTF!? What genius thought of that strategy? Me, being raised with good morals and ethics knew that I would be staying and finishing the shift, and likely beyond. Not to mention, I'm pretty sure I wouldn't get a great reference letter from my Manager for any future positions if I just rolled out. So now, imagine this scenario, but with only a few members of our staff remaining, because the rest decided to leave. Literally, kill me!

Here is the word-for-word letter we received:

Dear Paul (Tony) A.:

This letter is to inform you that due to extensive water damage, XX Company, LLC, is closing the entire XX Hotel and restaurant located at XX, Washington DC 20007, effective July 12, 2012. It is unknown how long the Hotel will remain closed, but it is expected to be more than six (6) months.

As a result of this closure, regrettably, employment separations at the Hotel are expected to begin on or about September 13, 2012 and your employment will terminate on September 13, 2012. You are being placed immediately on a paid administrative leave until your employment termination date. During such leave, you should not report to the Hotel unless instructed to do so by management. You will be paid wages equivalent to your average weekly wages over the last quarter, up to a maximum of 40 hours of straight-time pay per week, less applicable taxes and withholdings. Additionally, you will continue to maintain your current insurance benefits on the same basis as presently and during your leave, will accrue any other benefits (e.g., vacation) for which you are eligible.

In connection with this shutdown, you will not have the right to bump or displace other employees working for the Company.

This information is being provided at present without greater advance notification because of the unexpected and extensive water damage in the hotel which was not previously foreseeable. The above dates are based on the best information currently available. You will be notified if there is any further change in this timetable.

Should you have questions or require additional information and assistance, please contact XX, Director of Human Resources at XX. Beginning on Monday, July 16, 2012, questions or concerns should be directed to our Human Resources hotline at XX.

Very Truly Yours,

Hotel XX

By

After we got this, only a few Bellman, Valet Attendants, and Engineers remained, and proceeded to go door-to-door to gather guests to the desk to make them aware of the bad news. If they were not there, they would slip a letter under the door (in case they were indeed in there) and deactivate the door key so the guests would be forced to come to the desk when trying to re-enter the room. I would then have to precede to give them the terrible news, and set them up at another hotel in the area, with their first night and transportation to the new location paid for in full. One humongous problem, there were only a few rooms available in all of Georgetown that night, and the price of those were out of this world, but that really didn't matter at this point. This meant we would have to send majority of guests across the city to other hotels. It was a mad-house, to say the least. Guests were fuming! Think about booking your hotel in a certain area because you had an event nearby, or planned to shop, or go to a club, or needed/wanted water access, or whatever reason, and then being told you have to go stay fifteen-to-thirty minutes away for just one night (paid), and then you can figure out the rest of your stay. Fuck that! Everyone was rushing the desk trying to figure out the dilemma, and demanded to stay. Obviously, they could not in this case. Go for it Ma'am/Sir, and have the five floors above you crash down on top of you while you are sleeping.

We literally had the Front Desk cash box just sitting on the desk to hand guests cash to taxi to their new hotel. The idea was to log it as we went, although it became complete madness, so the logging went out the window real quick! I would hand guests a twenty, thinking they would be happy, but instead they would be upset, saying that it wouldn't be enough for the cab. Fine, here, take forty! I honestly could have cared less at that point because no senior-level Manager was there helping, and I knew I wouldn't be working for them anymore. And frankly, I didn't blame the guests in that shitty situation.

With normal "walk" situations, the hotel would be overbooked (meaning more reservations made for the amount of rooms it had left), and we would have one, maybe two, hotels lined up that we had already spoken with in advance agreeing to take our guests for the night, and bill the hotel for that first night's stay. In this crazy situation, we had a whole list of options for guests to walk them to. We did this for two reasons. One, because as I said, Georgetown hotels were very close to selling out, and because some guests were heading back to the airport or train tomorrow anyway. In that case, we would put them in a hotel by Union Station, which was the main train station in DC, and they could get to the airport pretty easy from there. Our anticipation of people wanting to stay closer to Union Station was not as high as we were hoping, so we had a lot of angry guests. This resulted in us at the desk having to call a bunch of other hotels closer to the Georgetown area to see if we could walk the guests to their hotel. In reality, it turned into the guest saying, "How about Chinatown, or U Street, or DuPont?" I mean, if you were changing course for the rest of your stay, at least change to an area you wanted to visit anyway, right? It was the least we could do to help them.

You'll notice that our hotel would only take care of the first night at another property. There lied another big issue. If a guest had planned to stay with us for a week, and it was only their first night in town, they would then have to pay whatever the rate is at another hotel for the remainder of their trip. Fingers crossed, they got a cheaper rate. And if they booked through a third party site like *Expedia*, good luck ever getting that money back! To be honest, I have no clue how our hotel handled those because it would be handled at a later point. I think we told the guests that they would be getting refunded for their stay, but realistically, there would be a lot on the back end that would need to be done to accomplish that, and it would not be quick. Just think about this scenario: You booked on *Expedia*, and paid in advance for a week at our hotel. You already stayed one night and were told to leave the next day. So you have five other nights (because we covered one) that you would not be getting reimbursed for at that moment, and have to find a new hotel, and pay for the remainder of your trip. That, or try and change your flight to an earlier date, and I'm sure you would be charged additional by the airline for that. And, if you did decided to stay and pick another hotel/neighborhood, then having to try and change and/or cancel your excursions that you already booked for the week. A complete travel nightmare. *TripAdvisor* was about to be lit!

The poor guests that were checking-in that day that we couldn't reach in advance, were getting a lovely greeting of, "Hello, goodbye! You're being walked to a different hotel because this hotel is out of commission!" They probably weren't out of their cab from the airport for more than five minutes before getting turned back around. They likely wondered why there were no Bellman and/or Valet Attendants outside to meet them as they entered the hotel. They had peaced the F out! Once they got to the desk, I would give them no time to question. I would walk around the desk, grab their bags, and assist them to the nearby street corner to catch a cab. All the meanwhile, explaining to them the situation as we walked, not even giving them a chance to react. I would toss their bags in the cab, inform the driver which hotel to take them to, throw them a twenty dollar bill, and off the guests went, shell-shocked...with a smile on my face the whole time of course! Not to mention, I was literally praying to my favorite Hotel Gods that the hotel wouldn't collapse on me every time I entered and exited the building. I would then make sure to cross their names off of our check-in list so we would know when all of the arrivals had "attempted" to check-in. I know for sure that we didn't do that every time because of how chaotic it was. Safe to say it was the worst day of my life, and probably will continue to be that way for the remainder of my career. Here was a new addition to my already lucrative hotel resume…"Shut down an entire hotel with a half hours' notice." I was at this property for such a short period of time, that no-joke, I couldn't even tell you the names of one individual from my time there, besides Duskett. This comes to show you who makes impressions on you.

Who would have thought that once I left my first hotel in DC that I would be stuck looking for jobs again three weeks later? Not me! Goddammit! But oddly enough, I think it worked out for the better. I was able to take about a month off to go on a cruise with my family, and then a week long guys trip to Nags Head, North Carolina. This was much needed to clear my head before having to search for jobs again. The company of the hotel that shut down sent us listings of available jobs within the company in the general DC area, but none were positions I was interested, or was even qualified for. That sucked, but I wasn't too concerned about waiting for positions to open up with them, as I wasn't too thrilled with the company after that crisis anyway. I began to peruse jobs on *HCareers*. I began finding out that Supervisor positions were not only few and far between in the city, but my whopping three weeks of supervisory experience sure didn't add to my resume, but instead open up eyes of the interviewers as to how short-spanned my time was at the hotel. I ended up having to do the ultimate no-no that I told myself I wouldn't do, and look for positions below the Supervisor level. I started looking at Front Desk Agent positions because my three months of pay was fading away fast.

I ended up getting a call back for a Front Desk Agent position at a major chain hotel that happened to be just five blocks from my apartment! This was amazing, as commutes are totally underrated for sucking ass! It was a brand new property in an up-and-coming area of DC. "Brand new" stood out to me because the last thing I wanted was having to work in a shit-hole hotel again, and having to shut it down! I was called for an interview screening by a really calm, soft-spoken guy named Thomas. He was the Front Desk Manager. He asked me a few questions about my background and schooling. I remember after I rambled on and then let him speak, he said, "Soooo…you went to WVU?" I scarily responded, "Yes?" He followed with, "I went to Clemson…" Now, normally you wouldn't think much of this, as the schools don't have much history with one another, but in this case, the college football Orange Bowl game had taken place just months before, and West Virginia set an ALL-TIME HIGH record in scoring on the Clemson

Tigers. I am talking about seventy points...in a football game! A good old fashion butt-whoopin! I didn't quite know how to respond when he told me this, as he could be my future boss. He actually laughed it off, so it made me feel at ease. Sweww. Dodged that one, and he asked me to come in for an in-person interview.

I went in for the interview and had my first experience with this particular chain's intense interview process. Basically, it was a large packet of questions that I would have to answer in a "STAR" response format. This stood for the **S**ituation that occurred, **T**asks/**A**ctions taken, and my **R**esponse to the situation. I gotta be honest, me being the OCD person that I am, I loved the organization behind this interview process. It was way more legit than other hotel gigs I interviewed with previously. This one felt professional. Luckily, Thomas wasn't too strict with the process, as it was my first time doing it. He was a good ole Southern Gentleman. He had a southern draw (accent), and wore a very loose/prep-like suit. He was a big fan of golf, and I could already tell he was a polo-wearing, palm tree embroidered shorts, and visor wearing kind of guy. Growing up in the South, people tend to go this route.

So, I got the job! Woooo! Third damn one that year. Jesus! Off the bat, I realized that this chain had their shit together. They had systems in place, procedures to follow, collateral out the ass, and marketing and advertising all over TV, magazines, and the internet. I would turn on an NFL game and it would be plastered with commercials of my new hotel brand. I loved it! Finally, a hotel with organization for my OCD ass! This hotel was crisp and clean. The building was all-glass from the outside, with modern furnishings inside. Guests were met by a security desk on the first floor, where they would hop in the elevators to head up to the Front Desk and a limited-service restaurant. People could only progress to further upper floors with a room key. Genius! This kept the scrubs out of the hotel. However, some guests would complain that the security desk was not a good first impression as you enter the hotel because it gave off the image that it was in a bad neighborhood. It was pretty sketchy at that time. I would simply inform the guests that it is a nice neighborhood, and I actually lived in it as well. It's better to be safe than sorry, and I credit this particular hotel for that security feature. I wish my first hotel had this, as we had riff raff at the wazoo coming in and out of that place.

Perhaps, the best part about this hotel and new position was the fact that I was paid more than I had been previously in any of my other hotel roles. Hell yes! About damn time! It was paying seventeen an hour. Yes, seventeen an hour for a Front Desk Agent. Amazing! It was sad that I was paid more in this role than the Supervisor role I was previously in, and the Front Desk Manager/AGM role at my first hotel. My boy Thomas knew to start me at the top of the position's pay scale because of my experience, and the likelihood that I would not take less. So, as much as my bouncing around hotels seemed stupid as hell, at least my pay rate was increasing.

As I said earlier, this hotel was in an up-and-coming area in the city. Gentrification at its finest! The city was known for taking crummy areas and throwing in nice apartment complexes and office buildings to bring in the wealthy, and clear out the poor/homeless. Northeast DC wasn't exactly an area to brag about at that time. There were two sketchy night clubs within walking distance of the hotel, along with a metro stop. Metro stops were notorious for homeless hangouts. This neighborhood did indeed have a few government buildings, such as the Department of Justice, and the Bureau of Alcohol, Tobacco, Firearms and Explosives, better known as the ATF. You would think this would be a nice area, considering those were located here. The city renamed this area to "NoMa," short for "North of Massachusetts Avenue." Oooh fancy! A little hip nickname secret that New York City is famous for doing to their trendy neighborhoods. This put off a vibe that the city was trying to revamp it, and rid of the old name with the poor reputation. The neighborhood had added a brand new grocery store, sandwich shops, Starbucks, upscale pet store, and a few nice new modern apartment complexes. "If you build it, they will come." --- *Field of Dreams*

Our guests were very different during the work week than on the weekends. The work week was filled with mostly government employees, and during the weekends, the hotel was filled with club-goers or hotel employees using their great discounted rates. The rates at this hotel were usually really cheap because it wasn't exactly in the heart of the city, or in the nicest area. The hotel also faced the issue of being positioned directly beside the metro rails and train tracks. There were rooms that faced them, which became a lovely topic of conversation for guests checking-in. I had been in these rooms a hundred times, enough to know that you could not hear the metro or the train from them. Yet, time and time again, guests would come down after going into their room to request a non-train track side room. I learned to not even argue, and just switch their room. Not worth it. Half of our rooms were located on that side, so if we didn't have any available, I would have to put on the sales cap and sell the shit out of those rooms. I would even run up to the room with them at times, and sit there while the metro and train rode by to reassure them it was quiet. And honestly, those rooms had floor-to-ceiling windows, and were larger rooms than the rest, so I would be happy if I were put into one of those. Just throw on some light music while you sleep, and you'll be fine. As I eventually found out, it wasn't the metro or train moving along the tracks that was the issue for guests already staying in them. It was actually the horns that the train would blow at the ass-crack of dawn every damn morning. Apparently, the Train Drivers had to blow the horn when crossing a public road, or something along those lines. FML. Here, I learned that there is no such thing as a perfect hotel, old or new.

We had a pretty strong leadership team at this hotel. There was Thomas, who I already explained was a very calm-demeanored Manager who could handle any troublesome situation by making it seem ever so simple. It was like magic. He kind of reminded me of Anthony from my first DC hotel. Thomas was apparently a scratch golfer and aspired to be a Golf Course Designer, so this explained a lot. If you have met any really good golfers, they always seem to have this personality type. They have the patience necessary not to chuck their clubs in the lake after a bad swing (Dad). The company we were with had resorts all over the world, with state-of-the-art golf courses, so his vision was to get into that area. What a badass path to take in the hotel industry that I would have never thought of!

Then we had Micah, who was the Assistant General Manager. He was another great calm voice of reason. He was an African American man that acted whiter than me. He actually tore his achilles tendon playing tennis within the first few weeks of me working there. How much more white can you get!? LOL! He would have to hobble around on crutches for the next few months, after doing a short stint in a wheelchair. Hilarious! That is an injury you don't wanna mess with. Micah was great for our sketchy weekend crowd because they would oftentimes try and take advantage of us Front Desk Agents, and then here came Micah, the Assistant GM in full suit and tie limping in to reinforce. Micah and a few of us Front Desk Agents had one night in particular of some rowdiness. Let's just say many shots were involved, and a lot of memory loss the next day. Normally, I wouldn't go get sloshed with an AGM, but Micah was pretty cool and knew that anything outside of the hotel was truly outside of the hotel, unless of course you were wearing a shirt with the hotel logo on it and making a bad name for it.

We also had an Operations Manager, which was basically a fancy name for Food & Beverage Manager at this property. Kyla handled the small, limited-service restaurant, coffee shop, and she handled the catering for any small meetings. Really, this restaurant was closer to a full-service one. This brand had been trying to make the experience more like a full-service hotel. Kyla was a little more like me in the fact that she wouldn't put up with guests crap. They tried to feed her typical the BS, and she wouldn't take it. She might have come across as a bitch to some guests, but was actually a very sweet lady. I would stand by her at the desk and watch her do her thing, and just remember reacting in my head to things she would say to the guests like, "Duamn girl! Tell em!" She did not mess! Not sure this was the best approach in the world, but we all have our own styles. Hers just may not have gotten too many friendly *TripAdvisor* reviews. Either way, I liked Kyla as a Manager a lot.

Last but not least, we had our fearless General Manager, Chris. Chris was the man! This dude came in after our old GM got fired for underperforming (so we heard). Since this particular chain was very loyal to their employees, I was told she was transferred to another property that was much easier to run. Our hotel needed someone with proven success with numbers, and where else would that come from? A Salesperson! Chris had previously been a Director of Sales for the majority of his hotel career, so he was a great choice for this hotel. We also had an on-site Sales Manager, Samitri, who would work with Chris to get business from companies around the area. As I found out, she actually helped to pull through group business that was booked off-site by Sales Managers at our Regional Sales Office in Northern Maryland. The Sales Office would receive inquiries for meetings and/or group room blocks at the hotel, and they would price and attempt to close. Sometimes the client would indeed need to visit the hotel, so Samitri would be the go-to person for the client on-site. Here, she could find out the ticking points with the customer, and either close it, or let the Sales Manager from the office know, and they could close the sale. She was also the one who would set up any amenities, breakfast coupons, etc. for group guest arrivals. This company had a three-step sales process for the most part: Sales Executives that would go out and get the leads and send them to the Sales Office; Sales Managers that would try and sell those leads over the phone and/or email; and on-Site Sales Managers that would assist in closing the sale, and be there for any on-site issues for the group as they were staying or holding their meetings at the hotel.

This was a pretty cool side of hotels that I was way more interested in than working at the damn Front Desk. We had two small meeting rooms (as most hotels of this size have) where groups would reserve for a few hours, an entire day, or multiple days. At our particular hotel, it was the Engineers duty to set up the meeting rooms to the group's specifications, and the Operations Manager would make sure the restaurant prepared and executed any necessary food and beverage catering associated with the meeting. This would all be listed on a Banquet Event Order (BEO) that Kyla would prepare once the Sales Manager from the Sales Office would get a signed contract and turn over all the information to the property to execute everything. We had a Property Coordinator (basically a Sales Assistant) that would input the group's guest room information so that us at the Front Desk didn't have to do a damn thing besides get their ID, read any notes on file, and that's a wrap. Sometimes we would have to pass out meal vouchers at check-in and clear out any parking charges before they checked out. During the meetings, we would occasionally have to unlock the meeting room door for them, assist in turning the meeting room's temperature up or down, and/or maybe get some coffee sent to their meeting room. We were basically just the messengers for Engineering or Kyla to take care of these requests because we were normally the only one manning the Front Desk.

I was pretty much glued to the desk during my beginning few months at the job because I was learning my SIXTH Front Desk system in the course of a few years! God forbid any of these companies use the same damn system! Oh well, it expanded my resume. Always gotta look at things with a positive, or try to. Because this hotel was new, it had features that no other had at the time. It was setting the trend for others to follow. The Front Desk had three separate counters, or pods, as they called them, with computers to check-in/out at each one. This was a much more welcoming design than the usual long Front Desks that Agents are stuck behind. Here, Agents could walk around the pods and present the keys to the guest, or even have them come behind the pod so you can show them things on the computer, such as directions somewhere. It was great! It was not for the shy Agents who liked to hide behind the desk. No damn chairs or stools though! This Front Desk area did, however, have a little back corner area equipped with a small desk and chair where we could tuck away and sit for short periods of time, until we heard feet scurrying around the Front Desk pods. This didn't really serve much purpose for me besides eating some food real quick. One of our Agents used it for laying out her homework and working on it between helping guests. I don't know how the hell she could concentrate doing that. My head was all over the damn place at the desk, and could only imagine trying to read or crunch numbers in between.

The restaurant area off of the lobby was awesome! It had these cute little cubbies, almost like booths in a restaurant, and had their own little personal TV's in them. They were great for working the desk during those boring overnight shifts! Guests could come here, plug in their laptop, grab a bite to eat, and catch up on some *Oprah!* The bar/restaurant area served breakfast and coffee in the morning, and dinner and drinks at night. The guests would order, take a little number, and their meals would be delivered to their tables, similar to some of the fast-casual restaurants out there. At night, dinner tended to be a little more formal. The Bartender would tell them to sit where they wanted, and he would bring them a menu, take their orders, and eventually deliver to them. I don't think he was supposed to do this, but I am sure his tips reflected this extra level of service. The Bartender was a really cool Ethiopian guy, as there were tons in DC. In fact, at the time, I think it housed the second most Ethiopians in the world, next to Ethiopia itself! Who would have known? I even dated an Ethiopian girl at the time. She was naturally very hospitable, always wanting to make me food, and prepping strong Ethiopian coffee for me before my drives home late at night, or early in the morning. I remember the Bartender always looked tired as hell, and in talking with him, found out that he drove for this "little" car service company called *Uber*. This was back when they only allowed drivers to have a black luxury car, and the price was more expensive than taxis. Crazy how things have changed!

I remember the Bartender would always complain about the parking at the hotel. It was thirty-five to forty bucks for guests, and a whopping discount down to nine dollars a day for employees. But

Jesus Christ, nine bucks times twenty working days in a month is pretty steep! There goes like a day and a half's worth of pay, and that was just for my positions pay. Thank God I could walk to and from the hotel! Parking costs would most definitely fall into the "hate" category of working in hotels. It is absurd to me to think that your place of work makes you pay to park there where you are freaking working! I mean, I get it, there aren't that many spaces because it is in a city, blah blah. But was that my fault that they didn't take this into consideration when building the damn garage, especially considering this was a new hotel!? Now, don't get me wrong, if it was a thousand-year old building like my previous two DC hotels, that would be semi-understandable. But man, it really shows who hotels look out for, and it sure as hell isn't its own damn employees! SMH.

During the day, when the coffee bar was technically closed, us Front Desk Agents became Baristas when guests arrived looking for drinks. It carried the same products as a Starbucks. This was a pain in the ass, as we would have to leave our pods, and walk across to the bar to whip up a damn Frappuccino! This would leave any phone calls or guests at the desk stranded to wait until we were done. After making their drinks, we would then have to run back over to the pod to charge that guest for the drink, as the restaurant system was different than the Front Desk one. At this point, working in any Front Office, I learned to just assume I would always be short-staffed, no matter what hotel it was. Although, as much as I complained about having to be a part-time Barista, it was great, because I got to make free drinks for the cost of "On the house," as my best friend Scotty would say. Me and Iced Caramel Macchiatos became best friends that year. My GM, Chris, even taught me how to put the fancy caramel swirl in the cup, and pull half of the straw wrapper up and make a fancy twirl out of it. Legit AF!

Our uniforms were pretty trendy at this hotel. We wore suit pants and jackets with a solid colored dry fit shirt underneath. So no uncomfortable and sweaty button up shirt, and no goddamn tie! Amazing! We could wear comfy black slip-ons (like Converse style) too, versus stuffy lace-up dress shoes. This made it a much nicer work environment. This also saved us from having to pick out an outfit every day. You know how amazing that is!? Just wake up from a hangover, snag the same pants, shirt, jacket, and shoes, spritz on your cologne, and good to go! This enabled us to save on laundry, and not have to buy new work clothes. The outfits were comfortable enough for me to walk the five blocks from my apartment to work in them. I eventually learned to leave the jacket in my locker at the hotel so I didn't have to worry about that getting messed up. I would even leave my nametag on it so I wouldn't have to deal with that daily. I had the system down!

I must say, working at this particular hotel was a cakewalk. I mean, it had its issues, but as I was saying, between the uniforms, having great management, having the pods making handling guests super easy and quick, it never really being too busy to handle, it was a breeze! I guess I had done it enough at this point that I didn't really stress out anymore. Also, after the last insane hotel closing episode, I was pretty seasoned. You could call me a veteran. I think the hardest task at this property was re-stocking the cabinets in the lobby with guest supplies, like toothbrushes, toothpaste, deo, women's products, etc., and having to answer the phones, or having to check someone in mid-stocking. This hotel would even let us wear our favorite NFL team jerseys on game days while working the desk, since the brand was an NFL sponsor, as I mentioned before. And let me remind you, games were on Sundays, Mondays, Thursdays, sometimes Saturdays, and Holidays. So literally half of my time at the desk was spent wearing my array of *Cowboys* jerseys.

One obstacle we did face at this property was the fact that our brand gave it a name super close to the name of another one of our properties a mile away. Hotels will often use local attractions nearby in its actual names to better attract search results, but they would alter them a bit if they had multiple in that same area. For example, our hotel was called the "XX Hotel US Capitol," and the other was called the "XX Hotel Washington Capitol Hill/Navy Yard." Needless to say, tired businessman would hop in a cab and ask the driver to take them to the "Capitol XX Hotel," and they had a 50/50 shot of the cab driver getting it right. Tired businessmen/women arriving turned into angry businessmen/women real quick when they discovered they were at the wrong hotel, and would have to grab another cab and head to the correct one. Of course, it always seemed to be our fault as the Desk Agents. Your everyday friendly punching bag. You're welcome.

There was a lot of BS time between the Front Desk Agents if we had the pleasure of working the same shift together, but because it tended to be quiet, this wasn't too often. I remember in some downtime, the F&B Supervisor and I would stand there on the *GolfNow* app and try to find cheap tee times for our next day off together. That app was legitttttt! For us cheap-asses working in hotels, you have to know the bargains, and this was the spot for cheap golf. We were able to find dirt-cheap nine-hole offers, normally on off-peak times, and at crummier golf courses. We didn't give a shit, as long as being outside, boozing, and stogies were involved, we were in...especially when it was like seven bucks each person with the golf cart already included! That's just silly. This was also around the same time that dating apps were becoming popular and I remember in some of this Front Desk downtime helping create one of my coworkers *Plenty of Fish* account. The things we do in hotels! She is now married with kids. I wonder if that was a *POF* date? You're welcome!

I was learning more and more about this company as I worked there. Come to find out, the hotel discounts were insanely good! I could get on the company website and look up any hotel in the world and get a discount with my employee rate, and even offer discounts to friends and family members. The company offered half-off of these already great rates during the winter holiday season. We could get rooms for like twenty bucks! Insane! We also had a benefits site where we could go and order discounted items through regular merchandisers. We had cell phone service discounts, ticket discounts, you name it. This made me feel very appreciated as an employee. The best part of all the perks had to be that if we stayed with the company for twenty-five years, we would be able to stay at their hotels for free! Wait, what!? Yes, you heard that correctly. Suffer through this industry for a quarter century, and lay your head in Aruba on the cost of "On the house." Now there's some encouragement to stay loyal to a company, instead of hopping around like crazy, like I had been doing.

My friend, Luke, and I took full advantage of this discount one evening when we found out this EDM (Electronic Dance Music) group called Krewella was going to be playing at the Echostage in DC, which was right up the street from the hotel I worked at. Well, not exactly right up the street, but like a twenty-to-thirty minute walk through the hood. With a little extra booze, we knew it would be fine. We were young. I remember hitting the hotel bar before the show while waiting for Luke to get to the hotel. My *Uber*-driving Bartender buddy whipped me up some solid beverages, a few of which were free, and I tipped him very nicely in return. Us hospitality peeps gotta look out for one another! You could say this was an "unwritten perk" of working in the biz. I was getting pretty blitzed, pretty early because Luke wouldn't hurry his ass up. He finallyyyyyyy got there super late, as I was getting nervous we wouldn't make it to the show on time, even though it was only like 9pm. He threw his stuff in the room, and we headed out. Luke had recently started to really get into smoking weed. I mean, we had both dabbled in college, but had mostly stuck to the legal stuff. We would commonly sit on his porch on nice days after class smoking flavored tobacco from his hookah. Luke lived in the sticks of Virginia post-college, so there wasn't much going on out there, so why not take up a little ganja. About ten minutes into our trek to the club, we came upon a closed up U-Haul store with all the trucks sitting outside. There were no gates or anything, which seemed odd. I was just looking for a good corner to pee in as I had already broken the seal, whereas Luke was looking for something else. After I squirted one out, I turned around and Luke was nowhere to be found. I asked aloud, "Luke, you ready to roll man?" He was behind one of the U-Haul trucks, and said, "Let me see something real quick," and pulls the little lever on the back door of the U-Haul.

Sure enough, that bitch was unlocked. They likely all are because when people return them at night, they throw the keys in the little compartment in the office door, and because the trucks are empty, they leave them unlocked. Luke was on a mission to find a spot to smoke, and so he did! He and I hopped in, shut the door behind us, and hot-boxed the shiz out of that U-Haul. I will never forget, this was when *Snapchat* had just come out, and I took a *Snap* of us lighting up, and sent it to a few friends. All you could see was darkness, and a lighter meeting the little green nuggets in the bowl. My brother, Connor, cracks up over that *Snap* to this day!

Somehow, we managed to make it to the show on time, had entirely too much fun, and got separated, of course. I clung on to some cute EDM chick, and Luke, at some point pretty early on, headed back to the hotel. He was hurting. We had an energy drink on the walk to the show, and it seemed like that mixed with the smoking and booze didn't settle well for him. No worries, because I was very preoccupied, and having the time of my life. That was the first EDM show I had ever been to, and was like two rows back of the stage. It was amazing! I eventually headed back to the room solo after the show in that super sketchy area of DC. Probably not one of my best decisions, but oh well. Again, *Uber* was not prevalent, or cheap then, so that wasn't an option. I got back to the room, and was greeted with an all-too familiar scent. It reeked of pot! The bathroom door was closed, light still on, with the fan blasting, and hotel towels shoved underneath the door. That dumbass Luke had hot-boxed the bathroom. Fucking idiot! He was knocked out in the bed, so I couldn't even yell at him at the moment. Remember, this was the hotel I worked at! That could literally get me fired instantly. When you use that employee discount, it holds you accountable for whoever uses it, even if it was a family member or friend using it in another town. That dumb shit! Luckily, I was cool with the Housekeepers, Maintenance, and Managers, so I never heard about it again. Thank God! In my eventual next role, one of my buds didn't get so lucky with smoking in the room using the employee discount. It went on his record with the company permanently, but fortunately, he was able to keep his job. Whoops! Don't do drugs kids!

This chain also required you to stick with a non-management role for six months before being able to post for a new position within the company, so that drug offense could postpone you. I did my six months in this role, and was ready to bounce! This was mainly because I was hopping around so much laterally, that I was ready to start moving upwards, and like I was saying, I kind of mastered the Guest Services/Front Desk Department. Now, I was eyeing the hotel chain's Regional Sales Office. I was ready to put on my big boy pants and snag a Monday to Friday gig. Our GM, Chris, really caught my eye with his Hotel Sales background. I really liked his mindset, and saw myself going that route in the company. It seemed like there was a lot more success to be had and respect given in the Sales side of hotels. At the end of the day, the Sales Department is what brings people to the hotel, and brings in the money. Most people start in the Sales Office as Assistants, and after six months, move to Sales Manager roles. I applied to any and every Sales Assistant position that popped up, which as I found out, I probably shouldn't have done, as HR can see that I applied to all of those positions and it looks desperate. Crap! I wasn't getting callbacks worth shit, and wondered if that was why! About a month later, after I had given up, I ended up finally getting a call from what sounded like a really young and vibrant guy who informed me he was a Director of Sales at the Mid-Atlantic Group Sales Office. YAASSSSSSSSS!!! Let's goooooo!

CHAPTER 4: SELLING THE DREAM

The phone call was super casual, as this guy was clearly not your stuck-up, serious guy you would think of when you hear the title "Director." He told me, as a whole, that the office was super casual, and people wore "pastel-colored Urban Outfitters pants," and go to happy hours together, etc. Somehow we got on the topic of music, and he mentioned one of his favorite bands, Passion Pit. Oddly enough, my bud from high school who I grew up playing soccer with, just so happened to be the drummer for them at the time. This earned me some solid brownie points, and he eventually asked me to come in for an interview. This was after he told me that it is near impossible to get fired from the Sales Office. He literally started whispering to tell me that I would basically have to kill someone to lose a job there. Interesting. Don't ask me how that came up, but he was rambling on, and I let him. It pretty much sounded like I was good to go for the job before ever walking into his office to have to answer those fucking STAR questions again. I was six for six on my hotel interviews so far, so might as well go for lucky number seven!

I pulled up to this monster, all-glass, typical corporate looking building right on a large lake. I entered the FREE parking garage (fuckin' right!) and walked into this beast of a building. I awaited someone to let me into the hotel chain's private floor, as you needed a special key to enter it. Alright fancy asses! I was greeted with a few of the hotel chain's ginormous logos on a frosted glass, modern entranceway. Bad-freaking-ass! I had made it to the big leagues...or so I had hoped. I strolled through the cubicles in...you guessed it...my job-killa H&M suit, looking around at all the young twenty-something-year-old faces! I saw a couple decent looking ladies, which was quite refreshing. Not that there weren't any working at my previous properties, but this was next level, fancied up business chicks with the glasses. You know, the naughty librarian look. Fuck yes! Something I could get used to. I was dropped off by my escort at the middle offices where the Director's sat. I saw, I came, and I conquered.

Let's take a moment and reflect on what just happened. Maybe next to losing my virginity, or maybe scoring game-winning goals in hockey, this could have been quite possibly the most exciting moment of my life! I just locked in my FIRST "official" Monday to Friday 9-5 job since graduating college! After working shit-shift after shit-shift in my previous roles, the time had finally come where I was in the corporate world. Normal holiday days off, normal benefits, normal holiday parties, normal cubicles, normal office-wide emails, normal everyday being the damn same...basically the movie *Office Space* in real life. I craved it, which is probably odd to most that do that routine daily and want to kill themselves. No more having to wait until someone got back from lunch to take mine; or cover the desk and phones while our operator called out hungover; no more covering the desk while someone shot-up heroin; no more being any more guest's bitch; no more waiting for Rodney to quit socializing with guests to come help me at the desk; and no more acting like the basement rooms are our best ones straight to people's faces. Thank Christ!

I would now have an hour lunch at my leisure, a half hour of which was paid. A whole goddamn hour! I didn't know what I was going to do with myself. I went from taking fifteen minute lunch breaks working as a Laborer for my dad's masonry company growing up, to then not being able to take any lunches at all at the Front Desk, or force feeding myself ducking into the back office, to now having an entire goddamn hour! As *Food Network*'s Guy Fieri says, "That's just out of bounds!" I would now be able to go out to lunch with other coworkers, instead of by myself in a little crappy, smelly, employee break room, or messy back office at the hotel, with phones ringing off the hook. This may sound like a little thing, but it would make the work atmosphere so much better. I would actually be able to go home and grab a quick bite if I wanted, as I lived close to the office, or maybe walk to Potbelly's and grab my chicken salad on whole grain, or even walk down to the Barnes & Noble and look at another business start-up book. Living the life!

Along with the ability to grab lunch with friends because of these lovely new banker's hours, I was able to enjoy happy hours routinely with coworkers or friends that also had normal hours. God, you wouldn't believe how great that was! And weekends! Omg I had my weekends back for the first time since my first hotel gig! And those really didn't count because I was always attached to my phone as the Manager. I could finally go on trips without having to request off over a month in advance because working the weekend is standard at the desk. And thank God, because every friend of mine decided to start getting married around this time, and of course the weddings were held on weekends. I would finally be able to take advantage of paid holidays actually on the holiday. I could now enjoy the three-day weekend when a holiday fell on a Monday or Friday, or if I simply wanted to use my PTO, and take one off, I could. So being part of this "corporate" world was a very nice change. Shit, maybe the hotel industry was for me after all! Ha!

My actual position in the Sales Office turned out to be even better than I expected. The normal Sales Assistant position in the office entailed preparing proposals, contracts, and doing follow-ups for a few different Sales Managers. My role was to assist three different Director of Sales. Occasionally, I would also assist each markets' Team Leaders, and the entire office's General Manager. This was awesome because I was the right-hand man for the top people in the office. I got to sit through all of the leadership meetings, and hear everything that was going on before anyone else. I was able to hear about hirings/firings, new strategies that were in the pipeline, and even promotions that were in place. It was pretty cool. I ran reports to determine our office sales numbers daily, monthly, quarterly, and yearly. Sales Managers mainly only cared about their quarterly numbers, as that was what they were bonused on, and the Leaders seemed to care more about the in-the-year-for-the-year booking numbers, so one would assume their bonuses were structured around that. I never knew.

Working closely with high-level Managers also taught me quite a few things about the corporate workplace. I was able to soak up life advice, career advice, and even love advice from my Leaders. Taking that from people who have lived through it was worthwhile over friends my age who liked to think they knew what they were doing. I will never forget one particular situation where I had to be taught a lesson. This was really my first role using the typical *Microsoft Outlook* email, with access to everyone in the company. Most of my previous roles would only involve using the small email groups for our office, but the Sales Office was pretty huge. It entailed all of the Sales Assistants, Sales Managers, Team Leaders, Directors, and GM of the office. One-hundred plus people. Since I was the Executive Assistant for the Director's, I would often assist the Senior Executive Assistant of solely the GM with duties that took up too much of her time, or simply because I enjoyed taking on new tasks. One of these tasks was the office roster/database. This database had the teams, the positions, their contact numbers, and eventually pictures (which I added). It was balling as shit after I was done with it, let me tell you! Anyways, I would frequently shoot out emails to the entire office team, requesting information so it was up to date. I sent some email, and I cannot remember exactly what it pertained to, but one of the Director's called me into his office, and asked me to shut the door behind me. Oh shit. Luckily, he was cool as hell, so it was super casual. I think the conversation even started with a "Dude…" He continued to tell me that I needed to take a moment and sit back and reread my emails before I send them, because some of them came across as snarky or rude. I was shocked, because I never meant to be that way. I am very much a person of getting shit done and don't fuck around, so if it was an email for something like a form or something simple that was overdue, I probably was serious, but I could see how it probably came across as rude. Either way, it has made me look twice at my emails before hitting that send button ever since, and I suggest everyone to do the same. Very much like texting in this modern day, it is hard to gather someone's tone from digital words. Luckily, emojis in texts can help a bit, but you have to be careful, and I learned that in this role.

In this role, I was able to meet a slew of big wigs in the company, as our office was nearby the corporate office, and they would drop in often to host meetings in our space, or simply to see how we were doing. I was frequently introduced to them by my Directors or the GM, and occasionally assisted them with setting up their meetings. Want to talk about an easy way to get on their radar! I remember one particular instance when the CEO's son (yeah, the one whose last name was plastered on all of our hotels), who was in charge of the entire East Coast, gave a speech to the whole office, and after, our GM called me over and introduced me to him. He didn't do that for anyone else, just me. In the great words of *Napoleon Dynamite*, "Heck yes!" Although, I totally froze up, and didn't know what the hell to say, other than "Hi, nice to meet you." It was ok though because there were so many brown-nosers standing around that I was able to sneak away unscathed, and he likely appreciated me more because I wasn't standing there obviously trying to suck up.

Aside from just meeting the big-wigs, the Sales Office structure enables you to meet hundreds of people. I was able to meet everyone in the office, but also representatives from each hotel we sold for, and all of the Area Sales Executives that would pop in the office. Networking at it's finest! Everyone worked for the same company, with the same overall goal (to make money), so for the most part, everyone got along. It reminded me of a college camaraderie in that sense. Office bonding was a common trend. Because of the office's location, being situated around a lake with shops around it, it enabled us to take Starbucks trips on the reg, or just a simple walk around the lake to stretch our legs. I would go with coworkers I knew, and others I didn't really know, but would then get to know them on our trips. Walks like these were also a great opportunity to drag bosses out of the office and connect with them. Happy hours around the lake were also a great time for networking. There is no better bond with someone you are unfamiliar with than drinking and having thoughtless fun in a judge-free zone. I would repeat this weekly for the entire eight months I was at the Sales Office. Remember, we were able to post for new positions after six months in a non-management role, so naturally I became antsy to look for my next step.

Looking for my next step became much easier this time around because I actually knew more of how the hotel chain was structured. Working in a hotel, you tend to get tunnel vision for positions specific to that hotel. You don't consider or even know about all the positions in the Sales Department or corporate offices. The natural progression would have been for me to become a Sales Manager in the office, or maybe Event Manager for a property. But honestly, neither sparked my interest at that given time because I was ready to bounce out of the DMV (DC/Maryland/Virginia) area. After hearing enough about politics, about how crappy the *Washington Redskins* were doing, dealing with family drama, or being blasted with snow and twenty degree weather, it was time for me to get back to the Sunshine State. I was ready for the laid-back, drama-free lifestyle, with daily warm weather, and beaches in my backyard. I wanted to be back in Florida, but I didn't think I would be able to snag a first-time Sales Manager role multiple states away, in an unfamiliar territory. I concentrated on looking for Senior Sales Assistant roles instead, as I knew I was well-qualified for that, and this would enable me to be back working on property, but with that corporate Monday to Friday schedule.

My search actually started in Hawaii, then Southern California, as I had never been to either and thought it would be pretty cool to mix it up. Wouldn't you believe that I actually stayed with a former hotel coworker, David, that crazy mo-fo that interned at the boutique hotel I worked at in DC? I was able to stay with him FOR FREE and see if Hawaii was the place for me. It was indeed beautiful, but it wasn't for me. I didn't smoke pot, I wasn't too adventurous in the sense that I wouldn't jump off cliffs, and I didn't surf. Also, the housing/hotels weren't the vibe I was looking for. A little too tiki/laid back. Remember, I tried that in Fort Myers Beach, and it wasn't my scene. I like a little more of that city vibe. Next, I took a trip out to San Diego to stay with an old high school tennis buddy. He had been living there for like a year, and he spoke very highly of it. I did my research, and it seemed like a dope spot to live. I actually had an interview lined up at a huge marina hotel there as their Senior Sales Assistant. I knew I had that on lock!

This interview seemed way too informal to the point that it seemed they already really liked me, and decided I was the one based on my phone interview, resume, and references. That, or the complete opposite, and they already had someone in mind, so were just fucking around, enjoying time away from their desks, sipping on some free coffee with me. Either way, I kind of had my mind made up when flying back home and dealing with the layover, that San Diego wasn't for me. In fact, it further reinforced my desire to get back to Florida. San Diego was nice, and I am sure other parts of SoCal are as well, but that flight home was brutal. It was pretty long and expensive, and that was a flight with a layover. Had I bought a non-stop, it would have been even more expensive. So if I took a job there, going back home for visits, events, weddings, funerals, etc., I would literally have to take off an entire day off of work. Florida is literally only a two hour flight to and from home. Super convenient. And I loved that Florida is hot, hot, hot, year round. SoCal can get a little chilly in the winter, and the Pacific Ocean is always chilly. Not to mention, geez there were a lot of homeless people there! So, I narrowed down my search to either Tampa, or Miami, because I wanted to be in a city near the beach, unlike Fort Myers Beach. Sure enough, I found a Senior Sales Administrative Assistant role at a monster seven-hundred room hotel right on a channel off of Tampa Bay. I applied. I had a phone interview. I nailed it!

On my phone interview, they mentioned my beautiful resume and specifically noted that they loved how I had a hyperlink to my *LinkedIn* on it. They were able to stalk my beautiful face, online resume, and my go-to slim-fit H&M suit in my profile picture. I had that position on lock before the interview even took place! The interview included a few Senior Sales Executives, the on-property Sales Manager, and the Director of Sales. I would also be assisting the General Manager, but he was not present during the phone interview. He trusted their judgement, and they all loved me!

The pay in this new role wasn't going to be as great because it was indeed in Florida, which is considered a lower cost of living area than the DC/Metro area. This hotel chain had a four-tier payscale system based on regions, and Florida happened to fall in the lowest tier, a.k.a. the crappiest pay. Because of this, I would max out at a pay rate lower than where I was in the Sales Assistant role. Fuck it, I would be back in Florida, and out of Maryland. Technically, because it was a "Senior" role, it would look like a step up on my resume, so I took that as a positive step, regardless of the pay. No one had to know I was paid less, except for now. I planned to network, do my thing, and grow within the industry down in Florida, where I wouldn't be miserable. This time, I told myself I wouldn't ever go back to the DMV area. I might move around the state of Florida, but not going anywhere else, unless I hit the jackpot, and then maybe move to Aruba, or some other exotic, warm-weather climate island.

So I did what I did best, packed up my car, and drove down to Florida. Fuck that drive! Thirteen goddamn hours with shit rubbed up against me because my little Chevy Sonic Hatchback was packed to the brim. I decided not to stop and take a night's rest, but instead push through, and make the drive in one trip. I was that ready to get the hell down there. Nothing was stopping me. Although, this turned out not to be the best idea, as my body took about a week to adjust to the lack of sleep and the shitty fast food I ate along the way. Virginia—drive slow because the cops will pull you over for a fly on your windshield; North Carolina—bigger than you think; South Carolina—here comes the palm trees and the anxiousness to get to Florida; Georgia—more palm trees but with fields of orange trees; then finally, the monster-size confederate flag blowing in the wind (on God knows whose flag pole), poking out of the trees…welcome to mothafuckin' Florida!

The trek from the point you enter Florida to Tampa is still a long journey. People don't realize that the state is not as small as it looks on a map. I would have to pass by Jacksonville and Orlando to get to Tampa. Once you hit Orlando, it's smooth sailing, as it's only about an hour and a half away. I learned that for the first time during this drive. I finally hit the exit I needed to get to Tampa. Keep in mind, I had only been to Tampa once for a hockey game that I drove up to when I used to live in Fort Myers Beach, and it was at night. I had to cross my fingers that it was as nice as people said, and as it looked in pictures. Well, it was a great start as I got of the exit and the ramp was lined with beautiful palm trees. Ahhhhhhh! The best! Why the hell couldn't Northern states put this kind of effort into their exits? So refreshing! It's crazy how much attention the state of Florida pays to the beautification of its roads. In the DC area, there are a zillion exits, and I have never once seen them lined with pine trees, or anything of that sort to make it seem appealing. Overgrown grass is the most I have seen. #CmonMan!

Prior to moving down, I had done my research online to determine which apartment I wanted to stay at. I based it on price, location, and amenities. Amenities were pretty important to me this time around in Florida. I did not want to stay in a run-down beach apartment like I did in Fort Myers Beach. This time, I planned on living in an apartment complex with on-site laundry, a pool, hot tub, gym, tennis courts, etc. I happened to find a reasonably priced place about seven minutes from my new hotel, just outside of the city, about five minutes to the nearest beach. St. Pete Beach and Clearwater Beach were only a half-hour drive away. Both were (and still are) top ten beaches in the U.S. I'll freaking take it! The kicker was that I had to put a deposit down on the place without ever having looked at it in person. I wasn't a fan of this, but I really had no other options. I had flown by the seat of my pants up to this point in my life, so why not keep it going.

I rolled up into this apartment complex that had the appeal of a gated community, minus the actual gate. I was ok with that. It still served the purpose of safety, without the pain in the ass of having a

Security Guard calling you for permission for your guests to enter. I was met at the complex clubhouse with keys, and got a tour of the property and my new apartment. The lady greeted me with joy as she knew I just drove a zillion miles from Maryland, as we spoke prior to my arrival. I wanted to double and triple check that the place would be available when I arrived, because my ass would need to crash ASAP! My unit was on the third floor. God dammit! My body was depleted after that long drive, so lugging all my shit up two flights of stairs was not in my thought process when I arrived. The place was great though! It had Florida ceilings, which as you already know, are obnoxiously tall. It had a nice kitchen with new appliances, and thank Christ, it had a dishwasher! My Fort Myers Beach place did not. There was a balcony off the living room that faced a little pond and the pool. My bedroom was really spacious and it connected to the bathroom that also opened to the hallway area. Perfect little spot for me! I dug out my beautiful ten inches of memory foam mattress, lugged it up the two flights of steps, tossed it on my bedroom floor, and lights freaking out!

I woke up to finish lugging my shit up to the new spot. Once I completed, I was ready to bask at the complex pool and get my tan on. My Northern white ass needed it badly! I enjoyed that for a bit, and then headed back in to put finishing touches on my new apartment. After that, I was right back out to the pool area to get my *Hot Tub Time Machine* on. What a new life! Nothing better than unwinding after a busy day of straining your muscles, than in a 103 degrees of heaven with a jet blowing on your lower back! Stress free! I had to unwind a lot that weekend because I didn't leave much time between arriving to Tampa and starting the new gig. I arrived that Friday and started at the hotel on Monday. The hotel wasn't ready for what was about to come to it...or was I not ready for what the hotel was about to hand me!?

On Monday morning, I hopped in my car to begin the quick seven-minute trek to work. The drive to work was immaculate! I cut right across South Tampa to this famous road called Bayshore Boulevard, and took that into the city. Bayshore rides right along the Tampa Bay, lined with the longest uninterrupted sidewalk in the world, palm trees at the wazoo, and mega-mansion after the next. Across the bay, you have views of Downtown Tampa and more mega-mansions on an island across from the Boulevard...one being Derek Jeter's monster compound. The speed limit was a mere thirty miles per hour, but was absolutely perfect because with the windows cranked down, you could enjoy the warm breeze and smell of the bay (hopefully a good smelling day).

Tampa was great because it was a large city, but a not so popular one, so it tended to be very quiet. At the time, it was the fifty-second largest city in the US. When most people think of Florida, they think of either Miami or Orlando/Disney World. Traffic in Tampa was basically non-existent, unless you were driving from Tampa to St. Pete right before a *Tampa Bay Rays* game. It was really odd because as beautiful as the weather and city was, you would think it would be overpopulated, with loads of traffic, but instead, the exact opposite. You would drive on the highway at night and literally be the only car on the road. Creepy AF! It was like an episode of *The Walking Dead*, or the movie, *I Am Legend*.

When you got to the end of Bayshore Boulevard, you were greeted by Downtown Tampa. The skyline was made up of only a few tall buildings, like the Sykes building, which looked like a gigantic cylinder, and the light-up triangle-pointed top Suntrust building, that would sometimes illuminate a lightning bolt for the *Tampa Bay Lightning* hockey team. It was definitely not like a New York City skyline where buildings get lost in the mix. Then, to the immediate right of those buildings, you would see two other tall buildings standing alone, sticking out like sore thumbs. One turned out to be a rival hotel, and directly across from it, sitting directly on a channel next to the Hockey arena and convention center, stood my new beautiful monster of a hotel! I would take one turn at the end of Bayshore, and boom, I was entering "the" go-to hotel in Tampa! It was a short, easy, and enjoyable commute.

Upon entering the hotel for the first time, I was greeted with the "wow" factor that this hotel brought. It really is hard to put into words without experiencing it first hand. Once you passed by the crowded Valet out front with the all-glass porte-cochere above you, you entered the automatically opening front doors and are instantly greeted with what seemed like endless fifty-foot high ceilings with sunshine from the floor-to-ceiling windows in the back of the lobby shining in. Through those windows you saw a back patio laying right on the boat-lined channel. It was phenomenal! I had to step back out front and check the sign to make sure I was indeed at the correct hotel, as it looked like a top-tier luxury hotel. The lobby looked like it was straight out of a commercial, as this particular hotel brand was working on its new lobby concept. It was more of a lounge/business center vibe, with little tables, nooks, high-tops, booths, and modern set-ups all over. Every square inch had an outlet for business travelers to be able to plug and play. Wifi was readily available throughout, as there was still a charge to use it in the guest rooms at this time. Servers roamed the lobby to assist with any food and beverage needs of the guests. Just sit back, relax, get your business done, and grab a beverage and bite. Loved it! I already felt privileged to be working there. I think all of us in the industry can agree that working in a hotel that we can brag about makes a lot of the other day-to-day worries take a backseat.

My new domain would be in the Sales Office that was positioned behind the Front Desk, like quite a few hotels are as well. Some hotels will have their Sales Department located on another floor, likely near the hotel's meeting space, for easy access to check on groups in the hotel. I was excited, as I thought there was a chance I would have my own office, or at least a cubicle like in my previous Sales role. Unfortunately, this was not the case. Come to find out, my desk was positioned right in the front of the Sales Office, like a goddamn Secretary! Ugh! This sucked major ass. Not what I had in mind, but oh well. I guess that was my own fault for not asking enough questions in the interview, or prior to taking the role. But again, I'm pretty sure I would have taken the job regardless, even if they told me I would be working out of the damn boiler room! There was another desk up front as well, where we had another Sales Assistant. He was a cool-ass dude by the name of Rick. Rick was a young guy as well, and had been at the hotel for entirely too long. He was at the point where he was ready to go. He had been a Front Desk Agent, Phone Operator, and even Front Desk Supervisor. He got tired of the crazy-ass Front Office schedule, so switched over to Sales. I think he was more pumped than I was about me starting, as apparently the last few Admins were either old ladies, annoying chicks, or just plain not conversational. Rick knew the ins-and-outs of the hotel, so he showed me the ropes of the hotel, and I showed him the ropes of Sales. He was not too savvy with computer systems. He was definitely more of a blue-collar guy, and computers/technology were not his strong-suit. No worries, because it was mine! A perfect working relationship in the making.

I also met the Managers that I would be assisting for the first time. I had only heard their voices during the phone interview, so it was nice to match their voices to their faces. I would be assisting the GM, the Director of Sales, and three Sales Executives, and Rick would assist the other Sales Exec, the on-site Sales Manager (who worked with the Florida Group Sales Office, similar to the Mid-Atlantic one), and the Catering Sales Manager. I was finally able to meet the GM, who wasn't on the phone interview. He was a super cool and calm guy that didn't really ask me for much. Ron was actually relatively new to the hotel as well, as he had just come from a huge resort in Orlando as the Assistant GM. The Director of Sales was one of those very intimidatingly successful ladies that happened to be very good-looking as well. She seemed intimidating, but was harmless and very nice. She just liked results, and must have been good at achieving them, as she got a promotion outside of the hotel soon after I started there. The Senior Sales Executives were all really friendly. They were all middle-aged ladies that had been in the Hotel Sales game for quite some time. They seemed very happy to have another young, smiling energetic face in the office, and one with Sales systems knowledge.

This job transition was great because for once, I knew all of the systems already. Halle-freakin-lujah! What a relief! The company had recently undergone system changes to the Sales process, so a lot of what they needed at the hotel was help with updating their files digitally, and into the new system. The Sales Exec's were not exactly computer savvy either, and not too welcoming to the transition, as some of them literally had drawers stuffed with files waiting to be input into the new system. This role ended up being pretty cool because I was able to assist and learn the ropes of multiple positions within the company's Sales Organization. I was able to soak in the knowledge of Senior Salespeople that had been in the game for a while, and really knew their stuff. I would prepare reports for the Director of Sales, such as lost or turned down groups. Lost groups were those groups that the Managers either lost contact with, or were told they were going with a different venue for whatever reason. Turned down groups were those where the Managers denied the client of meeting space and/or sleeping rooms because the hotel didn't have space, room availability for the dates the client needed, or it just wasn't a good business fit for the property per Revenue Managers. These groups would be lost or turned down by the Sales Executives on property, or the Sales Managers in our Florida Group Sales Office.

I prepared proposals, contracts, and addendums for our Sales Exec's. I would give tours to potential clients of the guestrooms, meeting space, and hotel amenities, in place of the busy Managers. I would help prepare client events, whether it was setting up the transportation and restaurant reservations around the city, or even a little electric boat tour around the bay. And yes, sometimes I was able to actually join in on these events with the clients. I would also work with the Food & Beverage Department to prepare arrival amenities, like fancy beverages and/or hors d'oeuvres. I would prepare and deliver amenities to VIP group guests arriving, and of course log notes in the Front Desk system so the Front Desk Agents wouldn't accidentally move those rooms with amenities already in them. I had been in their shoes before, so I knew that the more detailed notes on the reservation, the better. I would pretty much do everything for my Managers besides actually negotiating the contracts directly with the client. It was a pretty badass role! The job was tedious, but it really was something different every day, which kept it exciting. And because the other Assistant Rick and I were pretty cool, we would share the workload no matter what Manager it ended up being for, and oftentimes venture away from our desks together to BS a bit around the hotel.

It was freaking great to be back in Florida, let me tell you! The weekends entailed going to the beach, paddle boarding, or doing some other outdoor activity. I was again surrounded by boats galore, beautiful weather, beaches, and yes, beautiful women. Tampa had a few big universities, so the female talent was off the chainnnnnn! These women were much different than Southern Maryland girls. The Tampa women had this sexy confidence in their style. They knew they were hot, and showed it. Because of the warm weather year-round, the outfits were rather small and revealing, to show off their fit beach bodies and strategically placed tattoos. Similar to the girls I saw when visiting Adam back in the Fort Myers/Naples area, but hotter. A few of my friends actually came down the same month I moved down there to visit, and they were ready to move down immediately because of the weather, beaches, and female eye-candy. Sure enough, one of my buds, Phill, ended up meeting a girl, moving down, bought a place, and is now engaged to that girl! The people living in Tampa didn't get taking used to either. Most of the people that lived there were from up North, so it was like I was at home, except near the beach and had warm weather year-round. People there loved to stay active, and were very involved in their sports teams. This was a relief compared to when I lived in Fort Myers Beach, when the only recreational activities residents were interested in was in a green plant form. The *Tampa Bay Rays* were actually located in St Pete, but going to games was a popular after work activity. The games were cheap, and you didn't really have to pay attention. Gotta love baseball for that reason. It was a great date spot! The *Tampa Bay Lightning* were a fairly new hockey team to the city, and the arena was located right beside my new hotel, so that was also a popular spot. Seeing as hockey was my all-time favorite sport, it was a great choice for a date, especially if I found a chick that liked it too! Go figure, the NHL decided to change up the divisions right before I moved down to Tampa, so I would only see my *Washington Capitals* once a year there. Boo!

The GM, who I said earlier was pretty low-maintenance and cool, happened to be a big sports guy as well. He was from Wisconsin, and was a die-hard *Green Bay Packers* fan. He was very active, and would often start health initiatives within the hotel. Perhaps my best memories from working at this hotel was the hotel softball team that Ron started. He had done this with the resort he previously managed, and wanted to keep it going at this one. Our hotel chain held multiple tournaments across the state (and even country) throughout the year. Me, being a huge sports guy, I was super pumped to hear this. The problem was that I hadn't played baseball since middle school, and had only played softball once ever, as a fill-in for my buddy Andy's team a few years back, and my performance was far from stellar.

We had practices every Wednesday at a palm tree lined field near work, with views of Downtown Tampa in the background. Freaking awesome! The practices were made up of hotel employees from every race. It was ironic because American Baseball is very much like that. Let the stereotypes fly. The little Chinese guy from Banquets would hit every single ball and speed his way through the bases! He was crazy when playing the field too, diving at every ball hit his way, regardless of whether it was hit directly to him or not. The big black guy from Banquets would get up to the plate and straight crush it like Big Papi, and then slowly jog, practically walk his way around the bases. The ripped older Cuban Engineering Manager would get up to the plate and absolutely rip the skin off the ball, making you think of Sammy Sosa in his steroid days. I was your average, run-of-the-mill white boy with some smarts and decent athletic skills, knowing not to try and crush it and get a pop-up out every time, but instead hit the ball to a hole, and run my little ass off around the bases. In-the-park home runs were my specialty, and because of it, I was named the lead-off batter, and pinch runner. Leading off was perfect because I likely had no one in front of me to stall me from running around the bases to home plate.

This was such an awesome bonding experience because the team was made up of people from all of the different departments in the hotel. Working in such a huge hotel, unless you've worked there for years and years, and various shifts, it would be nearly impossible to meet everyone there. A lot of the Banquet staff only work at night and on weekends. Overnight Front Desk Agents and Engineers never see the light of day, and with my spoiled bankers hours, I would never see them. Being in Sales, I would rarely ever deal with the Housekeeping Department unless I had to bother them to touch up one of the Sales showrooms. Apparently, this new bonding experience with all of us worked out really well because we actually ended up winning the first tournament we played in! Not only did we win it, but we came from behind in the bottom of the seventh inning (we only played seven) with eight runs to win it with a walk-off hit. It was unreal! I contributed not only with a double early in the inning, but was brought in later to pinch run to bring in another. There might not be a greater bond formed between people than overcoming a massive comeback on the same team in sports. We received a trophy as tall as me, and we all took pictures of it after the game to show to our hotel colleagues. We were able to display the trophy (per Ron's suggestion) with a signed ball from all of us in the fresh new break room in the hotel. Fucking right!

We later participated in a thirty-day squat challenge that Ron put together with one of our Group Room Coordinators. It was a pretty standard routine of knocking out a set number of squats daily that would increase over time, so that by the end you would be able to do a ton of squats with no issues. We would do our scheduled daily squats at home per the schedule, and meet once a week to do that day's together to make sure we were all keeping pace. We did the squats up on the pool deck, where hotel guests would be watching. I could imagine it was pretty entertaining to watch us because some of the Managers would be getting their squats on in their work attire. Most would pack their workout clothes, but others would be cranking em out in their slacks, and even heels! Let me tell you what, for someone who didn't normally do squats, those bad boys were tough, especially at the fast pace we were going. I developed leg muscles and abs that I had never seen before in all my years of staying active with sports. Squats are the real deal! I see why the challenge exists, and why crossfitters make such a big deal of them.

Although this hotel was full of positives, it came with its fair share of drawbacks, like most. First and foremost, I went from working with two computer monitors at the Sales Office in Maryland, to only one here. Not possible! We work with multiple Sales programs simultaneously, so when working on only one monitor, you literally spend half the day shrinking and maximizing each program over and over again. I had to build the biggest case possible to make this happen here, and by doing what I came to find I do best naturally...selling! Rick was totally on board, as he had been working off of one monitor forever, and said he had asked multiple times before giving up. I pride myself in the area that if I want something to get done, it will get done, even if I have to bitch and moan to get there. As you will recall from my first ever hotel, I mastered that! Call me annoying or what they will, but sometimes that's how you have to be. I bugged the living snot out of our Director of Sales and GM, and eventually our IT guy, who just so happened to be one of the ringers on our softball team. He ignored my request time and time again, so what did I do? I got my ass on *Craigslist* and bought myself a ten dollar monitor from some sketch-ass dude who had hundreds stored in a shitty old garage. When I arrived at his place, it was like a scene out of a horror movie, and I thought for sure the *Texas Chainsaw Massacre* guy would jump out from behind a pile of his monitors! I didn't question as to why he had so many because I just wanted my damn second monitor and GTFO of there! I was practically sacrificing my life for this second monitor! And if I figured out how to get mine to work successfully, I would sacrifice it again to get one for my boy Rick too.

When I brought the monitor into work to plug-and-play, it figured that it would end up needing a special part entirely to be able to work on our hotel computers properly. As my good friend Elizabeth would say, "Fak!" And guess who would have to order this part? The one-and-only IT guy. Those fucking Hotel Gods, I swear! So the plan backfired, or did it? Because of this little mission I pulled, the IT guy finally gave in and said he would order myself and Rick second monitors. Hallelujah! Of course, it took about a month to get, and we thought he was lying when he said he ordered them, but we did indeed eventually get them. We anxiously opened those puppies up when they arrived, filled with joy and excitement, and as it turned out, they were only about 12-inch screens. Are you fucking kidding me!? It was barely bigger than my Samsung Galaxy Note 3 screen. Unreal! However, we made it work, and didn't complain (except privately between Rick and myself). Of course, everyone else in the Sales Office would come up and laugh hysterically about the small size of them. I would take the higher road, bite my tongue, and shake my head with a smile on my face. Choose your battles wisely!

Another drawback was working back on property in general. Paying for parking being one drawback. At this Tampa property, I would only have to pay $36 a month, and thank God because I had to drive there, unlike my properties in DC where I could bike or walk to. I remember I about shit myself when discussing salary with the Director of Sales before getting the job, and she mentioned parking was thirty-six dollars. I thought for sure that she meant daily, because that wasn't far fetched for DC hotels. My heart sank because I instantly would have had to turn down the job. An extra thousand bucks plus per month for parking, a.k.a. twelve-thousand a year! Nah, I'm good. She laughed at me as it was only thirty-six per month, which is absolutely absurd how low the parking garage charges for that. They were robbing themselves at that low price!

Another downfall about working on property was the fact that everyone, no matter what position, was expected to pitch in and help when needed. It didn't matter if you were a Front Desk Agent and are asked to unclog a toilet, because you signed up to be a team player. Sometimes this could be a great thing, as it was nice to mix up your daily tasks, but other times it sucked major ass! For example, Rick and I would get "voluntold" to assist with major group events, mainly with the Valet Department! This hotel had a pretty large porte-cochere where guests would pull up their cars, hop out, Valet would hand them a ticket, and then take their vehicles to a garage that was located about two blocks up the road. Sometimes for major events, the entrance would fill up quick, and there would be a line of cars down the street, awaiting to get their cars valeted.

The Resident General Manager, who was in charge of the rooms portion of the hotel, would come running into the Sales Office from outside, and shout, "Rick, Tony, c'mon!" Not that we weren't in the middle of building a monster block of space for our Managers or anything important! Goddammit. At first, this was a thrill. Hopping in cars that I would never be able to afford and take them for a joy ride over to the garage, and whipping around the tight turns up a few floors to park them. It brought me back to my Valet days in Fort Myers Beach. I would then have to mark down the spot number that I parked in and run back (yes, I said run back, as it was a long two blocks away) to the hotel to drop of the keys and hop in another car, and then do it all over again. This was fun for about a minute, until the Florida humidity gets to you and you're sweating profusely through your suit pants, dress shirt, and shoes, and it hadn't even hit lunchtime yet! Then, you had to sit there all disgusting for the rest of the day, smelling like you just ran a marathon. And to top that off, try doing this on days where it was pissing down rain, and smelling like a wet dog for the remainder of the day. Not cool. The struggle was real.

Other than that, the only other real negative at this particular property, like others, was all the corny shit the hotel (per company requirements) does to make the lower-level employees feel like something. As much as I love some of these large chains, they know they have the upper hand, and can get anyone to work for them, so they pay garbage, but attempt to offset it by making the employees feel "special!" This particular hotel called all of their employees "Hosts" (eye roll). Other hotel chains have other names for them, instead of just simply calling them "Associates" or "Staff." They feel the need to give this false sense of entitlement. Properties like this one also tend to hold these cheeseball "All-Host" meetings, normally around Christmas, where they give out awards and make you feel appreciative to be working there. Now listen, I am all about happiness in the workplace and what not, but at these events at every property I have worked at, the recognition awards always seem to coincidentally go to Housekeepers, lower-level Engineers, or maybe the Cafe Workers. I am one-hundred percent not arguing that they play a huge part in the success of any hotel, but are you going to tell me that the Front Desk Agents who literally have people screaming in their face on the daily, aren't going to get any of these awards? Hmm. The hotels give away corny-ass prizes like blenders, small gift cards to some basic-ass stores, or sometimes, if you are super lucky (sarcasm), a 32-inch TV. Then, to top it all off, once you win that award, they make you sign an agreement that you understand that taxes will be taken out of your paycheck for that prize that you just won. What in the hell? Here I am complaining about hotels giving us free shit and making us feel better. This is what hotels does to our heads...makes us loco!

A nice perk at this hotel was the fact that I could enjoy meals provided daily by the Food and Beverage Department for just a few bucks a day. A lot of times, it would even include top of the line entrees and desserts that were leftover from an event that was taking place at the hotel. Only a dollar fifty for a full plate of food, with anything and everything on top and a drink included. It wasn't free like the one hotel I worked at for a short time period in DC, but I'll take it! Andddd I could finish off my meal with a little plastic shot glass full of tiramisu (or the like) that was left over from a Banquet lunch going on upstairs. This worked out to be way cheaper than buying and packing my own lunch every day. It was cool too because this lunch purchase would come right out of my paycheck, versus having to dig out cash or a credit card every day.

Sadly, after six months of these cheap meals and assisting Sales Executives, I was ready to move up and do some management work of my own, and actually get paid the big bucks to do so. Well, big bucks in hotel terms, which isn't exactly big bucks. Regardless, I needed to be making more than I was as an Assistant. I was bringing in $13.99 an hour (around $26,861 a year), and as a Sales Manager, which would be my next step up, I would start at $40,000, but be working fifty-hour work weeks instead of forty, with bonus eligibility of up to thirty-five percent of my salary. So, taking into account that fifty-hour work week, it worked out to be around $16.67 an hour before taxes. Technically, the way it worked with that company, it would be $14.11 an hour for the first forty hours, and the last ten hours would be considered overtime. Super sketchy if you ask me. Damn slave labor! Although, in essence, if you can hit your bonuses, you can make a substantial amount. I would be making more money, and climbing the ladder in the company, and I couldn't argue with that!

The great part about that company in particular, and hotel career field as a whole, is that they encourage advancement. It's one of the few career fields where people don't necessarily frown upon a lot of movement between brands/companies. This company encouraged job shadowing. Here, you could shadow people in the position that you are interested in, and see what the job entails before you actually got into it. This would naturally filter out people that think they are interested, and then realize it is not what they thought originally; or it is indeed what they want to do, and will pursue a future in that position. Luckily, I already knew how the Sales Manager role worked because of my time at the Mid-Atlantic Sales Office. From what I knew, it sucked severely, and you were heavily overworked for little pay. Great encouragement, and one of the reasons I didn't show interest in the Sales Manager position in that office, or even when initially transferring to Florida. But here I was again, and my options were slim at this point. There comes a point while working in the hotel industry when you realize that your resume only reads hotel jobs, so you will likely not be able to get a job in another field. Your reality check! I had my Director of Sales reach out to the Sales Office in Miami to see if I could come shadow with some Managers there. Sure enough, the General Manager of the Sales Office, whom I had met briefly a few weeks earlier at the hotel, reached out to me and put me in contact with the Director of the Full Service Team for Tampa and Orlando. We agreed for me to visit the Miami office on Labor Day Friday. This way, I could drive to Miami, and stay for the weekend to not only check out the Sales Office, but also the area, as I had never been. I had heard the stereotypes of Miami, and see them on TV, movies, and music videos, but it was time to see it in the flesh, and boy, it did not disappoint!

CHAPTER 5 - THE TRIFECTA: BEACH, CITY & SALES

I packed up a little weekend bag, filled with bathing suits, fresh going-out gear, an outfit for the Sales Office visit, and a floaty. A floaty? Yup, a floaty. I found out that there was going to be a Floatopia going on the weekend I was there. This basically just involved thousands of people that show up to the world-famous South Beach with their favorite floaties, booze, drugs, whatever the hell else, and have a good ole time! I happened to find a cheap spot on *Airbnb* right on Ocean Drive, close to the famed Clevelander and Mango's bars, and I actually used my awesome employee discount at a hotel close to the Sales Office the night prior to my Friday workday/shadow session. It cost me a whopping twenty-nine bucks that night! Twenty-nine bucks for a hotel in Miami! Insane! This enabled me to do my shadowing for the day, and then head over to the beach after and chill for the weekend.

I went into the office bright and early on Friday. I parked in the FREE parking garage, and went up to the highest floor in the building next door. I was greeted by a huge, neon backlit company logo on one side (sound familiar) and on the other, a monster, modern, all-white kitchen/living room area, overlooking the entirety of Miami. Holyyyy shit! The view here kicked the pants off of the first floor views of sidewalks, roads, and pine trees in Maryland! I was greeted by the Full Service Core Team Leader. She was ultra-friendly (almost too much so), and was very excited for me to come and check out the office, and meet lots of people, as I could end up being a future member on their team. She set me up with a few experienced Managers on multiple different teams throughout the office. The office was set up just like the Mid-Atlantic one, with cubicles all over, and the Directors' offices around them. These were a little flashier (more "Miami") than the ones up North, sporting neon greens and purples, and the Director's doors had floor-to-ceiling glass sliding doors. The cubicle desks here had nice wood surfaces (versus a cheap plastic) and they had newer phones and monitors than the Maryland office. As a whole, it seemed much nicer than the other. Upgrade for sure!

After sitting with various Managers one-by-one, I learned that their roles were not at all different than the Managers in the Mid-Atlantic Office. The only major difference I noticed was that half of the bookings here were for wedding room blocks, family reunions, or company leisure trips, mostly due to the year-round nice Florida weather. The Miami Office actually had an entire team dedicated to resort bookings. It was really cool being at the office because I had emailed and ran many reports at my hotel involving the Managers in this office to check their productivity. When I would see their name on their cubicles, I would introduce myself, and get a big hug and kiss in return (from the females), or bro hug (from the dudes) because I had helped them with a lot of things. A lot of times, they would reach out to me to assist with a group that they booked at my hotel, since they were not physically there. I would deliver amenities for them, get a last minute contract addendum signed, etc. It was like I was already at home with all of the connections I already had at the office. The kissing on the cheek thing I would have to get used to, as we weren't that affectionate up North, well maybe with my New York family. Latins are very affectionate! There were definitely more than a few Latin people in that office, pretty Latinas included! Cubans, Puerto Ricans, Colombians, Brazilians, you name it. Super cultural. I had never heard more Spanish speaking in one place in my life, except for maybe when I was in Cozumel, Mexico on a cruise stop. It definitely fit the stereotype that a lot of people had told me about Miami before arriving there.

As I mentioned earlier, the view was amazing! As I walked around the office, I saw that it literally had a 360-degree view of the city. It sat right on top of a lake, surrounded by other corporate buildings, and you could see the Miami airport, Coral Gables, Downtown Miami, the Beach, and more. The free parking garage was great, but even greater was the fact that it had a covered walkway from it to the building. This was something the Mid-Atlantic Office could have used to save me from the rain and fucking snow! The break room was stocked with everything, including an entire coffee machine taller than me that allowed you to make any coffee and chocolate drink possible, FOR FREE! The Vanilla Latte was bomb! The living room area had two modern white couches with huge flat screens, and dual Wii's! A few of the guys in the office were getting super into it while I was there. The Mid-Atlantic Office had a Wii as well, and actually a foosball table, but they were in an awkward place and no one really played them, besides maybe my boy Josh. I think it was that conservative/professional atmosphere that the Northeast has, versus the casual, laid-back vibe of Miami. There was also a colada machine that I was unfamiliar with. This machine could whip up some infamous Cuban coffee, a.k.a. crack! This stuff was intense! One shot of it and my white-ass was buzzing. Locals would need a few to get them going. A few of the girls in the office would regularly make this, and come around with a stack of little plastic shot cups that they would pour for everyone around the cubicles. Super cool and super hospitable! I could get used to that!

The Director who brought me there was also super hospitable. She treated me to lunch at a nearby Cuban restaurant, and we discussed my career goals. The problem was that there were no positions open in the office at that time, but she hinted to me that there might be some openings very soon. With any luck, I would travel back to Tampa and a position would open up as soon as possible, so I could move the hecht on! She actually put me in touch with a Manager on her team who lived on the beach, and happened to be from Maryland as well. Not only the Director, but a few other people in the office told me that I should reach out to her that weekend. I managed to slip out of the office around 3 p.m. to head to the beach. I took the MacArthur Causeway Bridge across to Miami Beach, passing the crystal blue waters of Biscayne Bay, and the multiple cruise ships docked up along the way. The views were breathtaking! You could see the tall beach condos and hotels in the distance, as you passed by palm tree after palm tree lining the bridge. In my rearview mirror, I could see the gorgeous downtown Miami skyline. It truly was like you see in all of the movies and TV shows. I was getting chills of anxiety to get to my *Airbnb,* and get to the damn beach! "I'm in Miami Bitch!" --- *LMFAO*

Once I got over the bridge to Miami Beach was when the excitement really set in. The people watching turned on in full effect! I turned onto the famed Collins Avenue, and it was quite the beautiful site! The all-white buildings with ivy strategically growing on the facades, and splashes of pastel colors mingled in. A style that Miami is famous for, called Art Deco. Old time cars were parked on the streets, and supermodels walking all up and down the sidewalk. Tall, skinny Europeans, and curvy Latina's dressed to the nines. Helloooooo! Mingled amongst them were the obvious tourists, carrying their fresh shopping bags that they just filled up at Lincoln Road Mall. There were a few homeless and creepy dudes trying to hit on all the model chicks mingled in. The place I was staying at was in the perfect spot! It was a little sketchy getting up to the apartment, but I knew I would only be in the place to sleep, as I would be out exploring what South Beach had to offer. I had printed out *Wall Street Journal*'s *36-hour guide to Miami Beach,* and decided to check everything out on the list. That night, I decided to walk along the famed Ocean Drive, with the neon-lit hotels and restaurants facing the beach, the exotic sports cars lining the street, tables set outside, and beautiful women everywhere! I learned really quick that Miami was a free-for-all type of town. Girls wore whatever they wanted (or lack thereof), and guys were expected to be uber forward with the ladies. The music was pumping, and lights shining bright! People were drinking on the streets, and women with nothing but body paint on greeted you outside of the bars. What in the hell!? Where was I? Heaven?

I entered this super neon-lit place called Mango's Tropical Cafe, and that was quite the interesting place. I would have thought I was in Latin America somewhere! It was full of Latin people, Latin music, and Latin dancing! The walls and bars were painted with super bright blacklight paint. The female workers barely had any clothes on at all, and the men had on the tightest black shiny leather pants with no shirts on. I was very confused, and a bit uneasy to be honest. I would have thought this place was a strip joint featuring both sexes if I didn't learn otherwise. Next thing I knew, the Bartenders (guys and girls) were up on the bar doing a dance routine. No, not naked. Weird, but fun! They would grab microphones and start singing Latin ballads, and even some popular songs by American artists like Michael Jackson, or even Rihanna. It was a very vegas-like show atmosphere. All the meanwhile, some people were trying to eat at the tables right in front of them while performing. I'm not sure if I'd want body sweat or dirt flying from their dancing landing on my food, but to each their own. Welcome to Miami. Nothing is out of the norm here.

I then walked over to the Clevelander, which has a reputation from movies and shows. As I was walking up to the bouncer to get in, I noticed there were two smoking-hot women dancing on these raised surfaces above these small ponds, and they were wearing nothing but bikini bottoms and heels. Their tops were painted on. Dear Lord! It made my gringo-ass blush real hard! That's something you would never see in Southern Maryland, or better yet, anywhere I have ever been in the States. After picking my jaw up off the ground, I ventured over to a bar that was positioned right by the pool. The pool was covered up halfway with a stage, where people were dancing the night away. There was a DJ playing all kinds of house, EDM, and hip hop music. It was definitely the fun atmosphere you hear about in Miami. I actually took it pretty easy because I was alone and had a big day of exploring ahead of me the following day. That, and I wanted to be able to remember how the hell to get back to my *Airbnb* in this foreign town. I had a ten dollar beer or two, with a nice eighteen percent gratuity already included, as I found out was common for the beach. A ten dollar beer!? Yikes! You can drink for the ENTIRE night in Southern Maryland and not even rack up a ten dollar total tab. Thank you Green Door!

The next day, I got up bright and early to hit this place called The News Cafe. It was a quaint little spot along Ocean Drive, with little tables facing the ocean. There was a really nice beach breeze, which is very helpful in the South Florida heat. I wore my bathing suit, and had my beach bag with me so that I could head straight over to Floatopia after. Upon finishing up reading the paper and sipping on my cafe con leche (coffee with milk), I headed to the beach along with other people that started to flock over, carrying floats of all sorts: Alligators, whales, ten person party floats with cup holders, blow-up cabanas (yes, they exist), and the ever-loving blow-up dolls. The group that posted up in front of me on the beach were ready to party! They came equipped with not only a blow-up doll, but the torso and head of a department store mannequin! What the!? I wasn't quite sure what was going on there until I saw them pouring shots into the mouth of the mannequin and were taking turns with their mouths wrapped around a tube coming from the mannequin's privates. It was a makeshift beverage funnel. Freaking classic! They were in much more of a party mode than I was. I was still in more of an "observing, taking in South Beach" mode. There were people that brought speakers, blasting spanish and house music. There were even people that brought their own instruments. Drum circles were formed, and people were drunkenly dancing like crazy. I remember walking over to this loud crowd that had formed to see what they were surrounding and cheering about. There were a few drummers in the middle playing along to the beat of the music with this little skinny white dude (imagine the kid from *The New Guy* movie) getting twerked on by a larger, much larger, black girl, with very few articles of clothing on. Good times! South Beach has a reputation for some of the best people watching in the world, and it did not disappoint during Floatopia. Ninety percent of the women were in thongs, and a few were topless, as if it was no big deal. It was hard to tell if they were European, or just confident Latina Miami girls. Either way, it was pretty crazy to me as no one does that shit up North (well, it's illegal there)! It was a fantasy land, and I wanted to be a part of it!

I left Floatopia to head over to The Clevelander to watch the *WVU/Alabama* football game in their ESPN Zone lounge. The Clevelander was jamming out! I was not used to seeing bars going so crazy in broad daylight, then again I was indeed in South Beach.

My favorite dancers were there again, except this time with painted on football jerseys and cute little matching thong bikini bottoms, and of course, heels. Wow! I made sure to get a pic with one before I left, and obvi posted on *Instagram* with the caption "Sorry Mom." #DidItForTheGram. *WVU* put up a good fight against the defending champs, but my mind was elsewhere, instead of focusing on the game. I was already thinking of where I planned to live in Miami, assuming I got a job. Maybe South Beach, or closer to the Sales Office. I was leaning towards the beach, being that I was young, single, and kid-less.

The Sales Manager from Maryland that lived on the beach that everyone at the office recommended I meet up with ended up coming to join me at The Clevelander, and she became my tour guide after the game. We went to a cool spot called Monty's, where we watched the sunset, listened to live music, and sipped on some cocktails and got to know each other. She chauffeured me in her little Mercedes convertible. So Miami! We talked about the Sales Office, and mine and her futures. She was very independent like me and was looking to either move back home, or take a job on a Caribbean island, which meant her position would be available really soon. Perfect! I think this was why the Director wanted me to hang out with her so bad, because she couldn't technically tell me there was a position opening up on her team soon, but instead let the Sales Manager tell me that she planned to leave. We later rolled to another divey bar in South Beach where we drank, talked, and danced the night away. Good times, and it further motivated me to want to move to Miami permanently.

The next day, I woke up and ventured over to the famed Lincoln Road that I read about. I was able to scope out some famous hotels along the way, like the Delano, Loews, Shelbourne, The National, and many more. The Art Deco style was awesome, and I highly suggest you check it out if you have never witnessed it. It's crazy how the buildings have this old historic feel to it, but Miami has a way of modernizing them. Lincoln Road was packed with tourists, as expected. Just imagine one gigantic walkable street with stores on either side, and in between were tables with either trees or artsy awnings to shade people while eating. It's technically an outdoor mall, so naturally, the dining experience and people watching was great. It was your typical mall people-watching, but with the addition of the beautiful models and tourists of South Beach. The perfect combo!

At the end of Lincoln Road, there was a rooftop restaurant and bar called Juvia. I read about it in that *Wall Street Journal* visitor guide, and man, am I glad I did! This rooftop view was spectacular! It literally had 270-degree views of Miami Beach. Breathtaking! It was filled with whites, wood grains, and ivy draping everywhere with these beautiful purple flowers popping out. To match, the workers wore all-white with a touch of purple on their collars. Very contemporary. It felt super upscale, and I had no business being there. I sat down for some food, pretending I was some fancy-ass Miami local. The cheapest drink on the menu was twelve bucks, and cheapest meal (including appetizers) was seventeen. Guess what my cheap hotelier-ass got? The twelve dollar mimosa and seventeen dollar waffles with fruit and whipped cream! But regardless of them being the cheapest items, they were both amazing. I was totally getting the cold shoulder from the Bartender because of my cheap food and drink choices. Fuck her! Although, I guess I couldn't blame her for wanting a bigger tip on that automatic eighteen percent gratuity. Sadly, after this little Lincoln Road visit, I had to head back to Tampa because I worked the next goddamn day! Ugh. Back to the real world. How depressing!?

Sure enough, about two weeks later, guess what opened up!? That Sales Manager's position! Score! I applied immediately after an email from both her and the Director telling me that the open position was posted on the companies job site. I had people on the inside fighting for me! Her position was actually a second-level Electronice Leads Sales Manager, so I wasn't sure I was qualified for her position. That kind of made my heart sink because I thought she was an introductory Sales Manager. Normally, you would start in the office as a level-three Sales Manager on the Phone Leads Team. Oddly enough, that next day, a third-level Sales Manager position was posted. Whoops, because I had already posted for her position. I decided to call in the big boys and find out how to handle. I dialed the mothafuckin' General Manager of the Sales Office, Mike! Boom! Mike was actually the one who originally allowed me to visit the Sales Office, and seemed to really like me. I asked him if I should go ahead and apply for the lower-level Sales Manager position as well. This was also my sly way of calling to tell him that I already posted (applied) for a position. He told me not to worry about applying again, as they would pool all of the applications together and see who was qualified for what level position. Later that week, I received a call from the job recruiting company used to do the hiring, and I answered all the pre-qualifying questions to land an interview. I was invited to do a phone interview a few days later, as they knew I was located across the state. I had to suffer through those stupid-ass STAR questions AGAIN for the interview, but luckily I saved my cheat sheet from my previous interview in Tampa, and was pretty much able to read straight from that. I later interviewed with the Director and a few other Leaders from the Sales Office, and nailed it. Miami time!

Now the fun part began, when they sent me the offer for the new position, and I got to see how severely underpaid I would be. Welcome to the hotel industry! You can try and negotiate all you want, but they won't budge because your coworkers are all getting paid dirt cheap, and they don't want you making more than them as the newbie. Also, as I have mentioned before, in this day and age, they can hire a kid right out of college for the lowest pay possible, with only hotel knowledge from what they learned in hospitality school and maybe an internship. The difference with me was that they would be banking on my previous hotel experience and systems knowledge, even though I didn't have any actual selling experience. I was offered exactly what I expected...a fifty hour work week at $40,000 a year, with the opportunity to earn up to thirty-five percent of that salary extra in bonus. Key words being, "opportunity to earn." Like a baller, I countered the offer at $45,000, because...why not. Denied! Boo! But you know what, it was more than what I was making at the time, I would be advancing my hotel career, and living in fucking Miami! I could think of far worse decisions I made throughout my adult life.

The beauty of a management position in this company was that you were finallyyyy treated like a legit employee. This was probably similar in most companies. From the get-go, I was treated like a boss. They informed me they were going to pay for my relocation from Tampa to Miami....say whattttttttttt!??? This was totally unexpected, and honestly I would have taken the job either way. This was awesome because in the past, I had sold my furniture before moving, and then bought new furniture at my new destinations, and a lot of the times the exact same furniture. Thanks *Walmart.com* and Ikea! This was mainly because paying for movers and renting your own U-Haul were both expensive as fuck, and it worked out cheaper just to sell and rebuy. The company would cover the relocation costs, including the movers, food and gas on my commute over, a travel day of pay, and hotel accommodations until I found a place. How freaking cool is that!? However, I was so ready to be settled in and living in Miami that I actually took a trip there the weekend prior to look at places. This way, I wouldn't have to camp out in a hotel and live out of a suitcase for my first few months at the new job, even though they would cover the expenses.

So the movers came on a Friday morning, and I took off that day to take full advantage of the day of traveling pay. Two younger dudes showed up with gloves and back braces on, and full of energy to get me moved. I was able to roll out and do my own thing while they packed and moved my stuff into the truck. They would then call for me to come double check that everything was out of the apartment before they took off in the truck to Miami (or to other destinations to pick up more loads along the way). It was a pretty awesome process, as they literally wrapped every little thing up I had. It took less than an hour, as I went to the gym once they started, and before I was even done my workout, they were calling me to come give them the all-clear. They asked me where the load was heading, which surprised me that they didn't know. I guess they aren't told in advance. When I told them Miami, their eyes lit up! They were pretty pumped, as this meant they would be able to chill there for a night or two after they dropped my shit off. They had other stops along the way to fill up the rest of the moving truck, so they wouldn't actually arrive in Miami for a few days, even though it was only a four hour drive.

I went on my way with my little Chevy Sonic filled with just the necessities that I would need for the next few days, and let me tell you, I couldn't get there fast enough! I drove directly to the rental agency building to sign my lease, pay entirely too large of a deposit, and get my keys. Miami Beach, as I found out, requires your first month's rent, last month's rent, and security deposit. Talk about breaking the bank from the start! I found a dope little studio a block from the beach for just $950 a month. I couldn't even live in a shit-hole studio in DC for less than $1,500 a month. I would be about twenty miles from work, and the commute was opposite of traffic, so that worked in my favor. I preferred to live on the beach with a longer commute, rather than have lived close to work, and far from the beach. I mean, if I was going to be living in Miami, I was going to be living on the beach! Yolo!

This bachelor pad was in such a clutch spot! It was a fifteen minute drive to South Beach, less than five bucks to hop in an *Uber* or *Lyft*, and a free trolley ride if I felt like traveling with tourists and smelly peeps. I could always bike down there too. There were volleyball courts across the street from my building, right along a paved jogging path that ran along the beach both ways for miles and miles. And the beach…my God! Words cannot describe. As you crossed over Collins Avenue, you saw the crystal blue Caribbean colored waters peeking through the openings between the green shrubberies. When you got to the beach, kicked off your sandals, sank your feet in the warm, baby's bottom soft white sands, you could look left and right at the beaches, and see nothing but ocean for miles, with only the colorful art deco lifeguard stands along the way. The soft beach breeze hit you, and there was absolute silence besides birds squeaking, and the waves hitting the shore. Just close your eyes and take it in. Welcome to Paradise! Then, up and down Collins Avenue, stretched everything you needed. There were grocery stores, pharmacies, restaurants of every cuisine, and bars/lounges. The apartment was in a perfect little spot. I had no need to leave the area besides heading to/from work, or if I wanted to venture to another cool Miami neighborhood. If only my job was on the damn beach too!

Because of my dope location and working in the lovely paying hotel industry, I decided to host *Airbnb* guests on my couch to make some extra cash. Yes, on my couch, in my studio apartment. The lifestyle I wanted to live in Miami required another form of income, and there is no better income than rental income. I was able to get anywhere from thirty-to-fifty bucks per night during the off-season, and around eighty per night during peak busy season, which lasts a solid four months or so in Miami. Eighty bucks a night for letting them crash on my freaking couch, which I rarely ever used anyway! That, and I worked ten-hour days, plus the commute each way, so was only really there at night. The guests would likely be out and about grabbing dinner, drinks, and sightseeing in town anyways. Majority of the time, I wouldn't even bump into the guests during their stay, besides meeting them and letting them in initially. Some people think that it is super risky to let complete strangers into your home, but I relied on their good reviews on the website, and I needed fucking money! Had I been in a higher paying industry, I likely would not need to do that bullshit. However, I did meet some damn good people from all around the world, and was able to check out some cool new spots around town because I ended up playing tour guide with half of them. So here I was, working in a business that houses people for the night to make money, all the meanwhile doing the exact same thing personally. Hospitality was all around me! Can't escape!

Enough about my new place! Let's hear about the new gig, and what was to come of what I thought would be a great position! I entered the beautiful Sales Office and got my little cubicle assigned to me. I was surrounded by a few loud, outspoken Sales Managers who were really spunky and fun. I was the only guy on my team so I knew that was going to be interesting. I was able to hear the daily *Scandal* and *Empire* shows gossip, regardless of whether I watched the episodes or not. Spoiler alert on the daily (eye roll)! I got my training schedule, which happened to be a three-page, size-six font, excel sheet of online and live Sales and Brand Training computer-based classes that I would be required to take. Whelp, forget about selling for the first month, as I would be glued to a headset watching those damn things! I would end up being completely worthless to my team from the start because of this, but everyone has to do it. The training consisted of the usual corny-ass instructors cracking jokes and making our job out to be the most fun thing out there. Just rainbows and unicorns right? Fucking paradise! Part of my training was to physically visit the hotels I would be selling for, which was awesome! I represented the Tampa and Orlando markets, so I would get to head back to my old stomping grounds. One of the hotels I would be selling out of Miami was actually the one I came from in my previous role, which was cool, and likely one of the main reasons I got the job! That hotel was a money maker in that Sales Office.

I would take the hotel visit trip with another young, cool dude coworker that actually took a new position in our Sales Office. Danny was a Manager for the Select Service Properties Team, and made the switch to the Full Service Team. This was seen as a step up, as the full service properties were more substantial and entail more meeting space and catering options. We rented a car (company paid) and drove to all of our hotels in Tampa and Orlando. The hotels would set us up with free rooms, meals, and the occasional amenities throughout our stay, while we toured the properties during the working day. Not a bad set-up. My old hotel, of course, hooked me up with a suite, and my boy Rick had some alcoholic beverages prepped for me for when I entered the room! My dude! He hated working at that fucking place, but never lost his knack for good hospitality. It was a nice little getaway for the week away from work, even though it was still technically work. Gotta love management life!

At each hotel, we would get a tour from the on-site Manager, showing us all of the sleeping room types and meeting rooms, including outdoor meeting space, which was always my favorite. Being in Florida, the outdoor meeting space could be used ninety percent of the year. The only time you really couldn't use it was in the dead heat of summer. If you have ever experienced the humidity in the Florida summers, you can understand why. That, and hurricanes can be unpredictable. We were shown the hotel outlets as well, like the restaurants, gift-shops, coffee shops, business centers, etc. We took as many notes as humanly possible because there was no chance in hell that Danny and I would remember everything about each hotel by the time we got back to the office. For example, which meeting rooms had windows, which had bathrooms close-by, which had pillars, and all the shit that you honestly wouldn't think to take note of, but the customers would eventually ask us. Of course, most of that we didn't write down, but found out we should have once we got back to the office and started selling.

We kind of got the shaft on our site tours, or immersions, as they call them in the hotel world. Normally, the Hotel Sales Reps would give a firsthand look at the city in addition to the hotels. Like a little tour guide, they would take us out to local restaurants, bars, or events in the area to help us get a good sense of the area surrounding the hotel. This would also allow us to relay recommendations and such to the clients. They didn't on our visits because we really didn't have too much downtime between bouncing from hotel to hotel. The goal of this trip was so that when we were selling these hotels over the phone or email, the clients would assume we actually worked in the hotel, and/or at least worked in the same city of the hotel, and not across the state in a damn call center! This was a dirty world to clients. They prefer speaking with someone on-site. It gives guests a feeling of comfort I guess.

Danny ended up being a cool ass dude that could totally relate to me with my complaints on working in the hotel industry. He had never worked in the Guest Services side of hotels, but had been with the Sales Office long enough to realize the BS that goes on in the industry. We spent ninety percent of our drive together ripping on the industry, and discussing how we need to GTFO and start our own businesses. There were so many different things that lagged behind in the industry, and between the two of us, it was a matter of time before we came up with some big idea to better it, and make millions off of it, or so we hoped! I don't know, maybe write a book or something. :)

We made it back to the office safe and sound, just to be greeted with some more training and be given our first month's sales goals. Because it was a ramp-up goal, it was pretty tiny compared to the other seasoned Managers, but going from not having any goal ever to a $50,000 a month booking goal was scary. This, without having a clue of the influx of leads coming in, or not coming in. I didn't even make that amount of money in a damn year, and I have to book it in a month!? Yikes! The trickiest part about getting into any inbound Sales role has to be not knowing what kind of lead volume you are going to get. You just have to hope and pray that the goals are realistic based on past years, but you know the corporate peeps are always pushing for more and more, regardless of trends. When was the last time you've heard of a goal for the following year decrease? As I mentioned earlier, we had Sales Executives with the company that would seek out new business, and send us leads to the office to reach out and hopefully book. So we depended on them greatly to send us business! That, and we relied on the strong brand name and advertising that the company was doing to direct people to our hotels to book their group business.

The whole purpose of the Sales Office concept was pretty badass to me. Clients would call a particular hotel that they were interested in to host their meetings and/or room blocks, and the hotel would transfer the call to us. We would answer as if we were at the hotel. We represented multiple hotels in one particular region for the purpose of if that particular hotel was sold out, or didn't have meeting space, or the prices were too high, we were then able to cross-sell that piece of business to another hotel that had the space, or a more suitable price for their needs. Clients loved this most of the time because they were planning to call multiple hotels and shop around anyway. They were thrilled to find out that we represented many others. This kept the business within the company, and away from the competitors. Fucking genius if you ask me! At first, you would think, "Why wouldn't the Sales Team just sit on the property and sell just that one hotel?" Well, this was the exact reasoning, although some other brands and franchised properties still did it that way. We had our main cities that we were responsible and goaled for, but we were also equipped with information and resources on all others that the Sales Office represented around the state. We were able to cross-sell customers to other cities if a particular city wasn't a requirement for them. For example, some companies would host their yearly rewards trips, and they only knew that they wanted to host it at a hotel/resort in a warm weather destination, thus meaning they would be open to checking out other cities in Florida, other than just Tampa or Orlando. Again, they likely planned to call other hotels within the same brand in other cities anyway, and in-turn, get transferred to our same Sales Office and the same Sales Manager anyway. Might as well save them the phone roulette.

So back to getting started with my new role. I finallyyyyyy got access to my computer, as for whatever reason switching roles in this company was a goddamn nightmare! At least that was consistent! There were too many hands in one pot trying to get things switched over, which led to it taking about a damn month to get all the proper logins and programs installed. Go figure, when I was supposedly all set and had a goal, I didn't have access to the damn pricing tool! Yeah, the one you need every single time you create a lead to price! Sigh. This shit would happen at the last Sales Office I worked at too, but luckily in my role there, it didn't affect me. Now that it was about two years later, I would have assumed the glitches would have been straightened out. Nope. So for my entire first week of selling, I had to build a lead, and then bother another Manager on my team to assist me. A Manager who had a goal of their own to make. It made me look like a non-self-starter, which was so not me! But oh well, this was out of my control. My goal was to come in, kick some ass on my numbers, and make a good first impression to my team and Leaders. This couldn't happen my first week because of the ever-loving HR and IT departments. And to think they are the ones that get paid the big bucks. Hmm.

Anywayzzz, new team was made up of quite some characters! We had Detrice, who was a loud, always smiling, African American girl who cracked me the hell up! I think she might have been a comedian in her past life. This girl coined the term "Food Stamp Bookings," or in other words, crappy little $500 or less catering-only bookings without any sleeping rooms. These always tended to be super time consuming clients for such little revenue in return, and it would be frustrating to us Sales Managers because we had such high goals. Detrice was known for answering the phone, putting her microphone on mute, and shouting commentary to us about the client, as the client was continually yapping away. It was likely a Food Stamp Booking, a family reunion group, or sketch-ball trying to get a rate that was impossible to get at even a Burger King, if they had space. "Ma'am…Ma'am…Ma'am," I would hear Detrice saying to try and stop annoying clients from talking. Hilarious! As much as I loved Detrice, her, along with other Manager's loud volume would get old very quickly, as all of our cubicles were right by each other. Although, research shows that you learn a lot by listening to other Senior Managers on the phone and how they sell. Regardless, it was annoying as shit some days, whoever it was yapping away too loud.

We had another Manager, Jackie, who was also pretty loud. She was a spicy Miami Cubana! She had been in the office for a while, so knew the hotel game…overworked and underpaid. She tried her best to work the system with management, and was pretty damn good at it! Sometimes she got her way, but usually just sounded like a whiny you-know-what because she would often get shot down per this company's rep...cheap AF! I picked up quite a few Spanish words from Jackie, and some tips and tricks for closing on business, and the Miami Latinas. "Triple points" was Jackie's main trick, which was a ploy to close business by a certain date. Towards quarter end, she would offer customers the opportunity to earn double or triple hotel rewards points if they returned a signed contract by a certain date, and the bonus money would roll in. I heard her pull this trick so many times, and I remember mumbling quietly in a girl voice, "Triple points," and Danny, who was sitting on the other side of the cube from me would always crack the fuck up when I said this. Jackie was the queen of what I called "Sales fluff." She would chit chat with clients about anything and everything. I would overhear her talking with them about their kids and their birthday plans, blah blah. I was more of a straight to the point, get down to business type. I found it a little corny to be too buddy-buddy with customers, but it worked for her, and sometimes I would attempt the Jackie approach, but more often than not, I just felt ingenuine trying that.

Jackie was the one that came up with the "Tony for President" campaign. I believe this stemmed from a combination of my borderline-OCD, and my gringo-ass always doing everything by-the-book. This, as opposed to most people in Miami, who cut corners quite often. I became known for calling out properties that we sold for, as their information they provided for us to use to sell was outdated or incorrect. I didn't want to be selling a meeting room that claimed to fit twenty people when it could only fit ten in reality! We had an office contest where we had to decorate our team's section of cubicles, and fancy up one of those tri-fold exhibition boards that we would all use at science fairs in elementary school. Jackie, followed by our other team members, thought it would be creative to run with that "Tony for President" theme and have our other team members be members of my cabinet. We cut everyone's top half out of pictures, and placed them behind little podiums on the board, surrounded by lots of red, white, and blue.

We had red, white, and blue tinsel ribbon garland like you see during the holidays lining our row of cubicles. #Murica! You would enter the front of our row and follow the draping ribbons to the back wall where our display sat with yours truly at the top, reading, "Tony for President!" This always made me look like an all-star when upper management would visit the office and see my big smiling face at the top of the board. Good times!

Jackie and Detrice both very openly voiced their negative concerns with their roles daily, and it boggled my mind as to why they were still in the same damn position for so long! This as opposed to going for another position within the company when it came time for them to apply. They would instead sign on to stay in the same role for another year. It made no sense to me, especially for a measly two-to-three percent raise that they likely got from this company. From the sounds of it, they tried for other positions previously and were unsuccessful, so just said screw it, and took the small-ass percentage raise and stayed. I think it was circumstantial too, as they both had kids and the job kind of worked for them because they dropped the kids at school, and then headed into the office. Some people just get comfortable and lazy in their roles, regardless of how much they dislike it. These were the same two Managers that would either work through their lunches, or simply migrate to the great room and eat there. They wouldn't leave the damn office! It was like their second home, and as much as they complained, I think they secretly loved it...that love/hate! Me, on the other hand, I had to GTFO of that office during my lunch hour. No way in hell would I be working through my lunch, or stay there and try to be social with the same people I hear yapping away all day! I would either hit the little gym nearby that we had free access to, or take a walk to the local Starbucks or Burlington Coat Factory. This was a great time burner, and it would get me up and on my feet walking, as sitting for ten hours a day is ridiculously draining. Yes, this is coming from the same person that complained about standing all day during my days of working at the Front Desk. You can't freaking win in this industry! I'm telling you!

I was super excited to be back in the Sales Office atmosphere, as the Mid-Atlantic Office had a great vibe with young, single, and fun individuals who didn't mind grabbing the occasional after work beverage. This office...not the case. Miami is made up of quite a few Latin people in case you didn't know. Over seventy percent of the population to be exact. Their culture is known for having children at a very young age, and a lot of them! Most of the people I worked with had multiple kids, and a husband, or significant other that restricted them from post work events. They had to take the kids to an event, or make dinner, visit the grandparents, etc. That, or they were just straight up drained like I was after those damn ten hour days. The only post-work activities anyone would take part in were when our on-site Hotel Reps would come to the office to visit, and take us to our closest hotel restaurant for free cocktails and bites. This was great that they did this for us, but the shitty part was that it was off the clock for us Sales Managers. For the Sales Reps from the hotels, this counted towards their ten hours, but not us scrubs! Fuckers. I brought this up to leadership a few times, saying that maybe our team would be more motivated to go to these outings (as they were technically optional) if we left work early, and were being paid for it. After all, we talked about work the whole damn time as we ate and drank! These also sucked because the happy hours were always mid-week, and we all had to be in the office the next morning. There would normally be Supervisors and/or Director's present, so getting trashed wasn't an option. Although, we did always have that one rowdy coworker...Lourdes!

If we really wanted to step up the post work activities, we should have taken full advantage of the Miami scene. Let me plan the damn activities! We would have been leaving at lunch on a Friday and hitting up a Miami Beach rooftop pool, with a DJ playing, beach balls flying through the air, and models serving us cocktails in all-white, barely there bikinis. I mean c'mon, the office was in Miami after all! Or, how about hitting up the trendy art district, Wynwood, and release our inner-hipster. You want to "up the work atmosphere," let's up the social events, and make it seem like a place people really want to work. Help my *Instagram* cred out a bit. #WorkPerks.

My thoughts on the Florida Sales Organization being boring changed a bit when we had our annual Sales School. Here, Managers, Executives, Leaders, and Directors across the state would meet at one of our hotels for a week-long event full of trainings and themed dinners/receptions. You wanna talk about a great networking opportunity! This was the best because you ran into people from all across the state. You bumped into people that you previously worked with, people you currently worked with, people you had never physically seen in person, and completely new people. Here, I took a Revenue Management course that ran for three entire days. The other days I would take part in a variety of smaller, more general Sales classes. After everyone was done their class trainings for the day, we would all meet for the nightly themed dinners. This was great! We were able to unleash our outside-of-work personality with themed outfits on. We were able to mix and mingle with everyone, and sit wherever the hell we wanted. Awards were given out, speeches given, skits acted, and oh, did I mention...A FREAKING OPEN BAR! This was unheard of in the hotel business, because most of us are all alcoholics or pot-heads outside of work, and management would like to keep that outside of work. Sales School was a free-for-all. It was kind of a test though, because we would all have to get up for classes in the morning, so we would have to be semi-responsible.

We did what any responsible hotel employee would do...got wasted, mingled, danced, flirted, etc. on a nightly basis, for the entire week. Our Leaders didn't set much of an example, as they probably drank more than all of us, and were tied to a microphone all night, so it was a little more obvious. Classic! I may or may not have had a little hook-up with one of our hotels Event Managers in one of the floors hallways. This was after a bunch of us rolled out to a local strip club one evening, courtesy of the free hotel shuttle ride. Whoops! She happened to work in the Miami market, so it was a tad awkward seeing her in the future. The first night was a Miami

Chic themed dinner. I am probably the whitest M F'er in Miami, but donned the most Miami outfit I had. I rocked loafers, bright turquoise shorts, a white button up, maroon blazer, flashy watch, chain, and of course, orange reflective glasses. I clearly overdid it after seeing everyone else's attire that night. Oh well. Funny enough, at our breakfast with everyone the next morning, the MC, who was the Director of Area Sales, paused to make a special announcement. Everyone there looked hungover as hell, including me. He said they had to give out a special award for Best Dressed from the previous night's dinner. My immediate reaction was "Oh shit, this better not be my ass!" Everyone looked over at me and started mumbling my name. He announced the winner…and sure enough…it was my dumbass! As embarrassing as that was, it was pretty perfect because if someone at the Sales School didn't know me previously, they knew me now! Winning! Not a bad way to get on key Salespeople within the company's radars. There could be worse ways…a.k.a. throwing up, or slipping and falling in drunkenness, which others did.

Whelp, back to the real world in the Miami office. My selling skills were way better than I thought. I was just honest with people. I would tell them their options, price, and let them make the decision. If I recommended something, I would tell them and hope they take my word for it, being that I was a professional in the field. The kicker came when trying to sell some of the add-ons. When you are hosting a meeting, the "add-ons" such as wifi and audio visual equipment are truly a necessity. The problem was that our company priced them out of this world! "Oh yes sir, that will be five-hundred dollars for a projector for each day of your meeting, then a hundred-fifty for the screen, and fifty for the presentation clicker. Ready to sign?" What in the fuck!? "So you're telling me that the food and beverage minimum is X amount, and meeting room rental X amount, and then the projector is additional!? It doesn't come with the room?" "No sir. Oh, and the wireless internet is another hundred for the first device and twenty bucks for each additional device." The same wireless internet that is free at the Starbucks directly across the street, and literally downstairs in the hotel lobby for that matter. "Ready to sign?" Just shoot me! Seriously. Flip charts, markers for the flip charts, teleconference phones, microphones, lapel microphones, podiums, laser pointers, and more were extra charges. Tacky AF! This company was so dominant in the industry that sadly, they could get away with this. They rob you for your hotel room costs, then straight kill you if you are hosting a meeting, but people still booked with them like hotcakes! It still boggles my mind.

Another selling obstacle that I never knew about before starting my role, was some of our very own colleagues, the lovely Revenue Managers. I had no idea they would ultimately be the gatekeepers for us to quote business. This company had an amazing tool to help calculate prices to quote, but if you went outside of certain parameters, such as the dates, numbers of group rooms needed, food and beverage spend (or lack-thereof), then it wouldn't give you pricing, but instead a "Reach out to Revenue Management" message. Then, it was up to us as the Sales Manager to build a case to them that the group we were booking was worth it. In other words, why should the hotel allow your group to book, instead of another better one that may come along? Sometimes the business case wouldn't show as obvious in the computer. For example, if the group was booking that same event every single month, or at multiple hotels, for multiple years, it wouldn't show in one particular booking. You would submit a case to Revenue Management to convince them of the potential of the group beyond that one particular booking that was put in the system. I was relatively good at building my case and getting Revenue to approve. I learned that the more detail and reasoning you included, the more likely they were to accept your group. There were some Managers that would flip their shit when Revenue wouldn't approve their groups. It was easy to hate Revenue Management because you wanted to book anything and everything you could to hit your numbers and make your bonuses, but I am also very analytical, and can see where Revenue came from at times when they denied a booking. I made sure to never get on

Revenue's bad side, and it seemed they rewarded me for it by accepting the majority of my requests.

The office politics started to get a little out of control. From Day 1 when I started, the Leaders were preaching, "Be ready for change." They would constantly ask everyone during our morning stand-ups, "Are you guys still ok with being open to changes this year?" No one knew what the hell they were talking about, so would just mumble, "Sure." Clearly, they were trying to shake up the work atmosphere, so I was honestly all about it. It needed it. So out of the blue one day, new office seating charts were released, and our Administrative Assistants were also changed. Oh shit. I actually didn't mind the Assistant I had, as I didn't use her all too much anyway. Some people had been sitting in the same seat for years in that office, and had the same Assistant the entire time. Now they would have to switch both, and this did not go over well for a lot of people. Some didn't care, like myself. I literally only moved up one seat, and my Admin stayed the same. Then, a few months later, we switched seats again to move closer to our South Florida Hotel Managers (versus just Tampa/Orlando). I was not a fan of this change because it was already loud in the office, and now we would be closer to other Managers yapping away. Oh well, my headphones would get some more usage at this point in between calls. It was cool in the sense that we could become more familiar with those hotels, if for some reason we had to cross-sell them. Also, the team comradery picked up. We would joke and laugh more, but because of that, the volume got louder and distractions more frequent. This is how I got situated in the cubicle on the other side of Danny, like I mentioned before. He was on the South Florida Team. Michael sat across from Danny, who was another cool young dude. One of the boyz, as they say. In fact, myself, Danny, and Michael put together the best Halloween costume basically ever...three members of World Championship Wrestling's *NWO* (*New World Order*). It DOES NOT get much cooler than that! Period.

A lady by the name of Lourdes was the queen bee when it came to office noise, and she sat directly behind Danny. Fuck us! Loved this lady to death, but my God I think the whole office heard every one of her phone calls. She was at the point where she was ready to get the hell out of the office, so most of her calls were quite funny to listen in on, and her comments after the phone call were even better. She was a sixty-year-old Cubana, who looked, and dressed like she was in her twenties or thirties, and she could pull it off! As I always preach, gotta love Latin women! I would say fifty percent of her comments off the phone were sexual in some way or another. Luckily, everyone around her were just as perverted, so it worked out. It was just the volume that drove me bananas. Lourdes was famous for taking full advantage of the after-work events free booze. As I explained earlier, it was tough to get rowdy because the events were normally on a work-night, and the bosses were present. She didn't give AF! Her perversion and volume would increase as the free booze continued to flow. She got cut-off from alcohol at a few events that I took part in. Hilarious! We loved her for it. Management learned to just expect it, so she never really get punished for it, just cut-off, and life went on the next day. Surprisingly lenient if you ask me. I know other companies that I worked with where that would have been enough for immediate terms for dismissal.

After the musical chairs at the office, management then released the most annoying thing on the planet to better track our leads. They titled it DQI. Who the hell knew what that stood for!? Data Quality something, I think. We just knew it was a royal pain in our asses! Not to get into too much detail about it, but it was basically a series of reports that would be run weekly to see if us Managers were filling everything out correctly (or at all) in our booking system. This was insanely time consuming and definitely didn't help us close any business. Complete waste of time and energy. Management sure loved to bug the hell out of us to complete it though, because their Managers were looking at it as well. So naturally, our lack of completing it reflected poorly on them. Regardless, it was just one more damn thing to try and squeeze in our ten hour day in the midst of answering non-stop leads all day. Shoot me.

At this point, I had been at the Sales Office long enough to become bonus eligible. Wooo!! This was great because in my first three months, I killed it with my numbers, but wasn't able to get shit in return for doing so. I killed it again in my second quarter, and was super pumped to see what I would be cashing out at for the quarter. I tried to calculate how our bonus worked by myself, and soon realized I needed a damn PHD in mathematics to figure that shit out, so I decided to ask my other team members how it worked, and go figure, they didn't know. I asked my Leader...didn't know. Asked his Leader...didn't know. What the fuck!? The people that were tracking and paying out our bonuses had no idea how it was calculated. What a cluster. I remember that I coincidentally asked on the exact day of the four year anniversary of the Sales Office's existence. Four years, and no one knew how our bonuses worked. Dios mio (Spanish for OMG)! Are you kidding me? So I kind of figured it out myself and made a half-ass calculation tool in Excel, and just bit my tongue. Biting my tongue became a skill the hotel industry really trained me to master. I'm surprised that thing is still intact.

I did practically bite it off for another situation that occurred not too long after this bonus fiasco. So when I was originally being interviewed for this position, I was told how it was great because I could hit my goal two quarters in a row and become eligible to work as a part-time remote Manager. This meant I would work from home three days out of the week, and pick any two days to come into the office. Hell-fuckin-yeah! This was amazing because at home I would be able to sleep in, not have to worry about getting all dressed up, and not having to commute to the office. I could do whatever I wanted at lunch without being tied down to what was in the vicinity of the office. I could take a nap, go for a jog, jerk off, whatever I pleased. I wouldn't have to fight rush hour traffic heading to and from work either. There would be no distractions from other Managers or office visitors. I would have my own personal bathroom, and could knock out home chores in my downtime, such as laundry or dishes. I could sit at my desk at home, the couch, bed, or even better, my balcony, enjoying the Miami Beach breeze. Now that's what I'm talking about! My work-life balance would grow exponentially with this remote option, and would make the job ten-times more enjoyable!

Shockingly, I hit my goal two quarters in a row at 111% and 129% (percent to goal). I was sooooo pumped because I could post for that remote status. As I found out, it wasn't actually a guarantee because they would review your numbers and phone review scores, and make sure you would be good on your own. Well, cue the Hotel Gods! I was talking to another Manager and told her how I was pumped to be able to go remote as the quarter was almost done officially, and she tells me, "Oh, you can't because you have to be a Sales Manager 2 to be eligible." Remember, I was a Sales Manager 3, which was one level below. My heart dropped to the floor. I told her that couldn't be right because they not only pitched that to me when I was hired, but even confirmed it with me at a later point because I was worried I wouldn't be able to since my first quarter I wasn't at a full goal. They said that would still be ok. Sure enough, I talked to the Leaders and HR after talking with my coworker and being at least a Sales Manager 2 was indeed a requirement. I was fuming! This was literally my motivation from Day 1 in this position, so to find out I would then have to wait an additional six months to be eligible for SM2 and go remote, I was not a happy camper. I can't say that I was all that surprised though because it was the famed hotel industry. Just like the show *Big Brother* (CBS) says, "Expect the Unexpected!"

Just when I thought all of the surprises had run out, there came more. I explained earlier that we had a Phone Leads Team, which I was on, and an Electronic Leads (E-Leads) Team. We had literally just taken our employee surveys where we praised management, and how things ran in the office. Then, leadership called us in for a random team meeting, which was not normally a good thing, unless it was to announce a new hiring. The meeting began with, "Remember how we said to keep an open mind this year?" Oh God, here we go. Another fucking desk move!? Nope. This big announcement was that in two weeks we would all become combined Phone and E-Lead Managers. No longer would we have separate teams. We would handle both, and the leads would be distributed evenly amongst us all. I had actually heard that this was in the works back when I worked at the Mid-Atlantic Office, but at the time, I didn't exactly realize what kind of difference it would make since I was just an Assistant at the time. Honestly, it sounded like it would make more sense, so I didn't see the harm in it. I mean, shit, at least I can get a bit of work done without the phone ringing non-goddamn-stop.

The change was just too good to be true of course. There was one major issue from the start. Previously, the Phones Team had been seen as a starter position in the office. People without any experience would be required to start on the Phones Team, and then their next position would be an E-Leads Manager, although there were a few Senior Managers that preferred the Phones Team (don't ask me WTF shit they were smoking). Our team had a Manager that had literally just been promoted to an E-Lead Manager about a month prior to this announcement. She was enthralled at the time because she finally wouldn't have to answer the phones all damn day anymore. Whelp, she got majorly fucked with this new change. Poor girl. But it also sucked for us Sales Manager 3's because we would now be taking on a more senior role without the extra pay. Those sneaky ass Leaders! They tried to give us the work-around that when you went from Phones to E-Leads that the extra pay was just for the year-long commitment to stay in the position, not the actual position itself. I called bullshit on that one! Did I mention that this change was going to start just two weeks after they made the announcement? I made sure to stress to our Leaders that us Phone Managers would need some refresher courses on E-Lead Management because there were a lot of different lead response sites and methods that we did not face with phone leads...because like I said, it was a more intense role, hence the seniority that had previously been associated with it. SMH.

I gave this new system a try before I whined too hard, because who knows, maybe it would be better. Wrong! Let me tell you what...it blew major ass! Not to mention, my team was already short a Manager. Then, the Manager that had just gotten the promotion and then had to put up with this new shit ended up getting a role outside of the company. She was over it! I couldn't blame her. So make it two Managers that we were short now, along with this new workload. Fuck us all! Just imagine getting clobbered with E-Leads which were much more substantial leads for multiple hotels that we would have to respond to, and then having to answer incoming phone call leads all the meanwhile. The brain does not function like that. Putting whatever you are working on hold, and giving full attention to the phone call, then going back (if you remembered) to what you were working on previously. Insanity! I was not a happy camper, and neither was anyone else, and we expressed this, but it was out of our Leaders' hands, as this was now the future for the company. No bueno! I instantly got on my favorite *HCareers* site and began perusing for something better. I was ready to go.

Along with the new bull shit we were going through, management decided to crack down on that damn DQI even more-so in regards to how we sent our proposals/contracts, and how we noted things in the computer system. Pain in the ass! We were also being pushed by corporate to let clients know about a new *Pinterest*-like site they created for meetings. It was a really cool site. It would show examples/pictures of things we could do for our clients' events. For example, how we could set their meeting up in more of a lounge style setting, with couches or even bean bags. Also, they could have desserts or entrees served in unconventional ways, such as in a modern popcorn-like brown bags, or fish bowls, etc. It was a great idea, and would set us apart from the competition. Here was the issue...we were already overwhelmed as Managers doing our daily tasks trying to sell the business, and now we would have to try and sell an entire different idea and face possible questions that would set our timing back even more, hence losing possible good leads all the meanwhile. Sounds draining right!? Because it was! We were not equipped with any pricing information for ideas on this fancy new site, so the client would ask us how much it would be to do a certain set-up from the website for their event, and we would have no clue. Like I said, great concept, but corporate didn't think this one all the way through first. So basically, as a result, none of us Managers would even mention this new site to clients to save ourselves from questions and concerns that none of us would know the answers to, or want to take the time away from our other things to find out the answers to. Sorry, not sorry.

We were being micromanaged to the tee. We clocked in and out and would be grilled if we were a few minutes late or early. Yes, clocked in and out for a management role. We would also be grilled if we were running a few minutes late from our hour lunch and didn't give out Managers a heads-up. It was like I was back in elementary school all over again. We also had to log into the phones daily because that is how we received our phone leads on rotation. If one or two Managers were logged out and the phones got busy, they would ring non-stop to your phone. Our Leader could see who was logged in and out at all times, so it got to the point where the Managers would call us out if we were logged out when we weren't supposed to be. There were a few times where I would get yelled at because I was simply going to the bathroom or filling up my water bottle. It was pathetic. I so badly wanted to yell to my Leader in response, "Sorry, I was taking a shit!" Because we were on that rotating phone system, we couldn't all just take lunch at the same time. You wouldn't want to have three Managers on your team taking lunch at once, and leave you stranded on the phones getting plastered with calls. We had a lunch time schedule. Tony had 12 p.m., Jackie had 1 p.m., etc. Annoying AF! This sucked, because unless you pre-planned lunch with someone from another team, you were flying solo. It was definitely different from when I was an Assistant and could take breaks/lunch whenever the fuck I pleased, and have other people join me. That freedom was gone.

In addition to all of these negatives, here was the determining factor for me to decide it was time to look around. Every other management position I could apply for from here on out in the company also required that same ten-hour workday. Every single one. Every Sales Office, every hotel, every outside Sales position. So the same old bullshit, just a different day. Sales Manager 2—ten hours; Sales Executive—ten hours; on-site Sales Manager—-ten hours; Revenue Manager—-ten hours. What the fuck kind of company was this? For being ranked a "Top 100 Company" to work for year after year, you would think they would catch on to the fact that no one wants to work beyond an eight-hour day. It has been proven that people aren't productive working beyond eight hours. It was a no brainer for me to get out while I could.

At the same time all of this BS was happening, I started to get callbacks from some of my job applications, and I started to interview immediately. I had to take half days here and there just to squeeze an interview in normal hours (8 a.m. - 5 p.m.), because our asses with those ten hour days would start work before everyone else, and leave after everyone else. At your service! Anyways, I had an interview with a property that had just taken over a major chain hotel located nearby the Trump National Golf Course. The brand was a fancier one, and had a Sales Manager role that was like a combination role of our company's Sales Manager, Sales Executive, and on-site Sales Manager roles. This was exactly what I was interested in! This way, I would not be stuck up in an office all day, and could actually interact with the clients I was working with. I could actually give them a pretty smile and a wink, instead of trying to portray this through the phone. I could actually wear my favorite H&M suits, and actually get respected as a professional for it. I killed ALL FOUR of my interviews with them, and received an offer. Hell to the yessssss! Finally, get me out of dis bitch! Not so fast...

I should have known this was too good to be true in the lovely hotel industry. It doesn't let us escape that easy! Wouldn't you believe it, the great relocation that my current company had covered from Tampa to Miami held me up. I knew I would have to pay it back if I left before my first year, so this wasn't the issue. The issue was that the small relocation (or so I thought) ended up being a ridiculous $3,000 plus payout. Damn, movers are expensive! This wasn't exactly pocket change for a low-paying Hotel Sales Manager. Not to mention, the way my Leaders held me hostage with it, it made me realize that I would not be receiving a recommendation any time soon from them if I split early. Goddammit! So, I decided to try for the impossible, and ask the company that offered me the position if they would pay for my relocation payback. I felt very uneasy about asking, as this seemed super sketchy to bring up after already receiving my offer from them. The company convened for a bit and got back to me. Unfortunately, they could not do that, so I had to turn the position down. If the industry didn't pay us shit, I probably would have paid the three-thousand without blinking an eye, but it didn't. Well shit, back to the grind for a little while until I wait out my year, so I can move on to possibly another position within the company! The problem was that even after my year anniversary, I would have to wait another three months to post for a new position because of those first three months of training. Yikes! Good thing our building didn't have rooftop level access, because I was ready to jump.

Right around this time, our office was about to receive a special guest. The former CEO, current Executive Chair, and son of the founder of the entire company would be making his rounds to all of the Sales Offices around the country, and a few hotels along the way. Holy shit! That was pretty cool to me. This dude was a living legend, and his last name was plastered on all of our hotels. His son would also be joining him, whom I had already met at the last Sales Office I worked at. I doubted he would remember me. This office would straight jerk it when we had a high level Salesperson come to visit, and basically everything stopped to make sure it was cleaned, appropriate, and ready for the visitor. So imagine that, times ten for this visitor! We were given exact instructions on how the office visit and tour would go. He was an older guy, so they tried to keep his visits short and sweet. We would go to the office kitchen/lounge area and form a circle so he could come around and shake our hands, and thank us for our work. Then, he would head to each team's cubicle areas and snap a quick photo with the team. We coincidentally had a professional photographer in the office that day taking our office team headshots, so he was also able to snap some pics during the visit. Wouldn't you know it, one of the few pics he got during the visit was of yours truly! I was crushing it in my H&M suit of course, giving the phenom a firm handshake, and looking into his eyes as he is looking into mine. Fucking beautiful! I was super lucky because there weren't a ton of pictures taken from that quick visit. I was able to *Instagram* and social media the hell out of that, and make that my profile picture for a good while. It was such a good picture that my dad, who hates pictures, asked me for the original image so he could frame it for his office. Little did he know, I was in the process of bouncing.

Aside from being besties with hotel celebrities, I kept on trucking and killing my numbers in the office. I bit my tongue on the political bullshit for the most part, but would still voice my concerns from time to time because I knew I would be leaving soon. I figured someone might as well do it for the future betterment of the team. Just when I was coasting along and getting in the busy rhythm, another hiccup came about. Another one!? Like why, just why!? The quarter had ended, and I hit my individual revenue goal and my ADR goal...or did I? I get an email from my Director stating that I would get the low-end bonus of my ADR goal. What the!? Did I miss something? My goal was only a ninety-nine dollar ADR for the quarter. I was killing that with a hundred-fifty plus room rates for most of my bookings. In the email, it even showed that I was averaging an ADR well-beyond ninety-nine bucks! But then, in a grid below it, it showed some other percentage calculations. Apparently, all this time, twelve months into my role, the ADR was actually calculated from a percentage of the rates I was quoting, versus the rates we were recommended to quote. Unreal. I sat down with the Director to go over this, and she shows me this grid and calculations that I had never seen or ever heard of during my time in that office, until that email. Twelve months in...never. Wow.

Then, to throw the icing on the cake, we didn't hit our team attainment goal either! Un-freakin-believable! I was there for a year (four quarters) and we didn't hit that bitch once! Goddammit. Time to bounce. #HotelIndustry

So this just about did it for me, and wouldn't you believe it, the Hotel God's decided to throw me a bone, and I received a call for an interview for a soon-to-open new property right by my apartment on the beach for a Sales Manager position. It was literally fourteen blocks from my place. I could bike or even walk there if I wanted. It happened to carry the same brand name as the one I was working for, but was owned and managed by a different company, a.k.a. it was a franchise property. This was totally ok with me, as I was learning that working for corporate wasn't as hyped up as I once thought. With franchise's, there seemed to be more freedom to make decisions on your own, not just what corporate was passing down. There was more leeway, and oftentimes better pay. Oddly enough, the Director of Sales that was interviewing me for the position was previously in my exact same role, on my exact same team in the Sales Office? He knew the gig, and knew it well! He knew the pain and suffering that I went through on a daily basis, and even knew all the good and bad coworkers I worked with daily. It was like an angel from above sent down to save me.

Of course, having that instant connection made the interview way more informal than it should have been, but either way, I was prepped for this interview with all the ammunition possible. I researched the hotel, the company, the local area, the Director of Sales, and GM's backgrounds. I was not, NOT getting this position. I had suffered through the Sales Office horseshit long enough. Like I said, this position was for Sales Manager, which was the same as the last position I was offered and then had to turn town. I would mainly be focusing on Group Sales, but assisting the Director with anything Sales related if needed. He was very happy that I was very computer savvy as he said he was not, and actually liked that I came from the brand background and wouldn't need to take any extra time training for it. The best part was that my one year (and three months) had finally passed in order to not have to pay back that damn relocation! Nothing was holding me back this time! I had this on lock!

I was actually planning to end the book here with a happy ending on how I got the job away from the corporate world, but still in the hotel industry, and lived happily ever after. Not quite. So I did indeed get the job. I was stoked! I was going to be a part of a brand new hotel opening, and be the "cover boy" Sales Manager, if you will. I would be the face of the hotel, attending every event, and visiting all local businesses, making people aware of this awesome new concept of a hotel. It was up to me to convince anyone and everyone to stay at our hotel, and hopefully book group room blocks and/or meetings/events so I could get paid! I would wear my name tag in honor, and send out material with extra oomph behind it because I would be proud of the product I was selling. This, as opposed to sitting in a cubicle, lost in an office building, selling every damn hotel in the state like an order taker. Sales Manager my ass! That was a Call Center Rep! Thank God that was done!

This particular hotel was part of the chain's extended stay brand, which entailed the rooms being equipped with kitchenettes that were fully stocked with china/glass/silverware, and the rates would drop the longer you stayed. Most hotels in this particular brand of the chain were older, pretty boring in design, and in random small towns or airport locations. Not exactly somewhere you would go for a vacation. They were geared towards project business where guests would need a home-like setting for a few weeks, or even a few months. Well, this particular property was located a block from Miami Beach's crystal clear waters and white sandy beaches. It was an all glass, very modern looking building that you would never peg as a hotel from this brand. It featured a huge, spacious lobby, with a large courtyard arboretum filled with palm trees and tropical plants, shining natural lighting into the lobby. It had a lobby restaurant and bar, which was unheard of with this brand. It also featured meeting space, a huge rooftop terrace, along with a rooftop pool and cabanas. If I were to tell you these features, and then tell you what brand of hotel it was, you would never in a thousand years believe me. This is what would make it so exciting to sell, because it truly was a first of its kind.

The Director of the hotel offered me five-thousand dollars more than my previous role, and I countered with ten thousand more…nope. I was, however, told about a bonus structure that would offer me the potential of making an additional forty percent of my yearly salary, with a portion of it uncapped. This would put me at a really nice figure compared to what I was making. Andddddd I would be eligible to make bonus after just my first quarter of working there. This was great because if you recall in my previous role, I had to wait until quarter two and the bonus was not as great. I signed the paperwork, and was ready to get the ball rolling on selling this new hotel. A few days later, I actually ran into a colleague that was an on-site Sales Manager at a recently opened hotel on the beach, and he gave me one big piece of advice. He said to make sure that I had my bonus structure detailed out in my contract before I signed anything. Whelp, I already signed it. The new contract had it written that I would be eligible for my bonus starting Quarter 1, but did not specify in detail the forty percent and the uncapped portion the Director sold me on. I thought that sufficed, and assumed a legit company would follow their word. I probably shouldn't have assumed this knowing the hotel biz.

I was super pumped to start the new gig! I anxiously reached out to my new Director before my first day to see when and where in the hotel I was to meet him on Day 1. He tells me to meet him at 9 p.m. at some location in Aventura, Florida, which was about twenty minutes from my apartment and the not yet completed hotel. I assumed this was a corporate office or something where I could do all the HR paperwork and what-not before getting the ball rolling at the hotel. As it turned out, I would be working out of that location daily until the hotel was complete enough for us to legally and safely be able to work out of it. It would take me twenty minutes to get there, and thirty-plus on the way home because of Aventura's shit-ass traffic. One of the main reasons I was so excited to take this new job was because the hotel was located so close to my place. Guess not. Ugh...seriously! Can I catch a freaking break!?

This extra sucked because every time I would need to give a site tour of the hotel, I would have to drive back towards the beach to the hotel right by my apartment. Then after, back to the office. And then, a few hours later, head back home to that same location (imagine the straight faced emoji). I would have to get to the hotel early enough in case the clients showed up early for the tour. I would then have to pay for parking to later expense because the hotel garage was not yet complete. Then, I would sweat my ass off in my H&M suit in the South Florida heat walking to the hotel, and checking the non-air conditioned and unfinished hotel to make sure it was in "site-ready condition." Clearly, that wasn't possible during the construction phase with dirt still on the fucking ground! I would hope and pray that the clients would actually show up for the site because if they cancelled for some reason, I would have to do the whole process over again, and waste more of my days.

Oh well, moving on. The hotel was supposed to open on February 1st of that year, and it was already the first week of January. I would just have to suffer a commute for a few more weeks...or so I thought. All four of us on the management team lived close to the hotel, so I don't know what genius chose this location for a temporary office. Actually I did...the Director of Sales & Marketing (DOSM) that hired me. Nothing came to surprise me at this place. If it didn't make sense, that was the exact decision leadership made. At first, it was myself, the DOSM, the GM, and AGM all sharing this office that was under three-hundred square feet. It was four adults all crammed in a small ass office with no cubicle dividers, making phone calls all day, just talking over one another. Just grand! And this was supposed to be an upgrade from my last cubicle gig. Fail! Not a great start.

Come to find out, this was only half of the crew that would be in the office, or should I call, closet? Soon after I was hired, the Housekeeping Manager, Food & Beverage Manager, and Front

Desk Manager shortly followed, and joined our office orgy. All three of the new hires were also young dudes in their twenties, like myself. I must say, it was pretty cool to see the team coming together. We literally started from the ground up. "Started from the bottom, now we're here."--- *Drake*. We had a Director of Engineering as well, but he mainly worked at the hotel through the construction. Soon after the new management hires, we decided to have little meetings to recap what was going on in each department daily. It definitely made you stay on top of your daily tasks because you would have to share with the group every morning. I remember a few days into these meetings, our GM announced that he expected us all to be clean shaven. Umm, one little hiccup here, myself and the Housekeeping Manager were hired with beards already attached to our faces, and were never told this in our interviews or upon getting hired. One of the many reasons I was excited to work in the Sales Office previously was because I could actually have a beard (because it was not customer-facing). Whelp, that was short lived. This didn't surprise me much because working on property in hotels, being clean-shaven tended to be a norm. Regardless, there were still quite a few reasons as to why this bothered the shit out of me. One, as I said, was because I was not told upon hiring that I would have to go back to my baby-face. Two, in our company's handbook, it is permitted (allowed) to have a beard, as long as it was well groomed, which mine was. Basically, as long as you trim the edges and it's not long and scraggly to the point where you look homeless, you are ok, or should be. Third, and the reason that it irked me the most, was the fact that beards were in style, and yes, in the professional world, and shockingly the hotel world! Anywhere you went during that time frame, especially in the cool/hip hotels that apparently we were competing with, the male employees were rocking beards, and even tattoos. Just picture the hipster look. If we really wanted to make an effort for our hotel to stand out from the typical ones in the brand, then this would be a great area to set ourselves apart from the pack. Nope!

So, like a good boy, I showed up to work clean shaven as I was told, because I am a follower of rules. It was depressing because the beard had been hitting it big with the Miami ladies! It made me look way less gringo in a sea of Latinos in Miami. Obviously my non-Spanish, country speaking accent didn't help my cause. It also made me look older, and it was much damn easier to maintain. I kept it clean shaven for a week or so, and then let it go a bit, but kept it trimmed up along the edges, hoping it would go unnoticed. Well, apparently the GM really, REALLY didn't like scruff or beards because he said something to my Director. My Director pulled me aside after a site tour one day and said there was something he needed to speak to me about. Oh Lord. He informed me that the GM said something to him about my scruff, and it needed to go ASAP! This little incident particularly made me mad because the GM had to cowardly tell the Director to tell me, instead of just coming to me directly. Like I said, we shared the same damn closet office, so it's not like he didn't see me every goddamn day! What an ass! I guess maybe he wanted the Director to handle his own department, I don't know. I shaved it again, and kept it shaved (besides on the weekends) from there on out. I was not looking to make enemies amongst my team. If it was really that important to the GM, I would follow his orders, because if I were in his role, I wouldn't want an annoying Sales Manager disobeying my orders.

Now, quick backstory on this General Manager. This guy was actually a pretty damn big deal! He opened quite a few big name hotels in the Miami area. He even worked with the world famous Ian Schrager to open a hotel in New York previously. Yes, the same Ian Schrager behind the genius Studio 54. The GM was nominated by *HotelChatter.com* (when it existed) as one of the hottest GM's in Miami one year. I'm going to assume it was based on his successes as a GM, and not his looks. In case you didn't know, *Hotel Chatter* was basically a hotel gossip site that was run by Conde Nast. It was actually one of my major inspirations to write this book. Thanks to Ted, my old Supervisor, for introducing me to it. Funny I mention Ted, because he had actually previously opened a major Miami hotel with this very same GM. Ted was one of the Front Desk Supervisors on his opening team. So of course, prior to working here, I reached out to him to see what he thought of the

GM, even though it sounded like I would be working more with the Director of Sales anyway. Ted's exact words were, "He's a douche." Whelp, up until this little beard fiasco, I thought the GM was a pretty cool dude, and I gave him the benefit of the doubt with everything because he had been around the block way more than me.

I put that little episode behind me and concentrated on selling the shit out of the hotel. I called every client I ever worked with in my previous roles, every potential client my Director suggested, every client in the area that would most likely have use for hotel rooms or meeting/event space, and even people that didn't, but spread the word anyway. Everybody knows someday that might have a use for a hotel. I was forced to circulate this shit presentation that the Director put together that I honestly thought one of my mom's fifth grade students created. The thing had sound effects and transitions for crying out loud! Wow. I showed my friend and ex-coworker Danny because he and I were very similar in our vision for good marketing/branding material. He died laughing! This thing was straight embarrassing. Again, we were supposed to be selling this one-of-a-kind hotel for the brand, and this certainly was not painting the picture. It painted the exact picture of the brands previous image: The plain, boring, family-style, airport or middle of nowhere hotel. So me, being the creative guy that I was, created my own presentation that was ultra clean, modern, direct, and to the point. The Director was the king of lengthy, descriptive wording to describe a certain feature. Remember how one of the first things they train us in school on creating a presentation is using bullet-points and not be super wordy with paragraphs? I think he was sick during that lesson. And how about the dude never even saved it as a PDF, so people could straight edit the document when he sent it to them right in *PowerPoint*. They would then have to find in *PowerPoint* where the "View Presentation" button was, which we all know is a task all on its own. At least using his method, his sound effects and transitions would work, as opposed to being a *PDF* file. LOL! I mean, really dude!? SMH!

So, I distributed the one that I created quietly to my clients instead (imagine the emoji with the sunglasses on). At the end of the day, if I was getting the same message across and I had to be the one representing it, I could not send a garbage product like his. Director of Sales & "Marketing" my ass! His presentation only included two renderings of the hotel and a few images of the inside of a guest room. It also had a crappy quality floor plan of the lobby, where if you didn't label it, no one would know what in the hell it was, and go figure, it wasn't labeled. I had to ask my Director where the rest of the renderings were, and he told me there weren't anymore. Timeout...we are selling this one-of-a-kind hotel and we don't have any renderings of the spacious lobby with a bar, the beautiful courtyard arboretum, modern meeting space, and/or rooftop pool!? What in the F!? These were all features that set this hotel apart from the rest in the brand. Nope, of course not. That would make too much sense, right!? Jesus Christ. Amateur hour. I later asked the GM when myself, him, and my Director went to lunch why this was the case? He claimed that this particular management company normally only opened hotels that just had sleeping rooms and nothing else. No Food and Beverage Department, no beachfront, no meeting space, and especially no fancy courtyards or rooftop pools. We would be THE premier hotel for their company and the brand. That was a lame ass excuse, but it made me cut the company a little slack. But then again, this wasn't rocket science. You spend money on renderings that will sell your product, not just a few of the outsides of the building and of the sleeping rooms that look exactly the same as every other damn hotel. Sighhhh.

This also prompted a question to my Director as to where our hotel fact sheet was. A hotel fact sheet is basically a pamphlet, card, or full sheet of paper that has pictures and facts on the hotel, also known as a rack card, or brochure. We didn't have shit! I was a little confused because the hotel had been in the works for quite a while by the time I got there, and the Director had been there for over six months, so I wasn't exactly sure as to what he was handing clients when meeting them in person. Normally, when selling a product (Sales/Marketing 101) and trying to gain business, you have some sort of collateral to hand to prospective clients, accompanied by your business card. Now, here I was, attempting to sell this unknown hotel, with no fact sheet, no chachkies to hand out, and no business cards. Keep in mind, I had been hired almost a full month prior to starting. I would think at least the business cards would be ready to go by then. *VistaPrint.com* can turn them around in like a day! He tried to blame the delay on "corporate." Yeah, ok bro. How about you either forgot to order them, ordered them later than you should have, or completely neglected to do so.

I was supposed to be attending every event known to man and spreading the word of the new hotel...empty-handed. When I brought up the fact that we didn't have a fact sheet or collateral, I was looked at like I had three heads, like it was a new concept. My Director's solution was for me to hand out his business cards at events. That's all. Are you kidding me? So let me get this straight, I am a new Manager at a new hotel, advertising a new concept, and am already approaching people that probably don't want to deal with me, and I am going to hand them someone else's business card and say, "Sorry, mine are on the way?" Now tell me how great of a first impression that makes? Unreal. I think the craziest part about this was the fact that none of this struck my Director as standard operating procedure until I brought it up. Like, helloooo!!!

In this role, I would join and attend events of big organizations such as the Greater Miami Convention & Visitors Bureau (GMCVB) and the Greater Miami & Beaches Hotel Association (GMBHA). They would hold various events around the city and I would attend and represent the hotel. Here is where business cards and other material would have come in handy. I was meeting new people and shaking hands alongside other hotel competitors. So I would have to explain that it wasn't my card that I was giving them, and take out a pen to put my contact info on it. Then, I wouldn't have any pictures on my phone to show them of what the hotel would look like because we didn't have any fucking renderings! Just shoot me. At least those events were great because I was able to squeeze in some free meals and happy hours on the company dime, and network for my own personal benefit for the future. These events were also super cool because I would run into ex-coworkers and catch up. The events were oftentimes at ballin' hotels or restaurants, with some killer views on the ocean or the Miami skyline. I was able to snap some killer shots for *The Gram* and make it seem like I was some big wig. Some of the events enabled me to have a few moments on the microphone and give a short intro and spiel about who I was and who I was there representing. I tried to zone out the lack of professionalism going on behind the scenes, and put on the face of "Our hotel and team is the best!" Our hotel was actually set to host one of these events after the opening, which we had to push back the date a few times due to opening delays.

Well, let's hope by the time we hosted that event that we had a display banner, and a display table with a decorative skirt with our logo, because we didn't yet. Again, I was supposed to be attending events, and lacked that as well. Exhibiting 101. I mean, seriously, had this dude [my Director] ever worked at a hotel before, or for that matter even gotten out? So, of course, I recommended it, and was viewed as annoying again. I started to second guess myself, and think that maybe I was just being annoying and a complainer, but I just wanted shit right!!! Is that too much to ask for? The Director was able to find out first hand why I was bugging him for these things when we attended a bridal showcase together. The venue supplied a table for us, and it was up to us to decorate our display. One problem, we didn't have anything! His solution was to print out flyers on regular printer paper, on draft setting (to save money), have his Windows tablet set up on its kickstand, cycling my favorite renderings (eye roll), and throw a few of our purple construction hard hats on the table. That's it. I mean seriously. It was straight embarrassing! It was a huge reality check and eye-opener for him, which was much needed. There were hotels, wedding venues, and vendors that had multiple banners, beautiful table skirts, plants, TV's, food, gifts, you freaking name it! The table to the right of us was serving wine, and the table to the left was grilling fucking food to give out! That might have been a bit extreme, but sure as hell grabbed my attention! The table across from us had models dressed in bridal gowns, huge bouquets, fancy lighting, and music playing. Models, I mean models!? Come on! And there we were, sitting with a blank, white, cheap plastic table (one of the fold-up ones we all play beer pong on in college), hard hats, shitty flyers, and a tablet that ended up dying, so we couldn't even use. Fuck us!

Sadly, it took the Director suffering through this embarrassment with me to realize that we needed a banner and table skirt ASAP! Also, some t-shirts or polos to wear, and client giveaways. We had our usual morning meeting, and of course the GM wasn't present on this particular day, and the Director openly admitted that "We didn't show well at the bridal showcase." No shit, man! I remember specifically the AGM, whom saw eye-to-eye with me on the Director's lack of experience/smarts, looking over at me with a grin on his face because he had heard me voicing my concerns daily, and getting pushed aside. Told ya! I had no sympathy for my Director. The awkward experience worked out good for me, because now I would get some shit that I had desperately needed since starting there.

Another huge topic that "annoyed" my Director when I brought it up was the fact that we had no catering menu for our events. Keep in mind, I came from selling fifty-five hotels for the entire state of Florida to just this one hotel. I knew a thing or two about selling catered meetings and events. EVERY hotel I sold for in the Sales Office was equipped with a catering menu. This would accomplish two main things. One, it served as the Sales Manager's tool to quote food and beverage minimums for clients. We would simply take the amount of people they were expecting and multiply it by the meals/breaks they were looking to have, and add it all together to come up with a minimum that the client would agree to spend to hold their meeting/event at the hotel. See the example program below:

10 attendees
2 full days of breakfast, lunch, and dinner

Breakfast (per person) = $15
Lunch = $20
Dinner = $30

10 attendees X $15 breakfast X 2 days = $300
10 attendees X $20 lunch X 2 days = $400
10 attendees X $30 dinner X 2 days = $600

Add it all together, $300 + $400 + $600 = $1,300

So in this example, I would require the group to spend at least $1,300 in catering in order to hold their meetings at the hotel. Sometimes we would add a rental charge as well for use of the meeting room or outdoor space, but sometimes waive it if they agreed to pay a higher food and beverage amount. The point I am trying to show here is that a catering menu is necessary to quote business. So here I was receiving leads, and had absolutely no base to be able to quote the clients. The second purpose of a catering menu is to show off what your hotel can do with its food options. If they are paying a premium to have their meals catered through the hotel, they better be getting something worthwhile, and would want to see ahead of time what it is they would be getting. Catering 101. I seriously should have quit at this point, and started a Hotel School for Dummies. My Director would have been my first student.

I would quietly continue to bring the need for a catering menu up to my Director, and eventually the GM right in front of the Director, to make it clear that we needed to get this thing going. Luckily, my boy Matt, the Food and Beverage Manager, was pumped to start prepping for what he was to be making from the menu, so he was behind me one-hundred percent to get that thing going. So go figure, what ended up happening? I created the damn thing myself! Not that I didn't have enough shit on my plate, but I had to have something as a base to quote business. I was tired of sounding like a dummy and telling clients, "We will get back to you with pricing." Especially when most other hotels were giving pricing on the spot to close the leads quickly. Common sense Sales closing. Do I dare say it? Closing 101! Apparently, our leadership didn't understand this.

I am quite design savvy and borderline OCD like I said before, so this was actually an enjoyable task for me to take on. I enjoy taking on new tasks, even if it may not fall in my job description, which was starting to become quite common at this hotel. At least I knew that when I was doing it, my idiot of a Director wouldn't make a piece of shit menu like he did with that hotel *PowerPoint*, and then I would have to act like he did a good job when I reviewed it. I started by downloading all of our comp-set's hotels menus, and a few from hotels that I used to sell for, to get an idea of the formatting, wording used, and price ranges. Thanks to the advice I took from the best book on the planet, *"Insanely Simple"* by Ken Segall, I wanted this menu to be as simple, basic, and as clean as possible. None of this clutter and descriptive wording shit that my Director was famous for. I wanted the name of the meal, sides, price, and that's a wrap! People don't need to know every goddamn spice that was used in creating it, or corny selling words like "Miami Beach Sandy Beach Burger" or some gay shit like that to make the menu forty-five pages long. I managed to keep the menu less than ten pages, and it looked sharp as hell! Breakfast, Brunch (huge in Miami), Lunch, Dinner, Cocktail Reception, Audio Visual Options, and that was it. Simple AF! It had a clean white background, with the text in a modern, crisp, brand-standard font that I researched and downloaded when I made the hotel presentation earlier. It was displayed in dark purple, and a sky/beach blue that meshed perfect together, because, get this, that was also brand standard, so a professional Graphic Designer made sure they did! There is so much that goes into branding, and I could write an entire other book on it, but the reason it was ultra-important for us to follow the brand standards at this particular hotel was because these standards were new to the brand. We were releasing the newest of the new concepts for the brand, so it was imperative that we followed the new standards, even in regard to typography. None of those old cheesy-ass reds and elementary school colors, with *Times New Roman* and *Comic Sans,* or whatever shit-fonts the brand previously used. Now it was modern, clean, sexy, and simple! This was another reason I was so pumped to represent this hotel and brand, because I loved the direction it was going.

I looped in the F&B Manager, Matt, to help in the creation of the menu since he would indeed be the one executing and ordering the ingredients to make the items on the menu. We fine tuned pricing and ingredients so that he could make sure we were in the right ballpark and actually execute the meals that I came up with. This was also because we had a super small kitchen to whip this food up in, so there were limitations to what we could do, especially for having to feed large amounts of people that events would entail. We felt very good about the menu we had come up with and were excited for the Director and GM to give us the thumbs up. Did you think it would be that easy? Of course not.

First of all, God forbid I bother them to review the menu so I could distribute and start pricing clients. You would have thought I was asking for a million dollars. They postponed this for weeks. Weeks! Like WTF!? I didn't ask for much (or maybe I did), and for heaven's sake, they could print it out, take it home, and look at while they were taking a crap! Just reviewing, that's all. When I was finally able to get them to take a look at it, of course they murdered the hell out of it with edits. The GM was very meticulous, and thought he knew what people like to eat in Miami. Not sure where he had been hanging out, but whatever. The Director seemed to think we had a Ruth's Chris Steakhouse catering our food, because the prices he wanted to list the meals at were astronomical. I mean, dude, we were still a lower-tier hotel, but just happened to be surrounded by luxury hotels. We don't want to price ourselves the same as them, or else it defeats the purpose of our company putting the hotel in the location it did, to attract people looking to spend less! I shut-up, fixed it up, secretly repriced it with the F&B Manager, and distributed it. Suck it! Done and done!

Another common piece of literature that Sales Managers will send to clients to accompany the catering menu is that lovely hotel fact sheet, which I discussed earlier. This hotel fact sheet would not only include all the facts about the hotel, but also detailed information about the meeting/event space, with a diagram and a grid that entails the dimensions of rooms/spaces, and the maximum seating for each arrangement that can fit into these spaces. This is great to have both digitally and physically, so you can both email to clients and hand to them in person as well. Eventually, the Director started to work on this, and asked for my assistant on the format and proofreading. He was finally getting the hint that I had been around the hotel block or two. It was funny because he initially sent the draft of the fact sheet to the GM to proof-read, and the GM replied, copying everyone, saying, "Please have Tony proof-read everything marketing related from here on out." LMFAOOOOO! Needless to say, from here on out, most of our marketing material was in good shape, unless the Director sent it out without my approval, or changed things after my approval. I'll take that new Sales & "Marketing" Manager title!

Along the way, I was to keep track of my expense reports. This accounted for things such as gas used for Sales trips, parking, event registration fees, etc. This was pretty easy in my previous role as we simply had a company card that we would use, and at the end of the month, we would review it before submitting to corporate. This was not the case with this franchised hotel. Here, I would have to keep all physical receipts, and paste them on a sheet of paper to scan in and save for my own good. Then, I had to send the originals to corporate. On an *Excel* document, I would have to list the expenses and it had an automatic calculator that would show how much I would get reimbursed. This was mainly for gas, as it was something like fifty-four cents reimbursed per mile driven. I would also have to search the route I took on *Google Maps*, screenshot it, and paste it in a Word document for each trip that month. Really? What an absurd fucking process! Absolutely ridiculous. Did they really think I would fudge my expenses as a Manager? Sigh. This showed how much faith they had in us.

Anywayz, I did it. I later found out that the GM didn't do all of this shit for his expense reports, but instead, it was the brown-nosing Director who forced me to do it for corporate.

Just when I thought the process couldn't get any more difficult, I would then have to have the Director review it before sending to corporate. Of course, I would need to be micromanaged first. He was legit so scared of corporate that anything remotely suspicious on one of my expense reports, he would say I couldn't expense it. Meanwhile, this dude was charging bottles of water to his that he was using to fill up the coffee machine with. God forbid he use sink water! I never really argued about what he would cross out because I already felt like I was captain whiner at this property. I remember one time in particular, I worked at a food truck event in the town that the hotel was located in. I set up our new table with new table skirt, new decorations, new stand-up banner, new flyers, and spoke with people about the new hotel. I bought a sandwich from one of the food trucks, and assumed this would be covered, as I would have never even gone to the event if it wasn't to represent work. Common sense says that this would be a work meal. Regardless, the Director said it was not, and wanted me to remove it. I later swung my ass by the GM's office and asked him about it because it really pissed me off, and he told me to expense that every time, without hesitation. BOOM! Suck it! I will never admit that I am always right, but I have common knowledge.

All the meanwhile, guess what I see my Director playing around with on his computer? New freaking renderings of the hotel! Hallelujah! But wait, they weren't new. It turns out he had them the whole time, and forgot about them! Are you fucking kidding me!? I must say, it almost didn't bug me, because at this point, nothing surprised me. The Director quietly tried to shun it off as the GM's fault when I asked about it, but I call total BS on that. This joker was just unorganized AF! It was probably buried in his six-thousand emails (not an exaggeration) that he had in his inbox, along with all the unanswered emails I had sent him. Guess what else was buried amongst these emails...blueprints of the hotel, including the meeting space layouts. Layouts that included dimensions with the number of chairs and tables that would fit inside. This was discovered by the genius of a Director after we went up to the damn meeting rooms and were on our hands and knees putting down masking tape to mark out different layouts in the room. Waste of fucking time! The blueprints also showed us a completely new area on the rooftop that we had no clue existed. There was a fenced-off, artificial grass area on the rooftop. This was located in the area that we had been advertising as one huge terrace to clients. So needless to say, we had been lying without knowing it. The most frustrating part about this is that I had been there around four months at this point and would have sold the shit out of that newly found space had I known it was going to exist. The GM knew all along, and the Director had the plans, but apparently skipped over that key factor. Even more mind-boggling was the fact that when the Director and I created the fact sheet, website edits, and such with the dimensions and maximum capacities and had the GM look over, he mentioned nothing about this mystery space. And come to find out, even the chairs and tables for the meeting space were already ordered! WTF man!? I was legit spinning in circles. I don't think it was the GM's intention to leave us hanging, but just mentally overloaded with the opening, and things he thought were a priority or not, were different than ours. I also think he trusted the Director to have everything Sales related under control.

Back to those lovely layouts that the Director discovered. As I mentioned, him and myself spent a solid hour up in the meeting space with two rolls of blue tape, on our hands and knees, laying out fake tables and chairs so that we could get an estimate of the different layouts and amount of people we could fit in the room with each setup. This idiot clearly had never taken part in a meeting before, or you wouldn't have thought based on his accounting for zero space for anyone to move. He came from a few years of experience as a Group Sales Manager (from a remote office) but also an on-site Sales Manager, so I would think he had a concept of meeting space setups. You couldn't tell! The guy was measuring tables right up against each other with no room for the chairs or

Banquet staff to walk through. I had to remind him that there were chairs and people sitting in them. He still didn't think they needed any space. I get it, he wanted to be able to advertise that we could fit as many people as possible in the room, but at the same time, we had to be realistic. Otherwise, we would have tons of complaints from clients when they couldn't fit in the room for their event.

As I said before, we found out in passing that apparently chairs and tables had been ordered by the GM already. At this time, we were only a few weeks away from opening, and we still didn't have anything. No high-top tables, chairs, rolling bars, AV equipment, or anything for the meeting space I was selling. No rounds, semi-rounds, and/or school room style tables. How big were the tables? Six feet, eight feet, or even twelve feet wide? Did they fold in half? How about linens, plates, glasses, and silverware? Were we going to have separate fancy banquet chairs? How big were the normal business meeting chairs? Do the chairs fold? If the tables or chairs didn't fold, I don't know where in the hell we were going to store these when they weren't needed in the space. Oh boy. We measured based on what we *THOUGHT* the GM ordered. Our AGM was the one responsible for ordering everything for the new hotel, and he straight up told myself and my Director that these items were not on his list of things ordered or to-be ordered like the GM said. He even reached out to myself and the Director secretly to ask us what to order because the AGM didn't want to see us having a group come in during the opening week (which was right around the corner) and not having anything. What a cluster! I'm getting stressed out just thinking about it again!

Another surprise popped up when the hotel started to come to opening shape. I walked into the back of the fresh new Front Desk offices one day, and noticed some huge signs with the new name of our restaurant on them. Prior to getting into the hotel, our management team voted on the logo and color scheme of the restaurant concept. These signs that I saw not only had the incorrect logos, but incorrect color scheme too. What in the hell? The GM claimed to have no clue what happened, but also didn't seem like he was rushing to replace them. Super sketchy. Even my favorite Director was super pissed about this one. The colors were blue and red, which were not at all the brand standard colors. Not at all the same colors as our presentation, or fact sheet, or catering menu, or hotel sign with our logo out front of the damn hotel. Nothing! My excitement of the hotel opening was declining by the minute. Matt, the F&B Manager was not at all happy either. He, like me, on multiple occasions would express his concerns about not working at the hotel much longer. It was becoming a very unprofessional and untrustworthy workplace. Come to find out, as the hotel started coming along more, the cabana drapes on the rooftop pool had red in them, and the umbrellas were all red. I think this was the idea of the restaurant color scheme all along, unbeknownst to us. Once I saw that, I understood more, but it still did not at all go with the hotel branding. This is what happens when you let the Owner's Artist friends handle the hotel design. Clearly, they didn't double check with the GM to see if there were guidelines to their design.

Let me just tell you that Matt and myself weren't the only ones losing our marbles at this place! The Assistant GM, Director of Engineering, Front Desk Manager, and Housekeeping Manager were all at wits end as well. So much so that the Director of Engineering peaced the F out! All we were told was that he put in his notice, but was told not to come back for his final two weeks. As I later found out by speaking with him, he was tired of the BS that went on at the hotel. Here I thought we were the only department going through that, but turns out him, and the other department heads were not fond of how things were going. Things were pushed aside and delayed, things went wrong, and the hotel opening would further be delayed. The Housekeeping Manager, F&B Manager, and Front Desk Manager and I would frequently have drinks and compare how shitty things were going, and also with the AGM, but not over drinks. Don't get us wrong, we knew there were going to be obstacles with a hotel opening, but quite a bit could have likely been avoided at this property.

I was getting entirely too used to brushing problems off to the point where nothing seemed to phase me at that place anymore. Even as I tried to brush things aside, the next issue seemed to be worse than the last. The opening was close, and we needed to get some freaking answers, so the "annoying Tony" was about to become the "royal pain-in-the-ass Tony." One topic that I had brought up multiple times to the Director was what duties are going to fall into my lap, and which will fall into the F&B Managers once the hotel opened? The reason this was important was because at most hotels, there is an Event Manager, or a Sales/Events Coordinator that manages the clients once the event is booked. The purpose of this is so the Sales Manager can book a client and then move on to booking more. "Always Be Closing"--- *Glengarry Glen Ross*. The Sales Manager would then turnover all the info to the Event Manager or Sales/Events Coordinator to then reach out to the client and set up the remaining details of the event they booked, including what exactly they want on that motherfucking catering menu! The Director continually told me not to worry about this issue every time I brought it up, and would get so frustrated for some reason when I did. Like dude, we were about to open! It's fucking go time! I didn't want to have our first event and it be a cluster. Again, common sense shit. Whelp, I was ignored, and when bringing it up one last time, I got yelled at, "Tony, I am going to ask you not to bring this up again." In that case, I did bring it up one more time, and I did in front of the mothafuckin' GM (imagine multiple crying laughing emojis)! Bam! Then suddenly, it became a topic of interest, and then brushed under the rug again, like everything fucking else. SMH, just SMH! And oh by the way, I was promised a Sales Assistant/Event Coordinator when interviewing for this role, and found out it would be no longer in the budget. Or, who knows, maybe it never was. This was the reason I assumed Matt would handle those duties, and why I would ask.

One thing the Director did finally kick into gear was the ordering of hotel giveaways, or chachkies. I guess you could say it was better late than never? Psshh. He had me research pricing and items that I thought would be good for the hotel since I was indeed the one attending events. I picked out ten items that were priced super low, but would be great to give to potential clients and hand out at events. I sent an email to our management team, asking them to pick out their top three. All of them responded, so I forwarded to the Director an email summary with the pricing and everything laid out on a silver platter, ready to order. Well, I have no idea what the fuck he did with that email, because not only did I not get a response, but he ended up ordering sunglasses, visors, bags, and pens with our logo printed on them. NOT ONE of these items were on my list that was voted on by our team, and all of his items were more than four times more expensive than the ones I researched. What the fuck man!? My items ran under fifty cents each, and he wanted to hand all of his items together in the bag…valuing over eight dollars a pop total. So in comparison, I could have handed my individual chachkies that I wanted to order to SIXTEEN people next to his ONE bag for ONE person. Explain to me who in the fuck is going to wear sunglass or a visor with our run-of-the-mill hotel logo on it? What an idiot. I'm all for a fancy gift bag for good potential clients, maybe during a hotel site visit, but not for every single potential client, and with shitty, useless things inside.

Anywho, we finallyyyyyyy made it into our Sales Office, which was located in the basement, while the rest of the management team were located behind the Front Desk. It was a long and narrow office, with a prison cell sized sliver of a window. This didn't concern me too much because my role was mostly out and about selling anyway. There were two large L-shaped desks in the office, and two small rectangle desks. I am very tidy and simple, so I didn't need much. I'll take one of those small rectangle desks all day! Give me a space for my laptop, wifi, access to a printer, and I'm good. Our favorite blueprints from before had our desks set-up in a certain manner, and that is how the furniture delivery company set them up to start. It seemed nice to me. I went downstairs one day and they had all been rearranged, with cubicle walls to separate noise between them. I dug it. As long as I was sitting as far away from the Director as possible, I was good with any layout.

The rumor on the street was that the GM was not fond of the new desk layout. Jesus Christ, what are we in fifth grade? But you know what, I agreed with him. The original desk layout was set that way intentionally for convenient access to all of the plugs and outlets for the internet, phones, and printers. Apparently, the GM had mentioned moving it back multiple times to the Director, and he brushed it off (his favorite thing to do). The Director told Matt, the F&B Manager, and I, not to bring it up and maybe it would slide by, but it did not. I got an email from the Director one Saturday when I was catching up on some work at a Starbucks, stating that Matt and I needed to coordinate a time to move the desks back because he was too busy to do so. Matt and the GM were copied on this email. He literally said in the email "He was too busy to do it." Rearrange fucking desks in a 10-by-20 foot office? Really? It was a super strangely worded email, almost making it seem like it was Matt and I that wanted the desks rearranged in the first place. That little fuck! Regardless, not a big deal to me. It was literally only four desks, and that carpet was easily slide-able. I sent a response to everyone that said, "Matt, want to knock it out tomorrow evening when I come in?" "Tomorrow," being a Sunday by the way. Like literally a five minute job. No big deal.

The real reason I was even there working at the Starbucks that Saturday was because the previous day, I had brought up my forbidden bonus structure again to the Director. This was another one of those topics he would get mad at me for asking about. I asked him why I had been there five months and there was still no sign of my bonus plan? Five months! I suggested talking to his boss (the Regional Director of Sales) about it because clearly he was not getting through to him, or understood the urgency of it. My idea was simply to try and work a different angle, not make him look bad. A good Sales technique. I told my Director that there was no reason to stay at the hotel when I was missing out on money I was told I could get. I reminded him of how I had been getting brushed off about this, and just because he was angry because he hadn't received his bonus since he had been there, it shouldn't apply to me. I reminded him that my salary was likely much lower than his, so my bonuses played a larger part in the income that I thought I would be receiving from the job. He freaked the fuck out and acted like a child, saying that we would do it right then. He printed out these BS numbers that he threw on an unorganized-ass *Excel* sheet. I informed him that I would like to take these numbers home and look at them before agreeing on anything. He said, "Nope, we are finishing this today!" So he stomps upstairs like a baby to the GM's office, and they call me up for a meeting a minute later. Oh here we go.

When I entered the office and sat down, the GM started off with a smartass attitude, asking what my concerns were. I got the vibe that he equally didn't wanna be dealing with this shit. I let him know that my concern was that it was month five of me being there, quarter one got passed, and I do not want the same for quarter two as I was contracted to be bonus eligible from Day 1. He kind of laughed it off, and told me he would pay out whatever bonus the Director came up with if I hit the metrics. He mentioned this at a stand-up meeting a few days prior, but I never received a bonus sheet or anything in writing for me to sign and us all agree on. He reminded me that he said this. You think I wanna agree to something that this inexperienced douche of a Director came up with. I expressed my concerns of having a professional document that we all sign, because no offense, but a quick mention of it at a stand-up meeting, I couldn't assume anything would come of that. Let's get some damn documentation like professionals (didn't say that aloud)! I explained to him how I had been told by the Director repeatedly to wait for a bonus structure from the Regional Director of Sales, as he was apparently in the process of creating one for me and the Director. So suddenly, month five, being told that the GM had the power to agree to my bonus structure this whole time did not make me very happy. So the Director throws the GM that half-assed *Excel* sheet, and the GM smart-assedly signs across the entire paper that he clearly didn't even look at, and throws it at me. Real fucking mature. My response was, "I will look this over this weekend and get back to you." The GM chuckled, and asked if there were any other concerns I had? Yes, yes I did, but I said no, just to GTFO of that office. Meeting adjourned!

This brought me to the Starbucks on that Saturday. Here, I could take a look at that bogus bonus structure the Director came up with. I ended up creating a legitimate, professional looking bonus worksheet like every other hotel chain (and company in general) does. It entailed the numbers I needed to reach to hit my bonus, and included the criteria I needed to hit along with making those numbers. The Director had been super vague with the criteria needed, so it still needed to be more detailed. I put signature lines on the bottom of the new, beautiful, and professional bonus sheet for myself, the Director, and GM to all sign and date. Again, not rocket science here. I certainly wasn't reinventing the wheel. I sent an email to them with the document attached, and asked a few additional questions about the criteria.

That same morning sitting there in Starbucks, I received about ten emails in a row from the Director. I guess this was to show-off that he was in the office that morning. Fucking loser. This was from the guy that would get absolutely pissed at me and have a chat with me if I sent him two emails in a row, because it was "overwhelming him." I answered every single one of his ten emails with mostly short, snarky responses because I think eight of his ten emails I had already sent him responses to previously, and they were just buried in his inbox. I hate unnecessary repetition! Time fucking waster! "Ain't nobody got time for that!" --- *Kimberly "Sweet Brown" Wilkins*. I got a sassy email back from him that pointed out my smart-assness. I honestly could have cared less, because to me, I had reason to be. The dude seriously needed to get organized and read his fucking emails. Most of my responses were, "I already sent you this," or "See previous email," or even attach the email that I had already sent him months ago with the answers. Dumbass.

Sunday came along, and Matt got swamped with F&B needs, so we didn't get to move desks. No worries, we could knock it out on Tuesday, because we were off Monday for a holiday...or so I thought. It turned out my Director expected me to come in on the holiday. I knew this was one of our few paid holidays, and actually enjoyed taking these being in Hotel Sales, so I was confused. I didn't fuck around arguing with him because we all know that would be petty drama, so instead, I just texted the GM directly and asked if we worked Monday. He said, "No, enjoy the holiday." I screenshot it and sent to the Director. Was that so hard to do? Nope. So Tuesday came along, and you could cut the fucking tension with a knife between the Director and anyone else. We had corporate IT people in the hotel setting up all the printers, phones, and computers, and they started questioning our modified desk setup. At the time, it was just the Director and myself in the office. He told them to hold off on the printers, and we would hook them up ourselves once we moved the desks. Well, this wouldn't work because the corporate people leave that afternoon and if they aren't hooked up and installed on our computers, which needed corporate passwords to do, we would be without them. We all know how dealing with IT over the phone is, especially if it involves trying to troubleshoot hooking shit up. No thanks. So I suggested to him that we just move the desks real quick. The corporate people were already distracting us from what we were doing, so it wasn't like we were getting any work done anyway. And like I said before, it would literally take a total of five minutes to do. The Director glared at me, and said "Tony, I really wouldn't try and spearhead this task." This was right in front of the two corporate IT people, and made me look like a total idiot. I responded, word-for-word, "Dude, then why in the fuck would you send an email asking me and Matt to move the desks? You SPECIFICALLY asked us to spearhead it!" The dude was off his freaking rocker! I got up and stormed out of the office. He was all upset about me bringing that up like it was a freaking "top secret desk move" to these corporate people. Such a freaking weirdo. I have no clue what went through that dudes head ninety-nine percent of the time.

I went upstairs to grab Matt and see if he had a second to move the desks since the diva Director was apparently "too busy" to take five minutes to move them. You would have thought by the way the Director acted, that we were taking a tractor, clearing out the dirt, then renting a crane to lift up the desks and move them. Like dude, they slide across the fucking floor! Four desks. Four! Not desks with top shelves or anything. Just two plain-ass L-shaped wood desks and two small rectangle ones. Jesus Christ! Low and behold, as I am talking to Matt, the Director comes up and doesn't appreciate me going to Matt about this. He said to me, "Can I speak with you for a second?" I said, "We can speak right here because last I checked you specifically emailed Matt and myself to "spearhead" this desk move, and now all of the sudden you don't want us to?" He stormed off in the other direction. The awkwardness was at an extreme level from this point forward in our Sales Office, with those freaking desks still in the same spot, and nothing connected. Positive thoughts Tony, positive thoughts!

One thing in particular I loved about working in hotels was the fact that when you work there, you treat it as if it's your very own hotel. You brag about it, and show it off. I personally loved to share my love for whatever hotel I was working at on social media. Of course, I would keep it clean because I keep everything clean on my personal social media, but also so that I wouldn't get in trouble for posting something on behalf of my job. I was always a free Social Media Manager for any hotel I worked at. My friends would always hit me up, saying how great of a place it looked where I worked, so I must have been doing a decent job. Whelp, you will never believe who was in charge of our social media efforts for this hotel…the goddamn Director of Sales & Marketing. Screw us, right!? Because of this, I had made sure not to tag our hotel on anything because I wanted to stay far away from people thinking I had any control over our social media accounts! At this hotel, we didn't even have an *Instagram* account that I knew of, and honestly, I was afraid to look. Unfortunately, I did, and goddamn, I wish I hadn't. I looked at our extremely too long user tag (five words bunched together to be exact) and there were only five freaking pictures! Five! Let me remind you that this hotel was days from opening, and had been in the works for over two years, and the Director had been in his role for over a year. What the fuckkkkkk was this dude doing!? I mean seriously. It literally takes a second to post anything on *Instagram*. Not only were there only five posts, but there were under fifty followers of the page. I think you get a free fifty when you sign up for Christ's sake. Just kill me now. I was so embarrassed. I had asked on multiple occasions to assist with our social media, as I truly enjoyed it, but of course was ignored. Our competitor hotel across the street was at over seventeen-thousand followers. Us...fifty. I mentioned this little statistic to him, and was told our target audience does not use social media. Good grief, this dude didn't even know our target audience. The average age at our hotel was in their upper twenties, and you mean to tell me that they do not use social media? Ok, tell that to the hotels with over ten-thousand followers in our comp-set. Idiot. How in the hell did this dude get in the position he was in again? Marketing 101. For the love of God, know your target audience, and what your comp-set is doing to succeed.

If you couldn't tell from the previous few pages, it was getting to the point at this hotel where I had to get the fudge out. I mean, I dropped the F-bomb on my boss for crying out loud! It had been a few weeks and I still hadn't received a response to that bonus email I sent. Why was I not surprised? I freshened up my resume and started applying all over the damn place in Miami. There were quite a few Sales positions open at the time. I started to land interviews left and right. I had to be super strategic and picky as to how I went about these because I was working for the micromanaging king. In the past, I would tell the interviewer that I am available whenever, but here it had to be first thing in the morning, maybe lunch if it was quick, or at the very end of the day. I really didn't like being sneaky, so this was not my favorite, but I was very ready to get out of that hell-hole. Let's just say, I took a few long lunches, and left early a couple of times. Mind you, if I did this, I was working longer that day, or started earlier. I am not the type who is going to skip work completely, especially since I was missing it to interview elsewhere.

Right around this same time, I managed to get into an accident and total my car. FML! You ask how, and are you ok? Well, buckle up for this ride. Go figure, it was a result from working at this damn hotel, and it just added to the signs from the ole Hotel God's above (or below) that I needed to get the hell out. So, I was working on booking this group that seemed like a great one. A lady had reached out to me from the Gulf Coast of Florida, and she was in need of around thirty sleeping rooms and possible meeting space or rooftop pool space. She was asking about possibly renting out the entire rooftop pool deck, which could lead to some great revenue. It was the perfect size group for this hotel that included rooms, space, and catering, which is exactly what all hotels want in a group. The triple threat! "Triple points!" Haha! The lady informed me that the reason for the trip was for a bunch of Promoters coming from the Gulf Coast to network and party with Promoters in South Florida. Shit, I wanted to go! She said their event was at Haulover Park, which was super close to the hotel. I sent her pricing, and then she went full ghost! I could not reach her again after various attempts. I assumed we were too expensive. Finally, a few weeks later, I was able to get ahold of her. She informed me that her colleague had already booked something at a hotel that I had never heard of, which I found odd, as I knew every hotel in that area, or so I thought. I kindly thanked her and went on to research this hotel, as it must have been a new competitor. Upon research, I found out that this was not only in a different city completely, but was also a nudist resort. Hmm. I felt it was probably a good idea to let her know this, in case she wasn't aware of what her colleague booked, as it could have been a mix-up. Sure enough, she was very aware, and told me that was the kind of group they were. She called it a "lifestyle" group. The reason they were originally considering our hotel was because there was a nude beach across from Haulover Park, and that's actually where their festivities were going to be. Well, holy shit! It was probably a good thing I didn't book them at our hotel because that might have gotten me in some trouble if they planned to hang out on our rooftop pool in the nude, with other guests in their rooms onlooking.

Naturally, I had to ask the lady a few questions about this "lifestyle" group, because it interested me. Being from conservative-ass Southern Maryland, you don't hear of things like this. In Miami, you do. I gave her my personal cell phone and asked her to reach out to me, as I was interested in finding out more, but didn't feel it appropriate to discuss over my work email. She texted me with some info and a link to join some lifestyle site. Apparently, the term "lifestyle" covers a wide range of things; everything from swinging, S&M, sexual fun, etc. It was anything goes, with no strings attached, and the site was filled with a lot of very open people looking to have fun, with some kinky shit along the way. Interesting. Not really my style for being a pretty shy, conservative dude. Miami, however, had changed me a bit. I had become a little more confident with my looks, pick-up lines, and overall outlook on life. YOLO is definitely a corny saying, but it is very true! We all have a bucket list, and we should always be adding to it, and crossing completed things off of it. The lady suggested I join the site and check it out, but I saw there was a membership fee involved, and I wasn't about to pay for something like this. I wasn't that interested, especially when I had been having plenty of luck with the ladies in Miami thus far. Then, she shot me another link, but this one was for a free trial. Fuck it! I joined.

I started to peruse through this site some more, and it was much like other dating apps out there. The main difference was that the pictures were much more provocative, I mean much more, and it seemed to be encouraged. It would show the member's relationship status, most of which were married, or with someone, scattered with few single folks. Most of the people were older, and not so great looking. It was definitely not a place for singles to go to find their loved ones. Eventually, in my perusing, I noticed a young, pretty girl, and holy shit...I knew her! It was a girl I had met at a Miami Music Week event an entire year earlier. It was at some point before or after Steve Aoki tossed a cake in someone's face. She was awesome, and we danced the night away together, but I remember her having a boyfriend, hence the reason I never pursued her. However, we did exchange numbers and added each other on

The Gram. Instead of sending her a message on this lovely website, I decided to shoot her a text and say, "Guess who I just saw on XXX site!?" She laughed, and then seemed super excited that I was on it. Like I said, she was one of the few young, good-looking girls I saw on there, so would imagine it was similar for her options of guys on the site. She said she would take me under her wing and take me to some of these lifestyle events. I was all about it because she was very cute. One small problem though…she was into all the S&M super freaky ass shit, which was apparently the reason she was on there. I asked her about a thousand questions about the lifestyle and the events and what not. She invited me to one of the site's events where I would have to wear an all-leather outfit. Yeah, no. Where in the fuck do I even find a leather outfit to wear to an event of this nature? She instantly threw me some links to some shopping sites. Damn, who knew leather outfits were so expensive!? A leather t-shirt was like sixty bucks! The hell!? I was broke as shit, so this wasn't happening. Remember, I was STILL working in the hotel biz. So that helped me determine that I wouldn't be attending those kinds of events. I told her I would pass on that one and maybe if she had another less-crazy event, I would attend.

I started to think this lifestyle thing was not for me at all, until a few days later when I was at the dog park with the pup, I received a direct message on the site. It was from a pretty good-looking girl. She was probably in her upper thirties, but could still very much get it. She was very sweet in the message, saying that she was trying to go to this event in Boca Raton and needed a date because it was a couple's swinger event. I was very hesitant because I could roll with two girls, but definitely not another dude! She asked for my number so she could call me, so I gave it to her. My nerves were already pumping. She called me and sounded surprisingly down to earth. Not sure what exactly I was expecting. I expressed my concerns to her, and she laughed and was very sweet in explaining that this was the perfect intro event for me into the lifestyle. She explained that it was at a public restaurant and they had the outside bar area rented out. It would be all couples and there would be no commitments to anything. We could simply walk around and meet people, and if she was into the guy and I was into the girl, then we could head somewhere and have some fun. My concern of course was that I did not want anything to do with "fun" with another guy. She laughed, and told me that's not how it works. The guys don't have to tango at all, and normally don't ever do. She said we would lay ground rules from the beginning. This made me feel one thousand times better about it. She said, worst-case, if we don't click with anyone then we could just go enjoy ourselves for the night. Mmk mmk, I can roll with that. YOLO! The event was actually that night, so I had to make an instant decision because I would have to go home, get changed, and head up that way, as it was forty-five minutes away. I told her, "Fuck it, let's do this!"

I was shaking as I hung up the phone because I was nervous as all hell. I grabbed little Mischa's leash off of the dog park fence and told her it was time to bounce! She was only a puppy at the time, so I couldn't be away from her for too long because her bladder was still super small, and she was still crate training. My ultimate plan was not to drink much so that I could drive back later that night, even if it was 3-4 a.m. so that I could be with Mischa. This would also work for a bailout excuse if things went south at the event. The girl told me to just dress like I was going out, with a button up and jeans. Perfect! This was much better to hear than being told to slap on some freaky leather shit! I quickly freshened up, and got comfortable in my car for the forty-five minute car ride ahead of me. She asked that I pick her up first and then head to the bar in Boca, which was only a few minutes away from her place.

I did some recon on my phone on the girl, as some of her pictures on the site were professionally done. My initial thought was that she must have done some modeling, which was common in South Florida. My second thought instantly gravitated to maybe she was a Pornstar, or Webcam Model. Whelp, sure enough, I found some nudies and one video online. Then, her screen name on the site started to make a little more sense. It was her stage name, not her real name. Oh boy. This should be quite the evening! I scooped her up and she was actually way better looking in-person than I was expecting. On dating apps, I was accustomed to expecting great photos and then lowering my expectations in-person due to all the editing apps and software out there. She was dressed very very sexy! Not trashy/slutty, but more elegant. This was refreshing because you just don't know what to expect. She smelt great, and acted very comfortable around me from the get-go. Just like on the phone, she was super down to earth and told me how it was.

We rolled into this cute little town which I guess was downtown Boca Raton or Delray. I wasn't really paying attention, to be honest. It seemed quite bougie looking at the stores, restaurants, and how well-groomed and maintained the little area was. This immediately made me think that the place we were going to would have an older, more established crowd. We found the place, and I had to Valet my car. Ugh! Damn South Florida and the need for people to feel "important." God forbid places put a damn parking lot or garage, so we didn't all go broke paying for Valet everywhere. We walked into the back outdoor portion of the bar, hand-in-hand to the check-in table. My date was practically a celebrity in there. The older people (like grandparents old) checking us in recognized her and gave her hugs and kisses. They commented that they hadn't seen her in a while. That made me feel a tad better because I am not sure how I felt about someone going to these things all the time, and swinging the night after night. After signing in, we immediately went to the bar for some cocktails. I deffffff needed one to loosen up in this setting. I was hoping the first round was free, or we got some sort of a discount on drinks due to renting the space, but nope. The organization literally just rented the space, and the rest was up to us. It wasn't too crowded when we got there, except for a few older couples, which like I said, I was semi-expecting. Couples slowly started to roll in, and the girls definitely seemed younger and better looking than the guys they were with, which I was totally ok with. And let me tell you, they were dressed to impress!

We sat in a little outdoor booth and drank and talked on our own for a while, which was pretty cool because there was no pressure. We just scoped out the couples to see if any interested us, and of course talked shit about half of them. I'm not all too picky, so I could have talked to any of the girls, minus maybe the grandma's, although I'm sure some of the good-looking younger ones were still technically grandmas because Latinas tend to be invincible to aging. Eventually, we got up to snag another drink and mingle. We talked to a few different couples, and it was surprisingly very casual and cool. It didn't feel like they were eyeing you up to bang it out, or do some other weird shit. I didn't get weirded out by the guys like I thought because I am assuming they were mostly straight as well. My date wasn't really feeling any of the guys there, so asked me if I just wanted to roll out and just have some fun between the two of us. I'm not going to lie, I was actually getting into the scene and definitely wanted to have some fun with a few of the girls there, along with the girl I was with. I was ready to cross this off my bucket list officially! Oh well, I was sure just the two of us would have plenty enough fun, so we bounced. I only had two tequila sunrises and then of course she forced me to take a shot of who knows what, so I assumed I was ok to drive. Slight chance I was risking it.

Well, just my fucking luck, by the grace of what had to be the Hotel Gods, when I was driving back to my date's place, I drilled the rear end of another car. I came around a turn to reach a stop sign in this small block-by-block town, and assumed the car sitting at the stop sign would stop, then go, since there were zero cars in the vicinity. Nope. That bitch stopped, and parked, like literally I think they were shifted into park. Well, stupid for me for trusting anyone's driving judgement in South Florida, I smashed right into the back of that motherfucker! Fuck me! I drove a little turbo hatchback that could stop and go on a dime, so I tended to accelerate quickly and stop quickly. That bit me in the ass here. Thanks *Fast and the Furious*!

I blanked out from the moment my car hit theirs to the time I was standing next to it talking to a Police Officer. The airbags deployed and all. The entire front end of my car was smashed in. Totaled. Before I knew it, my date was sent off in an ambulance, and I was stuck walking a line and doing the eye test with the Officer to see if I had too much to drink. I told the Officer from the get-go that I did indeed have two drinks, and the bartender could prove it. I guess I passed because he wrote the Police report and took me to the hospital in his cruiser where my date was taken. This posed an interesting situation for me because I had to figure out how the hell to handle my car, find out if my date was ok, and how I was going to get home to my baby, Mischa. The accident occurred around midnight, so I got to the hospital around 1 a.m. I was able to visit my date immediately, and she was in some serious pain! She was super frantic and crying for pain killers. This was a side of her I had not seen yet. The pain was in her chest so I assumed she might have broken a rib. It turned out she broke two, and had a few nasty bruises on her, along with a busted lip that she bit during the accident. I felt like such a piece of shit because I was left without a scrape, besides bruised knees because I am assuming they hit the car dashboard under the steering wheel. She was in some serious pain, and the Nurses weren't really giving her attention. It was almost as if they knew there was alcohol involved and they didn't want to give her the time of day. That, or maybe her records showed medication problems in the past. She was already synced up to pain medication and was screaming for me, and that she needed more meds. It sure made her seem like an addict, which for all I knew, she could have been. On the other hand, she could have really been in some serious pain. I've never broken ribs so can't speak for the pain, but have heard it's pretty brutal. What a fucking night, although sadly it wasn't over.

Eventually, I was booted out of her room by the Nurses, as she was moving to another room only allowing family to visit. I had to go find a place to crash for a few hours until 8 a.m. when I was allowed to visit her again. I wasn't trying to full on date this girl, but I am a gentleman, and felt super responsible for her injuries, so didn't want to just roll out. I just prayed that Mischa was at home sleeping, and didn't have to go potty. I would stay until the morning, check on my date, and let her know I would go home to check on Mischa, talk to my insurance, get a rental car, and then come back. I attempted to sleep in the little lobby area, but it had a bunch of stadium-like uncomfortable-ass seats, with a little TV on with the volume on full blast. No way in hell I was getting any sleep in there. I asked the guy working the desk if I could just go tell her I was going to head home. He asked for her name and I froze. I had no idea what her real name was, just the stage name she gave me. I described her attributes and explained that I met her online, so didn't know her full name. He helped me, thank God! Unfortunately, like I was told previously, I would not be allowed to see her until 8 a.m. Ugh! I found a vending machine to grab a snack and a water and rolled out to go find a place to crash for the night. I ended up sneaking into a construction site next door to the hospital, and passed out on an adirondack chair that was outside of the construction trailers. I didn't even care. Of course, it was a little chilly that night, so I was freezing my ass off, but was indeed able to get a few hours of shut-eye with no creepers, animals, or Security Guards coming to bother me. I ended up waking up around 7 a.m. and figured I would test my luck on visiting her, even though it was early. Sure enough, the old dude working the counter at the time, let me in without question of who I was, or that it wasn't quite 8 a.m. yet. I guess I finally had a bit of luck on my side that night.

I made it to her room and felt so bad for her! At this point, she was sleeping in a comfy bed with food and drinks provided by the hospital. She finally got some pain meds that she was pleading for. I let her know I would have to leave and come back. I ended up having to get an *Uber* for my forty-five minute car ride home. That was a nice forty bucks that my broke hotel-ass had to spend! I finally got home to little Mischa, and she managed to hold her pee for the whole night. Poor little babe! She was very happy to see me, although she didn't know I was only going to be there to shower and talk to my insurance company, and then leave her again. I gave my insurance company a call, just to get the worst news of the last twenty-four hours, and my life up to that point. The Insurance Agent informed me that it didn't look like I had collision insurance on my vehicle. Wait, what!? Well that couldn't be right because I bought the car new, with a loan, and I specifically remember having to increase my insurance plan to get full coverage because they required it. The Agent said she would look into it and get back to me, but took all the details of the accident in the meantime. I asked about how the rental car worked, and apparently I didn't have rental car reimbursement either, so all of that would be out of my pocket. Greaaattttt! The Gods (both regular and Hotel Gods) above were sending me a serious message that I should not be attending swinger parties, and shouldn't be drinking and driving, even if it seemed to be below the legal limit.

The only rental place open at that time in the morning was located back up North close to the hospital, so I had to hop in another forty dollar *Uber* back up there, get my little Fiat rental, and go pick up the injured bystander to take her to get her pain meds and drop her the fuck at home! Thus, hopefully ending that wack-ass previous twenty-four hours! I let her know that I would visit her in a few days to check on her because I felt like a piece of shit for what happened to her, and nothing to me. I headed back to work the following week and battled on the phone with my insurance company, and car loan company as to why I was just now finding out about me not having collision insurance. As it turned out, when I moved from DC to Maryland a few years ago, my coverage switched and I approved the updated paperwork online. Was I likely paying attention to the quick scroll and sign online agreement? Hell no! Does anyone? Regardless of whether I signed it or not, apparently your auto insurance company is supposed to notify your lender that you are without any collision insurance, and then the lender is supposed to notify you. I was definitely not notified! From my research, I found out that my insurance company did indeed notify my loan company, although they never included me on any correspondence. My insurance company was able to provide written proof to me that they did. According to the car loan company, I was a so-called "VIP" with them because my credit was so great when I initially took out the loan, thus not flagging them to notify me of any drop in coverages. Had I not been in this (what sounded like bogus) "VIP" level, they would have notified me, and offered me collision coverage through them. How nice, but they didn't, thus resulting in this cluster. Thanks a lot!

All this time, which was about a two week process, my car was just chilling in a tow lot, smashed to shit, and I would be responsible for that daily charge, the removal from the lot fee, and of course, my rental car. And for the real kick in the nuts, because it did indeed turn out that I did not have collision insurance, I would be responsible to pay off the remainder of my car loan balance before the lender would give me the title to the vehicle, so that I could hand over my car to the tow company. I owed TEN-THOUSAND DOLLARS! Just kill me! I didn't have that kind of money floating around. At this point, the whole scenario was just laughable. What started as a fender bender, turned totaled car, turned broken ribs, turned *Uber* fees, rental fees, towing fees, and motherfuckin' ten G's, what else can you do but laugh? All from a swinger date night! Classic! My credit score blew ass at this time, so I couldn't get a ten-thousand dollar loan from anywhere, and was forced to do the ultimate depressing thing as an adult, and ask my dad for financial help. I had never asked him for money besides helping me with a third of my college quite a few years back, and that was pretty much my mom that asked. He, like me, thought there had to be a way around not having collision insurance. I explained how I planned to get a Lawyer to see what could be done, but I needed that money up-front so I could get my car taken care of, and get a new one ASAP, in the meantime. Thank goodness, he was able to help me out, and we worked out a payment payback plan. Thanks Pops!

I ended up hiring a Lawyer through a friend's recommended, and he suggested we write a demand letter to both my insurance company and car loan company for the ten-thousand. He said it is unlikely that we hear back from either of them, but we can send them one a few times. It was a two-hundred dollar charge for him doing this for me, versus a long, drawn out, and expensive lawsuit.

I agreed that this would be a good place to start. We could always file a suit at a later point. I finally got the Police report from the accident, which takes way too long to get after an accident, and what it read was pretty interesting, yet not too surprising in South Florida. The driver of the other vehicle had no insurance, and was driving on a suspended license. WTF!? So in essence, had that driver not been on the road, which they shouldn't have been, the accident would have never occurred. Just my damn luck! I thought I had a case there, but the law states that if you are at fault in an accident, it doesn't matter the situation of the other driver. It could be a damn raccoon driving the other vehicle! How ridiculous is that!? I ended up later getting sued myself by the other driver for bodily damage, which was interesting to me because everyone in the other vehicle was up walking around perfectly fine after, but whatever. My lovely passenger also sued for injuries, as expected. Luckily, my insurance handled both suits because I did indeed have bodily coverage. Thank Christ!

I eventually got some new wheels, which was a tad frustrating because I felt more rushed and stressed to get one than excited like you normally are when buying a new car. I had to settle for a car that I didn't necessarily want because as I said earlier, my credit score was not exactly ideal, so my car payment was wayyy more than it should have been due to my high interest rates. As you can tell, the accident really set me back financially. Not only would I have to pay my dad back for the totaled car, but my new car payment would now be a hundred dollars a month more than my old one, and I would now need to add collision coverage to my insurance. I was literally only two years away from a fully paid-off car, and having all of my credit cards paid off. Whelp, that dream ended real quick! What a freaking experience huh? And remember, this was all because of a potential client at the fucking hotel! The Hotel Gods were hard at work with this one. They were telling me to GTFO! Run and don't look back!

Not too long after this crazy-ass event, the big brand that we represented sent a representative to our franchised property to run us through some of the proper systems/trainings that the brand wanted us to use. She had a checklist that she would run through with each department to make sure they were meeting the standards that the brand required in order to carry that brand's name outside of our front door. This was a pretty cool experience for me because I had never been on the franchise side of hotels, and a new one at that. We had tables and computers set up in our meeting room, which was crazy to see because we had been staring at an empty space for quite some time. The tables and chairs were nice, but definitely for business meetings, not catered social events. Tables and chairs for social events were nowhere to be found. Clearly, they hadn't been ordered.

The Brand Rep was really down to earth, yet straight to business. I was the only person from our Sales Team at the second day of the computer training, so she would frequently call on me for questions regarding groups and such. Majority of my answers were, "The Director handles," or "The Director won't let me handle," etc. After a few questions, she got the hint, and realized we needed to have a chat outside of the training, which we did. She knew I came from an extensive background with the brand, so knew the ins-and-outs. We instantly bonded in that way. That, and she was very fun, friendly, and genuinely looking to help us open successfully, and saw that I was in the same boat. I filled her in on all of the BS that I faced with the Director. She acted as if she already knew. I wasn't sure if another Manager filled her in already, or if it was just common sense as she ran through her department checklists and nothing was getting checked off for Sales and Marketing. She really appreciated my honesty and said she would try and do whatever she could to help. I just remember her reactions as I told her certain things that occurred and she would roll her eyes, laugh, or had her jaw on the ground, in awe. She was very much like me in the sense that if something needed to be done, she would get it done, and not pussyfoot around. Organization 101: When you put things aside, they build-up, and they will get missed, or done half-assed. You could tell the lady was going to take what she learned from this training back with her, and share with whoever at corporate she needed to in order to make shit happen. I trusted that she had the power to get people fired, and she even joked about it while she was there, as she was friendly with the top dogs in the brand.

Not too long after her visit, we had some corporate big wigs from the hotel's management company come to assist us with a Sales blitz, as the hotel was opening the following week. Finally! My Director called the Sales blitz, "Boots on the Ground," because we would have him, myself, and the corporate helpers going out and knocking on doors, searching for business and spreading the word on the hotel opening. The infamous Regional Director of Sales came, whom was the one supposedly working on my bonus plan for five damn months. He was actually a really fun guy, regardless of how much I wanted to unleash on him for this non-existent bonus plan. He had a great positive spirit and was so excited to finally see the hotel and crush some Sales calls. He was especially happy to meet me, as this was the first time in person. My Director, believe it or not, sang my praises to him in our weekly meetings. I guess this shouldn't have surprised me all too much because he portrayed rainbows and butterflies on those calls, even though we were a fucking train wreck!

Along with him, came three Director of Sales from other properties around the Southeast, US. There was one young guy from St. Pete, Florida and two ladies from Atlanta, Georgia. The young, hipster-like guy was rocking a solid beard. Yup, a beard! My GM's favorite (eye-roll)! He and I actually had a moment to ourselves after we started to click and get along, and he asked how everything was going. I told him the God's honest truth about the bonus, the obstacles, and the Director's lack of experience and knowledge in the field. He was shocked at how low I was getting paid, even without considering any bonus. This guy knew what was up! The one lady was a pretty blonde who was actually a Director of two hotels. She was a rockstar in Hotel Sales, and had apparently gotten multiple awards from the company to show it. I was actually chasing her for the number one slot in regards to *LinkedIn* views within our company. She was number one, and yours truly was number two. Errr! I couldn't catch her! I gave her shit for it, and she laughed and acted like she had no idea she was number one. Yeah okayyy! The other lady was an older, very quiet, Jamaican, with a super laid-back personality. She almost came across as super clueless, but must have had that soft, grandma-like vibe with clients because she had been successful in her role. It's crazy how many different types of people and personalities can be successful in Sales.

We all received an agenda via email at about 9 p.m. the Sunday night before starting the Sales blitz from the Director. I'm real glad I had time to prepare. Psych! He had set up three teams of two to make Sales calls on Monday, and then hit the streets on Tuesday with the Boots on the Ground. Monday morning I actually ending up having to drop off my puppy at the Vet before going in because she had gotten spayed the week prior, and needed her dressings (bandages) cleaned and changed out. The Vet opened at 8 a.m., and the Director had us starting the day at 8 a.m. Normally, we started our days at 9 a.m. Goddammit! But honestly, I didn't care because of his insanely late notice. I notified him that I would be late, and he seemed pissed, but there was really nothing else I could do. I rolled into the meeting room at around 8:30 a.m., and the crew was sitting around a table going through the hotel fact sheet and sipping on some coffee and bagels. Of course, the Director wouldn't get them Miami local Cuban coffee with pastries, because he knows nothing about good hospitality. Instead, he spends twice as much at Starbucks on the company dime, when he claims to be so money conscious about everything else. Anywayz, I said hello to everyone, and then the Director continued on, as if he wanted to show off that he was mad at me for coming in late and didn't tell them in advance. GTFO of here! Hated that guy. My plan was to be very open-eared during their visit, and try not to express my true concerns. I would bust out that old Front Desk Agent fake smile that I perfected in the first few years of my hotel career. I did have to jump in a few times though because the Director truly had no idea what he was talking about, but overall, I was quiet compared to normal. We eventually got to the discussion on the teams. According to the Director's agenda, I was set to be with the Dual Director from Atlanta, but before we even got to that, the Regional Director shouted, "I want to be on Tony's team!" and insisted on us changing the teams. I had the biggest grin on the inside because I knew that my Director intentionally did not pair us up because he knew I would bring up all of my frustrations to him, including how shitty he was. He knew I would sell his ass out, and you bet your ass I would! My Director totally tried to defend his original teams, but luckily, the other folks at the table started shouting out who they wanted to be with, so the new arrangements stuck. Ha!

Then began the process of making phone calls from a list that the Director made for each team to call. It was broken up by different areas around the hotel's location so that if we were able to set up a face-to-face appointment, we would tackle it on on the following day. It was cool because it was actually made into a competition. The winning team would get some sort of free weekend stay (of course the Director didn't specify when or where), and if that reward had the same validity as my bonus plan, we know that shit didn't exist! The Regional Director was pumped and kept encouraging me so that we would win. Great teammate. We all sat in different areas around the meeting room, and my teammate actually sat out on the terrace off the meeting space, which was starting to get some tables and chairs delivered and set-up literally as we were doing this Sales blitz. It was a pretty cool experience because I was able to overhear other successful Salespeople's selling techniques. It reminded me of the Sales Office I worked in previously. Some, I could totally see how they were in Sales, and others, I could not. Hmm, wonder who I'm referring to? The support team were all pretty quick learners. They were pitching a hotel, area, and clientele that they knew nothing about, besides from that quick morning briefing. "Here is your info, now go sell!" I was setting up appointments left and right, and the Regional Director as well. That next day was going to be quite the busy day with appointments and cold-call visits.

Later that evening, we all went for dinner and drinks at a local dive bar on the water. The GM made fun of our Director for choosing that venue out of all the incredible places in Miami, but should the GM have been surprised with any decisions that guy ever made? I had been there before, and actually liked it. It was more casual for Miami, but had a killer view right on the water. Although, the last time I went, I saw a few too many cockroaches running around on the back deck. It was South Florida, so it wasn't too uncommon to see, but I don't want to see those bastards near my food! Regardless, it was his show, and I let him run it. We got a big table with a nice water view. Everyone was ordering drinks and made it seem like there were going to be plenty more to be ordered. I felt super out of place to be honest. I was a few generations younger than all of them besides the young guy from Tampa, although he was an old soul. The Director was younger too, but acted like a sixty-year-old married man...dad jeans and all! I was freaking starving, and not looking to get trashed. When the Server came around, everyone just decided to order appetizers for the table to share, instead of individual meals. I hate that shit! I want my own damn meal! So this made me feel even more out of place. I think at this point, my head was dreaming of another job, with another boss, and a hotel (or not hotel) that gave a shit about me and my bonus plan, and my opinions would matter. I didn't feel like being social with other people that were getting their bonuses and probably each getting paid thirty grand more than me. I was over it. I took full advantage of the free food and drinks, and then bounced because my little pup was at home waiting for me. I was the first to leave, so of course the Director made some smartass remark about me meeting up with a girl. Don't even man, we aren't bros AT ALL, and don't suddenly act like it to show off to the corporate peeps. Ugh. Peace out.

Surprisingly, I was actually pretty pumped to start Tuesday off. I knew we would get some fresh cafe con leche and pastries to start the day because I was buying this time, and then we would hit the ground running! Boots on the mothafuckin' ground! The Regional Director got to the meeting space in the morning with his dry-fit polo on, ready to roll! Thank God because I jumped all over any chance I had to get the fudge away from my Director and his cornball ass! Everyone else started to stumble into the meeting room and the Regional Director was no-joke ready to roll! He asked if I was ready, and of course I was. He told my Director that we were going to get on the road. My Director was kind of caught off guard and asked the Regional Director if he could talk to him for a second. My Director seemed super nervous. He asked me and the younger Sales Manager from St. Pete to head down to the Sales Office dungeon and separate some collateral (pens and shit) into three bags for the teams to take on the road. When he asked the Regional Director this, I just knew he was going to inform him of my bonus concerns and such, so that he wasn't surprised and it didn't make the Director look bad when I voiced my concerns to him. As I said, he was mister positive, and would do anything to keep his record squeaky clean. Douche!

So me and the young guy headed downstairs and started separating the overpriced branded pens and ashtray USB chargers that the Director ordered for this Sales blitz. These chargers sounded like a great idea, but our logo was located on the portion of the charger that would be plugged into the car ashtray making it not visible. And once those are plugged into an ashtray, it will likely never be removed. Great advertising...not. The fancy pens served no greater purpose than the free ones that the flagship company provided us for free. Stupid. My Director eventually came down to the office and asked if I could come upstairs to chat with him and the General Manager. I'm thinking, "Jesus Christ." I exit the office, and as I was walking up the stairs with him, I say to him, "Really man, I am in a good mood, about to go sell the hell out of this hotel, and we have to start the day with drama? Can this not wait until after?" He seemed really awkward (more so than he normally was) as we walked up to the GM's office. Meanwhile, the Regional Director was hanging out in the lobby ready to bounce as we passed him. I knew this was going to be a "Tony, please keep your mouth shut about the bonus and anything negative things about the hotel with the Regional Director because we want it to seem like everything is positive and going great." Total BS, but they knew I spoke my mind, and would not hesitate from telling the truth about the place, because naturally, the Regional Director would ask me. I would likely destroy my Director.

We get to the GM's office and the Director shuts the door behind me. So official! I take a seat and the GM starts with, "Alright, we have to put some closure to this." I said, "Okayyyy." not exactly sure what he was referring to. I was assuming the bonus FINALLY because it had not been addressed since the email I sent a few weeks back. He goes on to inform me that he was giving me the opportunity to resign. Whoa! I responded, "Why would I resign? If I wanted to resign, I would have done so by now and wouldn't be sitting here today." He chuckled and said they would have to let me go then. WTF!? I asked why, and his response was, "We cannot have someone working here that is looking for other jobs." I simply replied, "Okay then," got up, and walked the fuck out! I gave no handshakes, no thank you's, just walked the fuck out. I was fuming, to say the least. I didn't know whether or not to clear everything off of the desks as I was exiting the office (as you see in the movies), or turn around and punch my Director square in his jaw as he was following me out. What a fucking coward! He clearly went up there because he was truly afraid that I was going to sell him out to his boss, the Regional Director. And honestly, I would have. Such a cry baby. I walked faster than ever, right past the Regional Director and the other Boots on the Ground team, and made my way down to the Sales Office. I took my company laptop out of my bag and put it on the desk (still not moved), grabbed the few things I had in the drawers, and headed out. I shook the young guy from St. Pete's hand and said "I'm outta here man. They just let me go." He shockingly reacted, "What the fuck?" Luckily, he knew some of the backstory from what I told him earlier. Then, my Director came in and stood there scared shitless. He tried to shake my hand, but that was not happening. The dude is seriously lucky I didn't clock him, and I had never done that to anyone in my life. Then, I see him telling the parking lot Security Guard that I am not to be allowed back on the property. Like, really dude? You think I am going to come back and shoot up the place? GTFO!

Mannnnn, you wanna talk about adrenaline pumping! After throwing my shit in my car, I decided to go back upstairs and pull the Regional Director aside to tell him how fucked up this situation was. I told him, "You have my number, call me. We have to discuss some things." I then peaced the fuck out of that cluster of a hotel. It was weird because it felt as if a weight was immediately lifted from my shoulders, but at the same time, I instantly freaked out a bit because I needed a new job. Luckily, I had already been driving part-time for *Uber* and *Lyft*, so had that as a fallback to make money in the meantime. I went straight home and let the fumes wear off a bit. This lasted less than an hour of just lying there with my pup and letting things cool off. I didn't have any family in Miami, so my pup was the closest thing to me. She snuggled me good in that time of need, and listened to me venting aloud. The best de-stresser ever! My emotional support animal! Everything that had just transpired just felt so shitty and wrong and I really didn't know the correct way to handle it. It was weird too because in a sense, I kind-of out in my notice back when I told my Director that I should start looking elsewhere a few weeks earlier, but didn't know it would be taken literally. I never formally put in a two-weeks' notice, so not sure if they marked that on their calendars and this was exactly two weeks from then, or if they truly got a reference call from another job that I had applied for. Whoops. So what was I to do? Naturally, I sat at my computer and wrote.

I needed to put all of this bullshit shadiness that I experienced at that hotel in a formal, professional, yet honest and raw email. This email would be sent to my Director, the Regional Director, the Senior VP of Operations, VP of Sales & Marketing, General Manager, Assistant General Manager, Front Desk Manager, Housekeeping Manager, and Food & Beverage Manager. Basically, everyone who had been working closely with us (including those Manager's I liked because they would likely get some fake ass story as to why I was gone from the Director), and also the corporate people who had visited the hotel and saw the cluster first hand. And guess what I have...the actual email wording that I sent! Enjoy:

I just wanted to take the time to thank all of you for your time at the XX Hotel. I built some great relationships, and have learned a lot during my five months at the hotel.

As you all should know by now, I am a man of honesty and integrity and when I give you my word on something, I will follow through on it.

Unfortunately, my direct leadership at the hotel did not follow the same traits. I was told upon my interviewing and hiring that I would receive a sales bonus for reaching certain sales goals (as all sales positions entail). I had asked multiple times since my hire date what was going on with my sales goals and have yet to get a straightforward answer. Keep in mind, I have been there five months already. Sales bonus' are goaled and bonused by quarters, and one (January to March), almost two (April to June) have already passed since I have been there and still no bonus structure for me. This is something that any and all hotels have---even hotels where openings get delayed---it's not the first one ever. I was given a low salary of $45,000 and told the bonus potential would be 40% of my salary (some uncapped), giving me the opportunity to hit $63,000+. Instead, nothing.

Alongside that, I was told we would have a Sales Coordinator to assist myself and Director of Sales with duties that overwhelmed us and held us back from the end goal of selling the hotel. This is much needed at a hotel like this because we do not have an Event Manager. I would then learn that I would be taking on the duties for this role at no extra bump in pay or incentive.

"One team, one goal" was our motto at this hotel, but sadly my direct leadership did not follow this themselves.

Regardless of all of this, I was given the chance to resign today, and I opted NOT to because I have continued and planned to continue to give 110% everyday for the hotel even with all of the above mentioned. I was turning and burning contracts, hitting the road to check out competitor hotels, and attending after-work events to get the word out about the hotel to the best of my abilities. I was taking on duties for my Director such as creating the hotel presentation, spearheading the ordering of both the hotel fact sheet, banner, trade show table, and many more (one team, one goal). I volunteered to take over the duties on the hotels consistently incorrect and outdated website, and the hotels pathetic social media presence. Both times, I was brushed off and the hotel is paying the consequences, whether it be incorrect parking charges, pet fees, old pictures, etc. (Daniel [the Front Desk Manager] also pointed all of this out in a lengthy email that was just recently addressed by the Corporate Training Lady when she visited two weeks ago), and an Instagram/Twitter/Facebook with less followers and posts than my grandmother.

Instead, I was released from the company this morning, as I was told because "I am interviewing with other companies." I just thought this needed to be shared and I hope that the hotel can correct it's path and get on the right track to success. Sadly, I will not be a part of that path.

BOOM!!!! Suck on that! Damn that felt good to get off my chest. I wanted to make sure I sent this immediately because I did not want the Director spreading false reasonings for my departure, as I am sure he would have. This way, everyone knew the truth, and anything he said would make him look like a total ass, because everyone liked and respected me as a person. The Assistant GM especially liked me, and was one of the few with a clue at that place. After sending that email, he sent me a personal text telling me how much he loved it, and to make sure I forwarded it to our senior corporate team, including HR, the CEO, President of Operations, and even mentioned sending it to the Owners of the hotel. Apparently the Owners were not fond of our upper management, the female Owner in particular. But guess who she did like? Yours truly! So I sent it to her as well. :)

CHAPTER 6: FALLING OUT OF LOVE WITH HOTELS

It was finally time for an upgrade…from my H&M suit to a Forever 21 suit. Ha! That big hotel money! Coincidentally enough, I had an interview scheduled that very same day for later in the afternoon. Being that the corporate people were at our hotel, I knew it was highly unlikely that I would be able to slip away to make the interview, so I ended up calling the Director of Sales who would be interviewing me on the way into work to tell her there would be no way I could make it and would need to reschedule. It was for a Group Sales Manager role at a ballin' hotel down in South Beach! I was worried that I was over and done with as a candidate because I had to cancel. That was the first time I had ever bailed on an interview. That's normally a big red X on your resume, but call me lucky, because I was able to reach her after getting dismissed from the hotel and reinstate the interview. This would become the first of many hotels that I interviewed with where I would have the awkward conversation of why "I left" the last place. I figured it would be easier to tell employers that I left on my own accord, and play it off so they wouldn't question, but made clear that the old hotel did not like my decision to leave. This way, the prospective employers wouldn't call them as references. I tried not to shit-talk that hotel. I left it professional, and pointed out the differences going from a corporate Sales position to Sales for a small franchise company. They lacked organization, professionalism, resources, and they were dishonest about their bonus plan. In the Hotel Sales world, people know that bonuses are not something you mess with, so everyone I would interview with totally understood my concerns there. Also, I was very tight with the AGM at the old hotel, so I was able to use him as my "Supervisor" and reference. DEFINITELY NOT the Director!

I applied for every Hotel Sales position known to man! I started out very picky as to where I applied because I did not want to end up in a similar situation, but after some time of not hearing back from places, I was scrapping for a job. I was applying for not only Hotel Sales jobs, but also other industry Sales positions. I figured this might be my long awaited exit from the hotel industry that we all dream of. Well, not quite. You didn't think the Hotel God's would let me out that easy did you!? I ended up going two solid months with no sign of a job, so I ended up making the decision to move back to my hometown of Southern Maryland, and apply for jobs up there, while staying with my parents for free. I couldn't afford the Miami rent and lifestyle while jobless. I packed up my shit and puppy, and hit the road for the sixteen-hour trek home. I sublet my apartment per recommendation of my friend Hector, which worked out great. This stalled me time to figure out what the hell I was doing. It enabled me to have the ability to move back to Miami if I ended up hearing back from one of the jobs I applied and/or interviewed with. There were still two or three companies I was expecting to hear back from.

Going to Maryland was a great change of pace for me. My parents had recently gotten a Golden Retriever puppy, so him and Mischa were able to play with one another. My mom and stepdad had recently bought a monster house on the water, with a ridiculously huge yard and pool, which the dogs frequented. It was located back on a farm...yes a farm. You entered on a few mile long dirt road, surrounded by hay fields, horses, donkeys, and lakes equipped with duck shooting blinds. It was as opposite as you could get from Miami. I would have the entire basement to myself, which had a living room, bedroom, game room, fitness room, and little bar area. It also had its own exit to the outside pool area, so I could take Mischa out and go about my personal business without interrupting my parents. The only issue was that they had this ridiculous security alarm system which made being stealth impossible. Gotta love home life! I was able to nab a few good interviews at hotels and resorts in Southern Maryland and the Baltimore area. I thought it would be great to live in Baltimore, as it was pretty cheap to live, fun, young, hip, and I had friends that lived around there. The issue with the Maryland hotel biz was that the pay wasn't great in comparison to Miami. However, the cost of living was a tad less, so it could work. While staying with my parents, I also knocked out the remaining interviews I had from Miami jobs over the phone, or Skype.

It was funny because during the interviews that I did attend in Maryland, I had this new, cocky feeling of "Yeah, I know my hotel shit. Do you want my experience and knowledge or not? Are we done here?" I had worked in the hotel game for seven plus years at this point. I had worked in hotels, condo-hotels, timeshare hotels, worked on the beach, in the city, and in the suburbs. I had done Front Desk, Concierge, Valet, Bellman, Sales, blah blah blah...just fucking hire me! This was different than in the past, because in the past, I would practically do whatever it took to get a job. I would normally get a fresh haircut and shave my beard completely clean, seeing how the hotel biz loves that clean-cut look. Nope, not this time around. My hair was growing long and strong (as much as it could with my thinning and receding hairline that I attribute to having worked in the hotel biz), and my beard was longer and wilder than it had ever been in my life. Fuckin rebel here! I simply trimmed the edges and called it a day. Fuck it. I would normally print tons of extra copies of my resume and research the shit out of the hotel I was interviewing with. Nope. I showed up with two copies of my resume, and briefly perused over the hotel and the area in my car before walking into the interview. By no means would I become an expert like I normally would. If they asked me questions I didn't know the answers to, I would either wing it (which hotels have trained me to do well), or straight up respond, "If I am offered this job, I would know more about the hotel/town/clientele than anyone else in the business before starting on Day 1." In Maryland, I honestly felt like they were my jobs to lose, and there weren't any other candidates better than me for the position. I would simply let my personality and experience shine through. I blame it on Miami. The people of Miami have this mantra of not giving a flying crap, and it had definitely worn off on me.

So wouldn't you know it, about a month later, I hadn't heard anything back from any of the interviews. None! What the hell!? I guess my Miami attitude bit me in the ass. All the meanwhile, I had been starting to get the itch to go back to the infamous Miami, or civilization in general. Don't get me wrong, I loved seeing my friends and family in Maryland, and enjoyed the more laid back, country lifestyle, but that lifestyle didn't fit me. I figured I would give it a try, and that's all you can do. Luckily, I was up there during the warm summer, so the weather wasn't a deciding factor like it was last time I decided to move back down South. I had to go with Plan C now. That plan entailed me going back to Miami and sharing my studio apartment with the person subletting it. Not exactly the ideal scenario, but my rent would be dirt cheap, and I could afford to live that way while driving *Uber* and *Lyft* until locking in a new gig. I would have to be less picky with the jobs that I applied for this time around, even applying to some restaurants as well, as I thought that would be a decent paying, temporary option. I packed my bags, said my goodbyes, grabbed Mischa, and went on my way back down to Magic City. My mom wasn't all too thrilled, but also knew that Southern Maryland was not the place for me. She was happy that I gave it a try. Mischa was not going to be too happy with me either because we were leaving her new best friend, my parent's puppy. They played non-stop every single day we were there. Mischa would miss the freedom of not being on her leash majority of time. She loved the pool and the bay where we played fetch a few times. She was actually able to join me on a few canoe rides. Living that country life! Nonetheless, we were on our way, and off to conquer Miami for Round 2!

After two long days of driving, we finally arrived to Miami. I unpacked, got my car cleaned inside and out, and jumped back on the road, driving for *Uber* and *Lyft* full-time. At first, it was okay. I was able to make my own schedule, which was pretty badass. If I wanted to wake up early and drive for a few hours, I could, or if I wanted to sleep-in and do a few hours in the evening, I could. Or, I could do both if I was low on funds. The beauty was that I was actually able to pay my bills, which I was worried about. It started to suck-ass after a while though because ninety percent of the riders in Miami didn't speak English, they smelled, were rude, didn't talk to you, and/or listened to music while riding. I would be reminded daily of how I needed to get a new damn job. My restaurant job search did not go too well because it was off-season, and none of the restaurants were hiring. Also, my odds of getting hired were limited because I didn't speak Spanish.

I mentioned a few stories earlier that had me thinking at the time that maybe I needed to get the hell out of Miami. Whelp, when I returned to Miami, the signs continued. Ugh! I told myself I would push through them this go-round. I was about thirty minutes out from my Miami Beach apartment and I got a call from a 301 area code. It was the motherfucking Director of Sales at a hotel that was right beside my dad's house that I had applied for, and it happened to be the same hotel chain that I had worked at previously, so I was super qualified! Just my goddamn luck! I had been trying to get ahold of this Director of Sales for weeks because they had a Group Sales Manager position open. And go figure, as I was talking to the Director, we hit it off big time, and it turned out my mom taught both of her kids in school. In fact, she was slightly obsessed with my mom. God dammit! I told her I was back down in Miami for a few interviews, but was still interviewing in Maryland as well. She was super excited and said the GM would be calling me for a phone/Skype interview in the next few days. I eventually talked to him a few days later, and the call went great, but my conscious said nope, I was back in Miami to stay.

After the call with the Director, we were nearing the streets of my apartment, and I decided to be a good dad and take the pup to the dog park before we even unpacked the car. I started to ask Mischa, "Want to go to the park!?" She was in love with the park and knew exactly what the "P.A.R.K." was, so when I mentioned the word, her head popped up with ears perched and did the infamous curious dog head tilt. Now that Mischa had completely crawled into my lap with excitement, we pulled up to the North Beach Open Space Park. I slipped my sandals back on and got out of the car with a big stretch and sigh of relief because we finally finished that damn trip. I walked over to the passenger side to let Mischa out and she hopped out in excitement. She happened to hop right on the

240

heel of one of my sandals, and the cheap-ass $2 Old Navy sandal snapped right in half! The thong portion ripped right off, and I mean ripped off. No chance of putting it back together. Fuck me! All of my other shoes were buried miles deep in the car. Whelp, guess we weren't hitting the dog park. So, within the first five freaking steps back in Miami, I got a sign to GTFO! Ugh. Then, a week or two later, my car got towed. Not once, but twice, in the same freaking week! How is that even possible!? That damn Miami cocky mindset convinced me to illegally park and run in to grab a six-pack real quick, and then illegally park it overnight at my apartment because I was too lazy to look for open spots. Three hundred bucks in cash for each occurrence to have my car released from the tow lots! Six-hundred bucks...gone. Six-hundred bucks while unemployed. Just shoot me!

Finally, about a month and a half of being back in Miami, I started receiving some calls for interviews, and then second interviews. I had three second interviews and received three job offers within one week. When it rains, it pours! One offer was for a freight transport company which seemed a tad sketchy because the interview process was way too easy, and the pay was super pathetic. It seemed like one of those, "work college kids around the clock, and take advantage of them" type of jobs. The second offer was from the largest hotel chain in the world that I previously worked for, but for their timeshare division. This sparked my interest because I was semi-familiar with the timeshare division because my dad and stepmom had three of them with that same company. The salary they offered was about as good as a McDonald's cashier, but the real money was to be made from commissions. I don't mind a commission structured job, but it would need to have a decent salary associated with it, unless I knew one-hundred percent that I could bring in good money with the commission, which I was not aware of in this role. The third offer came from a hospitality staffing company. Hospitality staffing...hmm...interesting. This sparked my interest because it was still kind of in the hotel business, but from a different angle. I was looking for an escape from the hotel industry completely, but you know how it is...there is no way out! The pay was great, it had a good commission structure, and killer benefits. My decision was made, and the choice was obvious. Finally, the wait was over. Four freaking months later!!!

The job I ended up accepting was a Hospitality Sales Representative for the South Florida region for a publicly traded staffing company. Here, I would work with hotels, restaurants, catering companies, stadium concessions, college cafeterias, and anything else hospitality related to get them to use our company for their staffing needs. So I would still be selling, but instead of selling hotel rooms and catered meeting space, I would be selling our company's staffing services. You might initially think, well why wouldn't companies just hire their own employees? The easy answer is that by using a company like ours, they avoid the headaches of hiring/firing, training, paying for workers compensation, and many other HR nightmares. Also, the company offered great benefits like health insurance and paid-time-off to our associates, so people would prefer working for a staffing agency versus the client directly in cases where they weren't offered benefits, and to avoid being laid off by hotels that tended to be very seasonal. It's also great for part-time work. On days off from people's regular jobs, they could work for a staffing company and pick up steady side work. Positions like Housekeepers, Banquet staff, and Dishwashers are common positions that hotels tend to need extra help during certain occasions or busier times of the year. In high (busy) season, some hotels might need fifty Housekeepers every week, whereas in the off-season, they might only need twenty. So instead of these hotels laying off the thirty employee difference year after year, they would use a staffing company like ours, and we would simply be in charge of finding those associates another property that might have a need for them, and just move them. It's a win/win. The hotels or restaurants would just pay us a small fee on top of the normal hourly rate they would normally pay the employee. The extra cost works out to be less than the total costs needed for them to actually hire and handle everything for these employees themselves. It's amazing how expensive it actually is to hire someone. We actually used a staffing company in the Housekeeping department at the hotel that I helped open, and that was the only exposure I ever had to it. I remember the GM not being fond of it, but my buddy Constantine, the Housekeeping Manager, convinced him it was a must have for a hotel opening since you don't have a good estimate of staffing needs from the beginning. Then, we could always phase out the temporary staff as we found and hired our own good employees.

My new boss was fucking awesome! In my first interview, he asked if I could pass a drug test, after he was clearly convinced I was his favorite candidate. Before I even responded, he said, "If you can't, just tell me, so I can delay it." He was young, hungry to succeed, and seemed like he was tired of dealing with BS from other shitty employees. He reminded me a lot of someone else I knew...myself! Take a wild guess what industry he came from...the good ole hotel biz! Just judging by his interview process, and speedy responses to me in our back-and-forth emails before and after the interview, I had already gotten a good vibe from him. He was a hockey fan, rocked sleeve tattoos, and wasn't afraid to tell it how it was. This company offered incredible benefits and pay! It was pretty pathetic that I worked for some of the largest hotel chains in the world, and this company's benefits were supreme to all of them. The hotel industry...SMH. The salary was pretty much the same as my last gig, but this position paid monthly commissions for sales, not quarterly or yearly bonuses like hotels did. And get this...they actually put in writing! There's a shocker! Here, anything I would sell, I would get a piece of. Not only would I get a piece, but I would get a piece every single month that the client would use our services. So in essence, I could book a hotel, and they use us every single month for a year, and I get commissions on how much they used us every single month. He bragged and showed me how some of his Sales Reps were making over $100,000 after commissions. I naturally assumed he was exaggerating until I saw the numbers in front of my face. He had a Sales Rep that had already brought in seventy-five thousand so far that year in just commissions with three months still remaining in the year. The previous month, that same Rep had made ten-thousand alone. Keep in mind, this was just their commissions, so add their decent salary on top of that! I think I could roll with that! I had never made even close to ten grand in bonuses, or even half of that in an ENTIRE year in the hotel biz! It was time to make up for that!

I received a monthly hundred dollar cell phone reimbursement and a $450 car allowance. Yes, you read that correctly...a $450 monthly car allowance! This was meant for gas, oil, or maintenance that may be needed because I would be on the road seventy-five percent of the time selling our services. But if I planned it well, I could hit hotels and restaurants in the same areas on the same day and would never come close to spending that much in a month. Most Hotel Sales jobs will instead reimburse for mileage, like my last gig. What a pain in the ass! This monthly allowance was so much better, and I didn't have to track jack shit! Both allowances would be added to my paycheck, so it was basically a $6,600 a year add-on to my salary. I would work mainly remote, and only need to swing by the office once a week to catch up with the Operations Team that sat in the office that did the recruiting and HR work. I would need to keep a close relationship with them, as they were the ones carrying through anything that I booked...basically just sending good people to work. The health insurance at this job for me was FREE! Amazing! The company had a killer company store similar to the large hotel chain I started working with in DC. I also received a laptop and a mifi card for places I couldn't get wifi, thus allowing me to work on the beach! It seemed like a dream job, especially coming from my previous gig, although I was still a tad cautious because I was promised quite a few things in the past too.

So was this it? Was this my official escape from the technical "hotel industry?" Well, not quite. The Hotel Gods seemed to follow me to the staffing industry, but not in the same sense. There was still plenty of drama, but the weight that seemed to ride on my shoulders while working in the industry seemed to be lifted. Staffing for hotels was almost like working for them, but from an outsider's point of view, without being caught up in the nonsense hotel day-to-day. It was like a contractor in a sense. I didn't deal with guests' bullshit, but instead the GM's, Directors, and other department heads. I was able to visit different hotels daily, some crappy box hotels like the first one I worked at, some cute boutiques like the one I worked at in DC, and some super chains that I was with for multiple years. I took my experience and knowledge from my hotel career and applied it to selling our services to those hotels and other hospitality venues. I was still able to attend Hotel Association and Convention Bureau events to look for potential clients, so I was still able to get my hotel networking fix in. Also, when I booked a hotel as a client, I was able to still get that bragging satisfaction of working at an uber-cool hotel, but instead of having just one hotel, I could brag about representing multiple. I had all of South Florida's hotels at my fingertips. It was great! I made it. I made it out of the hotel industry alive! Or did I?

It was November 9th, 2017, almost exactly one year after starting this gig, and I received a call from one of our Regional Manager's. He apologetically informed me that my position (and as it turned out, the entire hospitality division for our company) had been eliminated. You've got to be kidding me! Surprisingly, it barely phased me. Back to the drawing board. Back to updating my resume. Back to dusting off my H&M suit for interviews. And most importantly, back to applying for what I knew best, what I loved, and what I hated...back to applying for hotel jobs.

THE END

EXTRAS:

Who I Still Keep in Touch with and Who's Still in the Game

First and foremost is my main man Ray from my first ever hotel. He was the Chief Engineer if you remember correctly. I actually reached out to Ray for help with this book to see if he still had a copy of the resignation letter for that hotel, as I sent it to him right before I left to read it, laugh, and cheer. Unfortunately, he didn't have it, but I managed to dig it out of my email sent box. Ray was able to secure a job a few months after I had left the hotel with AAA. He had been itching like fuck to get out of that shady ass place. I grabbed drinks with him when I was back in town not long after he got the new job, and we shit talked about the old hotel and cheered to futures outside of there. I now follow his wife on *Instagram,* and see my main dude living a happy, hotel-free life from time to time.

Jesse, from my first Fort Myers Beach hotel is still a good bud of mine. I don't really see him as much as I'd like, but when I do venture through that area, I make sure to hit him up. In fact, he hosted me during Hurricane Irma, as I escaped from the initial predicted path of Miami. Of course, Irma decided to stray and hit us in Fort Myers dead on! Was this the Hotel Gods mad that we left!? Jesse still busts my chops on the regular on social media for posting selfies, and I bust on his homeless-ass looking beard he's so obsessed with growing. He still has that manliness obsession syndrome, but that's what makes him Jesse. Funny enough, I was scrolling through some old photos on my computer and came across one of Jesse standing in front of my car smiling in the headlights with a tire wrench in his hand. What the fuck, right? That was actually from one of our late-night ventures when I either hit a raccoon, or someone else had in front of me, and it was fluttering to the end of its life in the middle of the road. Jesse hopped out of my convertible, way too intoxicated, and investigated the status of the critter. He came back to the car and asked me to pop the trunk. He grabbed the tire wrench and helped the poor little guy end his misery. That crazy bastard! Anyways, Jesse escaped the hotel industry like a mother trucker. He peaced the hell out of that hotel we worked at together and went jobless for a while. He has bounced around a few other industries since, but still plans to run his own fishing charter business in the near future. Sitting behind a desk, answering phone calls, and dealing with whiny-ass people was not his forte. I mean, is it anyone's really? He hasn't been sucked back into the hotel industry...yet.

Rodney, Rodney, Rodney! I actually surprised good ole Rodney one of the last times I was in Fort Myers Beach. Rodney had gotten a job as a Reservations Supervisor at a prime-time hotel on the beach, far from the one we worked at and suffered together at the Front Desk. He got a bump in pay, more normal hours, and no bosses stealing his petty cash or looking at guests feet. I called his new hotel to find out if he was working, and sure enough he was. I was able to swing in and surprise that goofy, sweet redhead. He actually wasn't as surprised as I thought as I guess he saw me post something with Jesse the night before, as we drank our faces off into some shenanigans like old times. Nothing changed there. Rodney was in a much happier place in his new role, but still suffered from annoying-ass guests. That, you will never escape at any hotel or hotel position. Rodney and I follow each other on social media, so we still keep tabs on one another. I'm not sure if you remember me talking about that sweet older crazy lady, Nancy, from our old property, but Rodney later informed me after I left, she eventually passed away. This was one of those times when it wasn't a family member or best friend that passed away, but someone that touched your life just enough to really make you sad, and take a step back, shed a few tears, and think about life.

A few of the girls from the second hotel that I worked at in Fort Myers Beach are avid *Instagram*-goers like myself. I see them keeping super active in the Florida lifestyle. They have all moved around and some have gotten out of the hotel biz. Whelp, not too fast...one went back and just received some Manager of the year award, and another hit me up when I was working at the Sales Office in Miami, asking about jobs with my company. I told her, "Don't even think about it! Let me save you now." The ex-boss that I had that little fling with is also big on *The Gram*. She is engaged or married out in Cali and expecting. I don't think it's a hotelier baby though. Lame. She seems to be enjoying life, and still working her way up the hotel ladder. Dave, who was the Concierge/Valet guy whose position I took over when I started at the hotel ended up going back to work the same position soon after I left. He must have gotten bored, or broke living the retired life. That character would always tell me how he was ready to retire and start his own thing, and never ever work in hotels again. Whelp.

Perhaps the people I keep in touch with the most are those from the Front Desk Team at the boutique DC hotel. Ted, Tony, Jess, Josh, and John are all good social media buds of mine. John sends me random-ass *Snapchats* on the regular, as he actually works at a hotel now on some Caribbean island. Ted is climbing his way up the ranks as expected, but has bounced around more than a hooker on a Friday night. I can't knock him because I have done the same. Tony is one of the top Concierge Agents in DC now, and is constantly hitting up DC's finest events, and was even featured in a magazine! Touché! We would always give each other shit on social media as to whose hotel brand was better. We both respect the hotel game and love to hate it. Sure enough, another girl, Amy, who was one of my Assistants at the Florida Group Sales Office, just so happened to end up working with Tony years after me working with both of them. The hotel world is smaller than you think! The Cali girl who I had the one-nighter with actually married one of our sister hotel's GM, and fled to the West Coast with him. She is still in the industry as a Manager somewhere over there. She will do well wherever she ends up. Josh was actually my shadow for a while there. I had gotten him the job at that boutique DC hotel, and ended up later getting him a job at the Mid-Atlantic Sales Office as an Admin shortly after I started there. He fit in great and everyone loved him. What's not to love about a funny, seven-foot tall, die-hard hockey fan!? He eventually bailed from the hotel game to roll out to Denver and take part in some legal recreation. He is now working for some brewing company which sounded pretty damn cool compared to any hotel gig. The Concierge, Luis, that showed me around DC when I started at that boutique hotel, sadly lost his battle with cancer in 2018. RIP Luis! We love you, darling!

The Intern from Philly, David, who had bounced to Hawaii, actually let me crash with him in Hawaii for a week. He was still a crazy-ass mofo, but a great tour guide, as that was what he was doing out there. Jess moved back out West and apparently joined the military and got married. WTF? Tall, skinny, Taylor Swift look-alike in the military!? Interesting. Our PBX Operator from that hotel, Sardia, bless her heart, is still at the freaking hotel! Everyone rolled out one-by-one after I left because of the stupid politics that went on there. In case you didn't notice, I liked to take the lead on a lot of things, and a lot of people liked to follow. I may have sounded like a whiny bitch or douche in the process, but there was normally a good reason for it. Was it too much to ask for a place to just run smoothly? Enter, *Love Hate Hotels* Consulting.

From my third DC hotel (the one that had the interesting weekend crowd), I keep in touch with a few of my old coworkers. My Front Desk Manager, Director of Sales, Director of F&B, and GM have all moved up in the industry. They are all working for that same chain as well. I still use them as professional references today. I still credit the DOS for getting me into Sales, and the FOM for his calm demeanor rubbing off on me. I actually follow the DOS on *Instagram* and we like each other's pics from time to time. The Security Guard from that property who I would go out and rage with from time to time actually rolled out to Brazil for a vacation and never looked back to the hotel biz, or the USA. I still need to take advantage of that connect. I recently found out his brother who could practically be his twin, actually lives in Miami too. Again, small hotel world.

I still keep in touch with a good amount of people from the Mid-Atlantic Sales Office that I worked at, and every last one of them is still in the hotel game, with the same company! I still use two of my ex-bosses there as references, and I just found out one of them just took a promotion in Miami. Everyone is coming down! The girl that trained me, Cara, who I always joked was my life coach, is always an email away from a good *Redskins* joke, or if I ever have a lead for that market. The other Josh, who was my

Admin buddy that got in trouble for one of his friends smoking in a room, has actually become an even better bud since I left. We email, text, and *Snap* on the regular, and I met up with him the last time I was in the DC area. I fell in love with his sister, but unfortunately that didn't work out (long story), so we always joke about that. He moved up to a Revenue position at the company's headquarters office, making the big bucks, and working great hours with great benefits. He is still trying to recruit me there to this day, but I can't give in to moving back up to the cold winters. I just can't. Plus, the corporate office is out in the boonies of Maryland.

At the Tampa hotel, I keep in touch with most everyone. My ex-coworkers there became great resources for anything I needed at the hotel, since I did indeed sell that hotel when leaving for Miami. Rick no longer works there, but instead for a car dealership, so he is still in the customer service field. Apparently, he got so fed up one day, he rolled into the Director of Sales' office and pulled the, "Fuck it, I quit." Savage! Something we all dream of. One of the Event Admins, Brian, is STILL there to this day! How in the F!? I swear it's because of his beloved *Tampa Bay Lightning* arena being so close to the hotel. He is maxed out (pay-wise) in his position, so nothing else makes sense to me as to why he would stay. It's only a matter of time. Danielle (the Group Coordinator) left, but ended up taking a higher position at a neighboring franchise hotel. There was another Group Coordinator named Haydeliz, that I actually got a job for her with my staffing company but for the Tampa market. Everyone else is still at that property, and I pop my head in when I am in town. I also use them for references on everything.

At the Florida Group Sales Office in Miami, I literally keep in touch with everyone, likely because I left on my own accord on semi-good terms. It helps that I still live in the same town. Ninety-nine percent of them still work for the same chain, but most have bounced positions since. In the staffing industry, having knowledge of the people there is a huge help. This chain is all over South Florida, so it comes in handy to be able to name drop to potential clients, or use them to inform me of hotels that may need our services. Danny is one of my main dudes, and we meet for coffee or drinks monthly. My old Supervisor, Ricky, and I exchange funny, perverted memes on *The Gram* daily.

The hotel I opened of course had its fair share of bullshit, but I am really cool with some of the guys there still, in particular Constantine, Matt, Dan, and the AGM, all of whom bounced the hotel soon after me. I also got Constantine a job with my staffing company in the Tampa area. He would end up working with Haydeliz. Two of my friends from previous hotels in different cities now working together. How does this happen twice!? The hotel biz! Dan moved to Hawaii of all places. A New York Jew in the Aloha State. Crazy. I need to introduce him and David. Matt bounced back to the West Palm area where he grew up, and works in Sales now too, but not for hotels, so I frequently bump into him at networking events. The AGM recently wrote me an incredible reference on my *LinkedIn*, and is one of my top references on my resume and job applications.

Of course, there are those select few ex-coworkers whom I do not keep in touch with. You guessed it, the Owner and GM from my first hotel I worked at. I have not talked to either of them since leaving. I don't talk with the creepy foot-obsessed Manager that I had in Fort Myers Beach, although he was actually a nice guy and gave me a good recommendation, so I would totally snag a beer with him and catch up if the opportunity presented itself. I heard he moved back to Vegas where he was from. I do not talk to the Front Desk Manager from the boutique DC hotel. He just always rubbed me the wrong way, trying to be my bro, and stopped me from being able to post for a new position with that bogus late write-up. Although, who could blame him for wanting me to stay at the desk (dusting my shoulders off)? I would still say what's up and be cool with him if I ran into him. In fact, I actually follow his or his families bar's *Instagram* that's in New Orleans. It takes a lot for me to dislike someone. I might not agree with their business decisions, or more specifically hotel decisions, but at the end of the day, I'm cool with anyone and can let stuff slide. Drama free since '93!

I obviouslyyyyy don't keep in touch with my Director at the hotel I opened. After my exit, I remember chatting with an old colleague that was on my team in the Florida Sales Office that had worked with him previously, and she summed him up perfectly. She said, "That dude is weird." Well gee, thanks for the heads up before I took the damn job with him! One of my other good buddies, Mike, that worked in the office with him previously said the exact same. He said the guy always rubbed him the wrong way. I actually ended up running into that Director leaving the Starbucks by that hotel a few months after my exit. I knew it was a matter of time. I asked "How are you?" obviously not giving a fuck, and he replied, "Good, and you?" and I replied, "Good" and kept moving along. Great convo. But being the nice guy I am, a few months later at my new job, I had a client ask if I knew anyone for an Accounting position at their hotel. Oddly enough, the only person I knew was actually that Director's wife whom I met once at an event. I knew she had finished school in that field and was doing people's taxes and such. I sent him a text and let him know about the opportunity. He thanked me but let me know she was good with her current job, or something like that. God, I'm a nice guy.

I do associate with the GM from that same hotel. I remember chatting with him one day in the little closet of an office before the hotel had opened about how he was starting up this website for things to do in Miami. We shared the desire to start businesses, as I actually was going to start one very similar when I lived in Fort Myers Beach, and had about a thousand other business ideas in my head. I liked that he was very business minded like myself. He was in a successful-ass position in a hotel...the motherfuckin' GM...and still trying to GTFO! Hilarious! One of the interviews I had after being removed from that hotel was at a nearby competitor hotel, and sure enough the person interviewing me knew that GM very well on a personal level. Oh boy. He told me that he called him for a reference, and I about got up and left the interview. The guy interviewing me informed me that my old GM actually gave me an incredible recommendation. This made me further despise the old Director because my suspicion of him being the one that wanted me gone was basically confirmed. And because of this nice gesture from my old GM, I later hooked him up a few times with potential clients as he eventually started that business he told me about. What goes around comes around right? Also, sure enough, he later got sucked back into the hotel biz, and my staffing company was going to assist his hotel. You really can't escape!

Why Hotels?

You're probably asking yourself, with all of the negatives that I discussed in this book about the hotel industry, why in the hell would I still be anywhere near it today? Here is why:

Job Security: At the end of the day, it has to be one of the best, most secure industries to work in on this planet. There are way too many hotels, motels, condos, timeshares, hostels, and businesses that work with hotels to name. If you lose a job in this field, no problem. As I proved, you can easily find another, even if you have to settle for a crappy Night Auditor position, or Valet Attendant with even the shittiest hotel. If you have done it at one place, you can do it at them all. And just think about your retirement years down the road. You can easily work part-time at a Front Desk, PBX Desk, or even in Sales as an Assistant.

Networking: Networking in the industry is unbeatable. How many bars/restaurants do you know that have other profession-specific nights dedicated to people working in the field, like "Hospitality or Industry Nights?" Exactly. They offer discounts to our broke-asses! There are multiple hospitality events throughout the week, especially in major cities. There are convention bureaus, hotel associations, hotel openings, hotel re-openings, Christmas parties, brunches, etc. that offer many opportunities to meet and mingle with other idiots that entered the field. Off the bat, you know for the most part that the people you will meet at these events will be down-to-earth, social, or can at least fake a smile and make you think they are. And most certainly, they are all big partiers, whether that entails drinking, smoking, sexing, etc.

Overtime: Working in hotels, you have a great excuse to pick up overtime on the regular. If the hotel is busy as shit and they don't have enough people covering for their business demands, they expect you to stay extra. And let's be honest, these mofo's are always understaffed! Yeah, sometimes they will have you leave early on the slower days to make up for it, but a lot of properties won't, so act super busy all the time, and maybe you can slide in some OT money! It makes up for the shitty pay a bit.

Ability to Work Anywhere: Besides for maybe not knowing how to speak the native language(s) in certain areas of the world, you can literally work anywhere. You can live, work, and play where other people vacation. As long as you are willing to take the risk of moving to a new town, the flexibility is awesome in the hotel industry. As you have read, I did this multiple times. I didn't particularly go to any crazy exotic places, but the opportunities were out there, and still are, especially with so many hotel chains now going global. Build a good reputation with the one you are with, and transfer.

Benefits: Working in hotels normally does come with some bomb-ass benefits, other than the obvious health/vision/dental insurances. Each chain and brand are a tad different, but most have the following of some sort: Hotel discounts for yourself, family, and friends; employee meals, whether they are discounted or free; free gifted food from clients/guests/hotels; the ability to grow, or even shift properties after a short period of time (normally 6 months to a year); the brag factors (celebrity sightings, new hotel openings, special events held at the hotel, maybe staring at a killer view all day, etc.); and if you stay with whatever brand for X amount of years, you can get free or discounted stays for life, even when retired. The list goes on and on.

No Education Needed: Perhaps the best part about working in the hotel industry is that you don't need a PhD or even a college degree like most jobs these days. Hotel experience trumps any schooling you may have in the field. Keep in mind, this being the case, you can get stuck working under some clown-ass uneducated bosses! Not that being uneducated correlates to clown-asses, but sometimes people could use two-to-six years of maturity growth. Anyone can apply and work at a hotel no matter what your background. There are tons of departments with different skill sets needed, and you can grow within the property, or transfer to others. If you aren't computer savvy or presentable, apply for Housekeeping or Engineering, or maybe you just don't want to deal with people complaining all day. If you are presentable, well-spoken, computer savvy, and don't mind getting yelled at, then maybe Front Desk Agent or Server/Bartender at the hotel restaurant is for you. The opportunities are unlimited.

If I Were to Do It All Over Again...

Real Estate - As I mentioned before, if you happen to know someone ready to buy as you are finishing up your license, that would be ideal. This way you would snag commission immediately and can put that in the bank while you are building your clientele, and try to sell without going completely broke. Or, you can do what all the sexy girls in Miami do, and get a part-time restaurant, bar, club, or yes...a strip club job. I went to one in Miami, and half of the girls I met there were Realtors. Hey, I can't blame em. Or, I would wait until I had some solid money saved up in the bank, and then start my real estate career, or even after I retired, like my Aunt did. Point being, money needs to be in the bank, versus a broke-ass college graduate like me.

Restaurant Industry - As I have learned by working in Miami Beach, and other touristy cities, a restaurant Server or Bartender can make a fucking killing! Yeah, the hours suck, but they also do in most hotel positions, so fuck it! You might as well work in a field where you can make more based on how busy it is, or the amount of customers you will have, especially if you're at a place that has automatic gratuity. If you are a sexy girl, or even a decent looking girl with a nice figure, go to a city like Miami or Vegas, and you will clean house! You could easily be making a six-figure salary, and if you work at the right type of place where celebrities and zillionaires go, you can gain many other opportunities like free boat rides, cars, an automatic bank transfer, etc. Sky's the limit!

Hotel Industry - Surprisingly, I would choose the hotel industry again, but I would do it differently. I would start working part-time for a hotel at the end of my high school career, and then continue to work for one full-time out of high school. I would take a few college courses part-time, and maybe get some sort of degree, but know that it isn't necessary. As I've said, hotel experience farrrrrr outways any college education in the field. I would simply climb the ladder in Front Office up to Resident GM or GM of a hotel, probably a smaller, newer franchise property. From there, craftily transfer to Assistant GM or GM of a larger, more prized hotel that pays better. And then, eventually finishing with a huge chain that will have solid benefits. For example, a chain that offers free hotel stays after twenty-five years, as I mentioned earlier. Here, I would have saved myself over a hundred grand in college tuition, and been able to grow my experience for the four years that I would have been studying and partying. Instead, I would be MAKING over a hundred grand! I could have easily been a GM or even Regional Manager by age twenty-two, whereas I would normally be completing a four-year degree, just to graduate and go straight to a Front Desk Agent position, and then start to climb the ladder. Waste of fucking time, as I found out. But again, it wasn't my plan. I know people who took my [now] preferred path and I am pretty envious. Some were my bosses, and some were coworkers that I had actually fired, and they pressed on to become in these high-level roles. Think about it...

Age 17 - Part-Time Front Desk Agent

Age 18 - Full-Time Front Desk Agent - maybe take some night college courses
Age 19 - Front Desk Manager - maybe take some night college courses
Age 20 - Front Desk Manager, maybe Assistant GM - complete your two-year degree/certificate
Age 21 - Assistant GM, maybe GM
Age 22 - GM
Age 23 - GM, maybe Regional Manager
Age 70 - A Hotelier President of the United States ;)

Sounds easy-peasy, but if I had not lived it, loved it, and hated it every step of the way, I would not have known to take this alternate route. *Love Hate Hotels*.

To continue to follow and interact with myself and the *Love Hate Hotels, Inc.* brand, follow *@LoveHateHotels* on social media, visit www.LoveHateHotels.com, or even email me directly at Tony@LoveHateHotels.com. Until the next time my hotelier friends...and yes there will be a next time. It's already in production!

ABOUT THE AUTHOR

Founder of Love Hate Hotels, Inc. (recruiting & consulting), & Administrator of @LoveHateHotels, **Tony Matthews II** has over ten years of experience in the hotel industry, including employment with nine different management companies, & two staffing companies. He compiled knowledge & expertise of select & full service hotels, condo-hotels, timeshares, & sales office processes. He worked at hotels with rural, city, & beach surroundings, & mastered positions in Valet, Concierge, Guest Services, Front Office Management, Sales Administration, & Sales Management. He has experience closing down a hotel, opening one, & managing the staffing of entire hotels.

Printed in Great Britain
by Amazon